JUDICIAL INDEPENDENCE AND THE AMERICAN CONSTITUTION

Judicial Independence and the American Constitution

A DEMOCRATIC PARADOX

Martin H. Redish

STANFORD LAW BOOKS

An Imprint of Stanford University Press

Stanford, California

Stanford University Press
Stanford, California

Printed in the United States of America on acid-free,
archival-quality paper

Library of Congress Cataloging-in-Publication Data

Names: Redish, Martin H., author.
Title: Judicial independence and the American constitution : a
    democratic paradox / Martin H. Redish.
Description: Stanford, California : Stanford Law Books, an imprint
    of Stanford University Press, 2017. | Includes bibliographical
    references and index.
Identifiers: LCCN 2016047380 (print) | LCCN 2016048546 (ebook) |
    ISBN 9780804792905 (cloth : alk. paper) | ISBN 9781503601840
Subjects: LCSH: Judicial independence—United States. | Judicial
    power—United States. | Constitutional law—United States. |
    Democracy—United States.
Classification: LCC KF5130 .R43 2017 (print) | LCC KF5130 (ebook) |
    DDC 347.73/12—dc23
LC record available at https://lccn.loc.gov/2016047380

Once again, for Caren

Contents

Acknowledgments

This book represents the culmination of more than twenty years of thought on issues of judicial independence and American constitutionalism. For that reason, the chapters for the most part represent revised, modified, and on occasion reorganized prior publications. In certain instances, the original articles were coauthored with former students, all of whom deserve substantial credit for their enormously valuable contributions to their respective articles. These former students are Matthew Heins, Jennifer Aronoff, Colleen McNamara, and Christopher Pudelski. While the book draws significantly on all of these articles, it simultaneously represents a new synthesis of my previous thoughts into a wholistic theory of American constitutionalism and of the role of an independent judiciary in American democratic society.

As is true of any major scholarly project, this book could not have been completed without the substantial encouragement and support of many. I very much appreciate the Northwestern Pritzker School of Law and Dean Daniel Rodriguez for the support of my research over the last several years when I was completing the book. As already noted but worthy of repeating, I owe a great deal to all of the student coauthors mentioned above, who were my collaborators in the truest sense of the word. The final manuscript also benefited greatly from many valuable conversations with my Northwestern Law School colleagues: Steve Calabresi, Andy Koppelman, John McGinnis, and Jim Pfander. Also, the book would not have been possible without the efficiency, dedication, and good cheer of Juana Haskin, who has served as my faculty assistant throughout the entire process. Finally, my deepest and most heartfelt thanks go out to my family—my wife, Caren, and my daughters, Jessica and Elisa. None of my scholarship would matter without their love and support.

JUDICIAL INDEPENDENCE AND THE AMERICAN CONSTITUTION

Introduction. America's Contribution to Political Thought: Prophylactic Judicial Independence as an Instrument of Democratic Constitutionalism

The famed historian Henry Steele Commager once suggested that while "America has contributed little to formal political philosophy," it is also true that "[t]he generation that fought the Revolution and made the Constitution was politically the most inventive, constructive and creative in modern history."[1] "Its signal achievement," Commager noted, "was to institutionalize principles and theories that had long been entertained by historians and philosophers, but practiced rarely by statesmen and never by kings."[2] This analysis of the contributions to political thought and practice made by the Framers of the American Constitution seriously understates the important and unprecedented innovations they actually made. The American Constitution took important steps beyond its closest predecessor, the unwritten British constitution, by enshrining its fundamental principles in mandatory, written, countermajoritarian directives.

Perhaps the most unsung provision of the American Constitution is Article V,[3] which provides for a complex and difficult supermajoritarian process for amendment of the document's directives. This provision has been regularly ignored by many leading constitutional scholars, who believe either that the document's directives remain binding only to the extent that modern generations affirmatively accept them (though without indicating any process by which such acceptance is to be manifested),[4] or that the document may be amended by some vague notion of a "constitutional moment" where all somehow agree, implicitly and informally, that the document has been modified.[5] Both approaches, of course, completely ignore the unambiguous formal process for alteration required by Article V.

In shaping the American Constitution, the Framers synthesized the concepts of constitutionalism and legal positivism. More important for present purposes, the American Constitution adopted a system of separation of powers that added an innovative framework of prophylactic protections of judicial independence that were unprecedented in thought or practice, as a means of enforcing and protecting the Constitution and the values it was designed to guarantee. The Framers learned a lesson from past republican systems that had failed due to a lack of adequate checks designed to prevent dangerous aggregations of power that led inexorably to tyranny. The goal of this book is to explain the significance of these strong protections of judicial independence as the necessary foundation of our nation's form of constitutional democratic government.

The book's thesis, while relatively straightforward, is multileveled. On one level, my thesis posits that it is only by vigilant enforcement of prophylactically assured judicial independence that our constitutional democratic system can function effectively. Any constitutional system that fails to provide for such prophylactic protections of judicial independence is, in important ways, vulnerable to manipulation and circumvention by the majoritarian elements of government. This is simply because if those vested with the final say as to the meaning of the countermajoritarian Constitution are vulnerable to the pressure, intimidation, or control of the very majoritarian branches sought to be limited by that Constitution, then as a practical matter the document imposes no legal restraint on those branches. As a result of such a failure to insulate the judicial interpreters and enforcers of the countermajoritarian Constitution, the entire foundation of a constitutional system is potentially undermined and democracy threatened. This does not necessarily mean that those branches will regularly ignore the document's directives. But if they observe them, it will be either because those directives are deemed to have purely moral force or because the restrictions are politically acceptable to those in power. Either way, the document will have failed to serve its intended function of legally restraining the majoritarian branches. To be sure, a society may consciously choose a system that fails to impose binding, written countermajoritarian restrictions on majoritarian government, as the British have done. But for the form of mandatory constitutionalism our society clearly chose as a means of checking government and avoiding tyranny, prophylactic guarantees of judicial independence constitute an essential element of the system.

On a second level, however, it is simultaneously essential that the insulated judiciary maintain an appropriate degree of political humility, commensurate with its limited role in a democratic society. Absent grounding of its decisions in a principled construction of the text of a governing constitutional provision, the unaccountable judiciary lacks either moral or legal authority to ignore or overturn legitimately made political choices by the democratically elected branches.

When these two levels of analysis are synthesized, the result is that the judiciary's authority to check majoritarian government is, for the most part, confined to situations in which it is invoking provisions of the countermajoritarian Constitution. When it is performing another adjudicatory function, such as enforcing or interpreting a legitimately enacted statute, the scope of its independence is far more narrowly defined. In such situations, the integrity of the judicial function imposes certain protective limitations on the extent to which the political branches may manipulate the judicial process. But beyond those limited protections, it is wholly inappropriate for the judiciary to second-guess or ignore the political choices made by the representative branches of government.

While the book's thesis, stated broadly, is straightforward, its implementation as a means of resolving long-standing controversies about the scope and nature of American judicial independence gives rise to numerous complex issues. Before I can fully explore those controversies and how my approach to American constitutionalism would resolve them, it is first necessary to provide a foundational definition of the concept of the term, "constitutionalism," which I believe is the fulcrum of the American political system.

AMERICAN CONSTITUTIONALISM AS A CORE PRECEPT OF AMERICAN POLITICAL THEORY

American constitutionalism refers to the preeminence of the rule of law through a process of checking government's unlimited power over the individual, the government's relationship to the electorate, and the majority's unlimited power over the minority. This is achieved through use of a written, mandatory, countermajoritarian document as the nation's supreme law. While the inherently adversary nature of our form of political interaction is well established in American history,[6] the essential premise of our system is that whoever gains political power must remain accountable to the electorate and may not suppress the minority for no reason other than ideological disagreement or the desire to gain a competitive advantage in the political marketplace.

The concept of American constitutionalism links two distinct but intertwined levels of theoretical analysis. One is appropriately described as "macro" and the other as "micro." On the macro level, American constitutionalism refers to the core notions of a government confined, not solely by the will of the majority or the decisions of the majoritarian branches of government, but also by a binding, written constitutional structure, subject to revision, repeal, or amendment only by an intentionally cumbersome supermajoritarian process. Although this is admittedly not the only form of democratic government our society could have chosen, there can be little question that it is in fact the system we have selected. First, we chose to have our system of government laid out in a written constitutive document. Second, by its express and unambiguous terms the document's directives are framed as commands, rather than recommendations, suggestions, or pleas. Finally, also by its express terms, this constitutive document is subject to formal alteration only by an intentionally cumbersome supermajoritarian process. The underlying theory of our constitutional system in that fragile countermajoritarian constitutional structure must be protected by as many speed bumps to tyranny as possible. Paradoxically, then, an independent, unaccountable judiciary provides an essential protection of a democratic government.

On the micro level, American constitutionalism is designed to implement and protect the implicit social contract between government and citizen in a liberal democratic society. Only through a fair process of neutral and independent adjudication may government deprive citizen of their lives, liberty, or property.

Although the United States has built a strong tradition of judicial independence, careful examination of how the judicial power has evolved reveals a number of troubling situations where scholars or jurists have advocated or accepted restrictions on judicial power or independence that seriously threaten the judicial authority demanded by the precepts of American constitutionalism. In the chapters that follow, this book will seek to achieve three main goals. First, it will explain why strong judicial independence is so central to American constitutionalism. Second, it will categorize and define the conceivable forms of judicial independence, explaining which forms are demanded by precepts of American constitutionalism and distinguishing those that would actually threaten the American constitutional democratic system if adopted. Finally, it will explore and critique a number of areas of the law in which prominent scholarly theories or established judicial doctrine have had the effect of dangerously undermining the judicial independence central to our democratic system.

On the most basic level, one might reasonably expect the educated American citizen to be aware of both the countermajoritarian nature of the judiciary in American democracy and the foundational purposes that the independent judiciary is designed to serve. Surprisingly, however, many respected constitutional theorists have either failed to grasp the nuances and complexities of the nation's constitutional system or unwisely rejected many of the system's foundational premises, instead advocating recognition or adoption of such dangerous or misguided concepts as "constitutional realism," "popular constitutionalism" or "departmentalism." Even those courts and scholars who have both understood and accepted the basic premise of the essential intersection between judicial independence and the foundational precepts of American constitutionalism have struggled with troubling questions, which continue to surround that intersection. These include (1) what, exactly, are the scope and reach of the prophylactic protections of judicial independence? (2) How can the existence of these protections be reconciled with an appropriate role for processes of judicial discipline and removal? (3) What specific purposes of American constitutionalism are served by preservation of judicial independence? (4) Under what emergency circumstances, if any, may the guarantees of judicial independence be restricted or circumvented? (5) What are the specific constitutional sources of judicial independence, and does anything turn on which source is invoked? And, finally, (6) what are the limits implicit in our democratic system on the independence of the judiciary? Put another way, to what pathologies may invocation of judicial independence lead, if that concept is not properly defined and limited?

In this book, I explore and respond to all of these questions by examining the inherent intersection between the precepts of American constitutionalism and the requirement of an independent judiciary. The book includes in its title *A Democratic Paradox* because in it I explain the intentionally created paradoxical nature of our political and constitutional system: In order to preserve the essence of popular rule in which the governors are representative of and accountable to the people, a significant level of legal authority must be vested in a governmental body that has been intentionally and formally insulated from the requirements of representation and accountability. This is true not only in performance of the traditional judicial review function, but also as a necessary check on the elected government's ability to deceive the electorate by means of obscured or sub rosa legislative manipulation. This paradoxical form of governmental structure itself flows logically from an even more foundational paradox, this one growing out of the Framers' recognition of the inherently paradoxical nature of the human condition. On the one hand, a commitment to democratic government necessarily reflects a belief in the possibility of human flourishing and self-realization. Through participation in decisions directly affecting one's life, the individual grows personally, morally, and intellectually. On the other hand, simultaneously inherent in the human psyche is the tendency to authoritarian suppression of others. The goal of our paradoxical constitutional and political framework, then, is to reconcile the oxymoronic "skeptical optimism" about the human condition that the Framers so wisely brought to the task of shaping our young nation's new form of government with its simultaneous recognition of the potential for human flourishing.

Recognition of this structural paradox dictates acceptance, not only of a rigorously independent judiciary, but of one whose independence and authority are characterized by strong prophylactic protections, which are in many cases properly understood as far stronger than courts and scholars have traditionally deemed them to be. For example, in this book I will make the bold and controversial assertions that (1) the power of Congress to suspend the writ of habeas corpus recognized in Article I, section 9 of the Constitution is properly seen to have been superseded (and therefore rendered unconstitutional) by enactment of the Fifth Amendment's Due Process Clause; (2) the power of Congress to impeach and remove federal judges is properly restrained by recognition of the reasons why judicial independence was prophylactically protected in the first place; (3) the underlying theory of procedural due process, constitutionally enshrined in both the Fifth and Fourteenth Amendments, logically dictates the need for prophylactic protections of judicial salary and tenure in much the same manner as explicitly and formally imposed on the federal judiciary by Article III; and (4) as a result of this recognition of the scope of procedural due process, state judiciaries in which judges lack these prophylactic protections of their salary and tenure should be deemed violations of the Fourteenth Amendment's Due Process Clause.

It should be noted that it would be a mistake to place blind faith in the judiciary's ability to enforce individual rights or preserve democracy. All too often in American history, during so-called pathological periods the judiciary has failed to perform its checking function effectively.[7] But that unfortunate fact does not alter the basic point that must be made: Absent the availability of an insulated judiciary, there effectively exists no means at all of assuring those foundational American values. At least with an independent judiciary available, there is reason to hope and expect it will perform the checking function for which it was designed. Absent the availability of that check, absolutely no hope exists that majoritarian invasion of minority rights will be stopped.

From the opposite perspective, it might be suggested that, absent supporting empirical proof, there is no way to know whether the presence of salary and tenure protections actually assure judicial independence. While there does exist some level of supporting anecdotal evidence, it would be all but impossible to establish the superiority of judges protected by salary and tenure guarantees by means of some form of definitive empirical proof. But the question then becomes, on which side in this debate should the burden of proof be imposed? Common sense would seem to dictate the conclusion that judges whose salary and tenure are subject to the control of the legislature will be more restrained by political considerations than judges whose salary and tenure are guaranteed. Certainly, the Framers proceeded on the basis of this assumption, as Hamilton's *Federalist* No. 78 makes clear. Indeed, long before the drafting of the Constitution, the Declaration of Independence listed among the colonists' grievances with the English Crown that the King "ha[d] made Judges dependent on his will alone for the Tenure of their Officers, and the amount and payment of their salaries." As Hamilton reasoned in *Federalist* No. 79, "[n]ext to permanency in office, nothing can contribute more to the independence of the judges than a fixed provision for their support."[8] Though the book will advocate a revolutionary expansion of the scope and reach of judicial independence as an essential means of preserving the foundations of American constitutionalism, it also recognizes the need to sort out the specific types of decisional independence *not* appropriately exercised by an independent judiciary, in order to preserve the essence of American democratic principles.

The first two chapters of the book explain the concept of constitutionalism as it exists both normatively and historically in American political theory, which recognizes and develops the symbiotic relationship among three foundational elements of American political theory and structure: (1) democracy, (2) constitutionalism, and (3) judicial independence. These two chapters further develop the theory and structure of judicial independence, both as it has evolved and as it needs to be modified in the future in order to fulfill its foundational role in American political thought. Subsequent chapters, in contrast, focus on several of the most important practical implications of the intersection of these three elements. Some of these implications have already become accepted elements of American constitutional law, but others concern subjects in which courts and scholars have, for the most part, failed to grasp the logical outgrowths of our commitment to this tripartite intersection of political values.

In the first chapter I lay the groundwork for the remainder of the book by defining, structuring, and defending the principle of American constitutionalism, exploring how it not only coexists with but is actually essential to preservation of our form of democracy, and explaining why a vigorously independent judiciary is essential to the preservation of America's form of both constitutionalism and democracy. The chapter emphasizes what I deem American political theory's most important contribution to political philosophy: the concept of a prophylactically protected independent judiciary as the means of implementing and preserving the rule of law within a predominantly democratic society.

This chapter previews later chapters by emphasizing the need for final judicial authority to interpret and enforce the American Constitution (drawing on both historical and logical argument, grounded in what I deem to be the foundational premises of our form of constitutionalism), as well as the need for the judiciary to be insulated from political pressures. In doing so, it critiques the theory of "departmentalism," which, at least in its more extreme forms, would allow each branch to have the final say as to the constitutionality of its own actions.

The purpose of chapter 2 is to explain and contrast the different conceivable forms of judicial independence. This examination is necessary because the concept can potentially apply in a variety of situations, and not all of them are consistent with principles of either democracy or constitutionalism.

Chapter 3 explores the tension between the needs for judicial independence, on the one hand, and for checking judicial abuse through methods of discipline and removal, on the other. This issue has traditionally received at best limited attention, and this is as true of the Framers as it is of modern jurists and scholars. The thesis of this chapter is that while impeachment and removal are legitimate in truly extreme cases, it is vitally important to keep these possibilities extremely limited, lest the threat of impeachment or removal be so great as to completely undermine—albeit through the back door—the goals sought to be achieved by establishment of judicial independence in the first place.

Chapter 4 considers the role of state courts within the framework of American constitutionalism. State courts have always played an important role in the interpretation and enforcement of federal law. However, in judicial or academic discussions of judicial independence, state courts have always been the elephant in the room. The prophylactic protections of judicial independence embodied in Article III do not apply directly to state courts. However, the Due Process Clause of the Fourteenth Amendment guarantees at least a certain degree of judicial independence on the part of state judges. As it has traditionally been construed, that clause guarantees a "neutral adjudicator" before life, liberty, or property may be taken by the state. Although the Supreme Court has traditionally defined neutrality as the avoidance of "possible temptation to the average man as judge,"[9] the Court has been unwavering in its conclusion that in order to preserve such neutrality it is not essential that state courts possess the prophylactic protections of independence guaranteed to federal judges by Article III. In this chapter, I challenge that conclusion, and argue that, to the contrary, the adjudicatory neutrality required by due process must incorporate guarantees of salary and tenure.

In supporting this conclusion, the chapter will undertake three tasks. First, it will explore the meaning of neutrality for purposes of due process, in particular the Court's most recent application of the concept in *Caperton v. A. T. Massey Coal Co.*[10] I argue that the Court's holding in *Caperton* that a decision by a judge in favor of a large contributor to his campaign violates due process is anomalous, because the post-election gratitude focused on by the Court is far less of a threat to judicial independence than the chilling caused by a judge's fear that he or she will not be retained because of unpopular judicial decisions. Yet surprisingly, the Court has never found any constitutional problem with governmental structures in which state judges may be removed by political processes. Second, the chapter will explain why the current structure of state judiciaries is unconstitutional—not because of their methods of initial *selection,* but rather because of their problematic processes of *retention.* As long as judges possess no fear of loss of tenure or reduction in salary, how they are initially selected is—at least as a constitutional matter—of no great concern. Finally, the chapter will use the due process inquiry as a jumping off point to attack the poorly reasoned and extremely dangerous theory of "popular constitutionalism," associated with such leading constitutional scholars as Larry Kramer. The idea that final interpretation of constitutional provisions should somehow be vested in the populace as a whole is fundamentally inconsistent with the notions of countermajoritarianism that are essential to the dictates of American constitutionalism. Thus, to the extent the popular accountability of state judiciaries is somehow grounded in these concepts of popular constitutionalism, I argue that the process is not only misguided but also a serious threat to core notions of the nation's constitutional system.

In chapter 5, I explore one of the most significant functions served by a system of strong judicial insulation from public and governmental pressures: protection against legislative deception. Traditionally, the purpose served by an independent judiciary has been seen largely as the protection of minorities against majoritarian abuse, and there is no doubt that implementation of countermajoritarianism remains a vitally important function served by a system of strong judicial independence. However, judicial independence also serves an important majoritarian function, namely, assuring the accountability of the governors to the governed.

Judicial independence in this context assures that the political branches may not enlist the judiciary as an unwilling participant in the imposition of what amounts to a fraud on the public. To understand how such a scheme would operate, one first needs to keep in mind that the principle of "political commitment" is central to the smooth functioning of a representative democratic society. By this I mean that at least in significant part, representatives of the electorate are judged by the positions they take publicly on particular normative issues of social policy, often as embodied in proposed legislation. Thus, if a member of the electorate is in favor of Position A, and her elected representative voted against legislation adopting Position A, the democratic process enables her to demand an explanation from her representative or to oppose the representative's reelection.

While to a certain extent this is an oversimplification of the democratic process, there can be no doubt that dictates of accountability demand that elected representatives' positions on controversial legislation (and which legislation is appropriately designated "controversial" will of course vary depending upon the needs and interests of the individual voter, leading to the inescapable conclusion that *all* proposed laws must be assumed to be of such a character) must be made public to the voters. But even more pathological for the democratic process than secret legislative votes would be legislative deception—in other words, statutes that purport to enact "A" but, through the back door of procedural or evidentiary manipulation, are effectively transformed into "B" or even "Not A." At least in the case of secret legislative votes the voters are on notice that they have not been informed of their representatives' votes. In the case of legislative deception, in contrast, the voters are misled into believing that they are in fact aware of their representatives' political commitments, though the reality is very different. I argue that fundamental principles of separation of powers flowing from the formalized independence of the judiciary dictate the unconstitutionality of such legislative manipulation through interference with what I call "decisional independence."[11] Such interference occurs when Congress either (a) directs the judiciary to decide a particular case without simultaneously modifying the generally controlling subconstitutional law, or (b) directs the judiciary to employ procedural or evidentiary rules or devices that will have the effect of either preventing existing substantive law from being implemented or altering the underlying DNA of existing substantive law. The chapter will focus on the Supreme Court's cryptic but potentially significant decision in *United States v. Klein*,[12] as well as more modern examples of such legislative manipulation of the judicial process.

In chapter 6, I rely on the premises and insights of American constitutionalism to argue for a radically new position on the scope and force of the so-called Suspension Clause of Article I, section 9, clause 2 of the Constitution, which provides that "[t]he privilege of the writ of habeas corpus shall not be suspended, unless when in cases of rebellion or invasion the public safety may require it." While this clause has been the subject of a good deal of recent scholarship by leading federal courts scholars, none of it has taken the position taken in this chapter: to the extent that suspension of habeas corpus results in denial of a judicial remedy for violation of individuals' constitutional rights, the Suspension Clause is unconstitutional because it violates the Due Process Clause. The chapter argues that because the constitutional guarantee of due process requires adjudication by a neutral and independent adjudicator prior to the deprivation of life or liberty, inasmuch as suspension of habeas corpus will often result in deprivation of that protection, the Due Process Clause is violated by a suspension of habeas corpus that results in deprivation of liberty absent a hearing before a neutral judicial adjudicator. The chapter rejects the argument that the relatively contemporaneous enactment of the body of the Constitution and the Bill of Rights precludes the conclusion of a possible inconsistency between the two—an argument that has long been rejected by courts that have employed the Fifth Amendment's Due Process Clause as a limitation on congressional power to control federal court jurisdiction.

What is simultaneously so interesting and surprising about the thesis advanced throughout this book is the contrast between what should be the relatively uncontroversial nature of the foundational normative premises of American political theory advocated here—drawing on a commitment to democratic theory tempered by the demands of countermajoritarian constitutionalism—and the highly controversial nature of the specific insights I glean from those premises in a variety of jurisdictional, structural, and substantive contexts. Every chapter of this book advocates approaches to these specific issues that are either inconsistent with established legal doctrine, contrary to the dominant strain of scholarly thought, or (most often) both. In short, I argue that on the basis of principles of

American political theory that are widely accepted in the abstract, numerous doctrines need to be altered and numerous scholarly approaches advocated by prestigious scholars must be categorically rejected. The book's intended contribution lies in its effort to reshape the law of federal jurisdiction and judicial independence by returning to foundational, generally accepted precepts of American constitutional and political theory.

CHAPTER ONE

The Foundations of American Constitutionalism

INTRODUCTION

When we embark on the task of answering constitutional questions or teaching constitutional law, most of us start from the sensible position that our Constitution is interpretable positive law whose dictates must be respected.[1] This requires acceptance of three basic premises: first, that the written document is our supreme positive law; second, that the judiciary is empowered to interpret it; and third, that the judiciary's interpretation represents the final word as to its meaning. We *must* start here; otherwise, there would be no purpose in engaging in the study of our founding document and the rules of governmental ordering that it sets forth, nor could we place any faith in the study of Supreme Court case law defining and demarcating the boundaries of federal power contained within our Constitution. Upon this foundation we have built entire worlds of doctrine and constitutional theory.

It may come as something of a surprise, then, that a number of highly respected constitutional scholars have, in recent years, sought to undermine both premises.[2] These scholars are appropriately labeled "modernists" because they remind one of the architectural modernists who defiantly spurned tradition in favor of naked—and aesthetically displeasing—functionalism in the early twentieth century.[3] Architectural modernism was known for its determined rejection of history and tradition, free from the "idealization and imitation of some past era."[4] It disclaimed ornamentation and symbolism, which for centuries had been rightly understood as central to architecture's identity as a practical and necessary craft of urban design that was also, at its roots, an aesthetic practice steeped in artistry.[5]

Similarly, two sets of modernist constitutional commentators have proposed theories that reject the long-accepted tradition of American constitutionalism on the basis of different forms of naked functionalism. In one camp, self-described "constitutional realists" have variously claimed varying positions on one basic assertion: that constitutions are composed of those laws, norms, and practices that principally define the relationship between the people and their government and delineate the nation-state's power structure. On the basis of this premise, they argue, the American Constitution is simultaneously both more and less than the piece of parchment upon which our nation inscribed our supreme law in the late eighteenth century. It is less, insofar as there are provisions of the Constitution that are neither respected nor closely adhered to, and that have thus been effectively written out of the Constitution by oversight or indignity. It is more, insofar as other laws and movements—powerful and meaningful ones that the American public views as fundamental to our relationship with our government, but that were never codified in the document at the founding or thereafter by formal amendment—are nonetheless appropriately deemed to possess constitutional status. Surely no one can dispute, for example, that on a purely practical level, the Civil Rights Act of 1964 has had a more profound impact on social and governmental ordering in the United States than, say, the Third Amendment[6] or the Emoluments Clause.[7]

In another contrarian modernist camp are those scholars who, while not denying the unique supremacy of the Constitution, nevertheless challenge the premise that our constitutional regime provides for a judiciary that is uniquely empowered and specially equipped to serve as the final arbiter of constitutional interpretation. Whether by legal or originalist argument[8] or by observational or normative means,[9] these "departmentalists" and "popular constitutionalists" contend that the constitutional democracy the Framers devised was not built to support effective, enforceable judicial review. Departmentalists make the descriptive originalist argument that the Constitution envisioned all three branches as possessing equivalent power, and that allowing the judiciary's interpretation of the Constitution to bind the other two branches upsets the balance of coequal power. Popular constitutionalists, on the other hand, make the normative argument that judicial supremacy is deleterious to the democratic vision of American constitutionalism. Observing that judicial review and supremacy were not explicitly provided for in the Constitution, and that courts often act in concert with majority views, despite their freedom from democratic oversight, these scholars understand our constitutional system to accept majoritarian authority over constitutional meaning and enforcement.

This is uncharted territory to be sure; constitutional realists, departmentalists, and popular constitutionalists are nothing if not innovative. But there is a reason that this territory has remained uncharted for so long: those who would depart from the premises that have long served as the undergirding of American constitutional law fundamentally misunderstand the unique virtues of American constitutionalism. Our Constitution was specially designed with an eye to protecting the people against tyranny in all its possible forms (including the majoritarian form), and theories that either obscure the nature of the Constitution or misunderstand its structural guarantee undermine America's most meaningful and significant contribution to political theory. In this chapter, I urge a return to a sort of traditionalism because this view uniquely understands that our Constitution (1) was written down, (2) in a single place, (3) to enshrine a constitutional democracy that would effectively balance our competing interests in celebrating majority interests with the need to protect minority rights.

The traditionalist view of American constitutionalism, however, was a premise rather than a reasoned conclusion. Literature explicating the traditionalist view is sparse because it went without saying that our Constitution was . . . well, our Constitution. But if one asks, "What *is* the American Constitution?" we can find the answer by examining how it came to be and why the government was formed the way it was formed. What were its causes, and what were its aims? This ought not be an "originalist" inquiry, in which we seek to discern original intent or original meaning purely by way of excavation and historical research. An originalist inquiry inherently gives rise to often insurmountable archaeological difficulties, and would require a different kind of scholarly methodology than is consistent with our lawyerly training.[10] The historical origins of our constitutional system lend some clarity in defining the borders of our constitutional framework, but simple reverse engineering does more of the theoretical work. Traditionalist theory considers the broad animating purpose of the Constitution and concludes, based on an assessment of clues derived from historical context and the document's structural design elements, that the American method is a very particular type of constitutionalism, uniquely defined by its countermajoritarianism.[11]

One might properly describe this theory as "premodern," because it presents a defense of the traditionalist view that probably could not have been fashioned prior to the modernist revolution. Modernist constitutionalism presents arguments that American constitutionalism is not fundamentally defined by a singular written proclamation of the supreme positive law of the land, entrenched against majoritarian choices and pathology by inclusion of a prophylactically insulated judiciary empowered with the final say as to the document's meaning. But both types of modernism misconceive the nature of the American system. The premodern theory revives the traditionalist view, advancing its underlying values by considered rejection of modernist alternatives.[12] The premodern view fortifies traditionalism by articulating the essence of American constitutionalism through exploration of the logical missteps at the heart of modernist theories and the dangerous nature of the consequences that would ensue if their views were accepted.

The Framers made a conscious decision to write our Constitution down. This was an intentional break from the British tradition, and it represented an affirmative choice. Founding Era America's resolution to break from the British tradition of "unwritten" constitutionalism[13] was truly striking and should play a meaningful role in forming a present-day understanding of the American Constitution. America's decision to break from the British model has been hailed as the impetus for a great constitutional revolution, and many in the nineteenth century trumpeted the work of the Founders as out-of-nowhere, momentary brilliance.[14] But the truth is that, in the words of one scholar, the American Constitution came to be in a manner no different from other constitutions around the world: it was "a result of actual circumstances of the past and present, and not a product of abstract political theorizing."[15] In fact, the idea of employing a single written document has been attributed to the existence of state constitutions and corporate charters at the time of the framing.[16] The Constitution "was no empty product of political theory," but was rather "a growth, or . . . a selection from a great number of growths then before the Convention."[17]

The animating force behind this growth was the pervasive fear of tyranny. *The Federalist* paints a picture of a Founding Era obsession with the dangers of tyranny; Hamilton and Madison saw it lurking behind every corner and under every bed.[18] Each measure the Founders took in the course of building the new federal government was aimed at safeguarding the young nation and future generations of Americans from oppression in any form—tyranny of the majority, of the minority, of an aristocracy, of plutocracy, or of the intellectual elite. When the Framers gathered in Philadelphia in 1787 to reconstitute the federal government, they sculpted a constitutional document that would provide for checks and balances between the branches of government, would be entrenched against simple majoritarian change, and would serve as the supreme law against which the validity of government action could be measured. The written Constitution and the fact of its writtenness inescapably demonstrate the Founders' unique understanding of humankind's potential for both flourish and folly.

The Constitution is positive law. It does not merely set forth and structure the exercise of public power; rather, it establishes and imposes on the polity a set of rules and norms. Moreover, it designates enforcement mechanisms against both its subjects and its implementers. For a nation primarily concerned at the Founding with prophylactic avoidance of tyranny in a largely heterogeneous society, the writtenness and countermajoritarian entrenchment of the Constitution are both logical and fundamental. There was real structural brilliance to the constitutional regime that was created with the ratification of our Constitution. For Americans, the Constitution performs four vital and overlapping functions. The document is descriptive, aspirational, structural, and checking. The descriptive Constitution sets forth the aspirations and purposes of our constitutional regime. The structural Constitution sets up the processes of our government. And the checking Constitution preserves the democratic process through the supermajoritarian limitation on majority rule.

The prophylactically insulated judiciary is the beating heart of the structural brilliance that defines American constitutionalism. Indeed, once the nation chose to adopt a Constitution that was to be in written form, mandatory, and countermajoritarian, it was essential that the final say as to the document's meaning and the authority to enforce its provisions be vested in the insulated judiciary. It was thus no accident that a nation born of a revolution fought for political accountability chose to make one of the three branches of its fledgling national government completely insulated from public accountability: only by including an entirely insulated judicial branch could this democratic republic be protected from itself. Democracy inherently embodies a belief in human flourishing, in the people's ability to control their own destinies by participating and believing in representative government. But by establishing a politically unaccountable coequal judiciary branch, the Framers acknowledged that human flourishing could not be optimally accommodated if majorities were permitted to rule unchecked. Concerned primarily with thwarting the threat of tyranny in any form, the Framers created a Constitution that enshrined as supreme law a uniquely American form of what is best described as "skeptical optimism"—optimism that an empowered majority could achieve both great prosperity and personal growth, tempered by recognition that majorities tend to oppress minorities. To implement this skeptical optimism, the Constitution was structured around the political apparatus of countermajoritarian checking of majoritarian power. The choice to include an insulated judiciary was a meaningful one, and that judiciary's ability to provide prophylaxis was the key to achieving the Constitution's devised ends. Without a countermajoritarian judiciary armed with the power of judicial review, the entire design of our national government would be meaningless, or worse. Without the insulated judiciary authoritatively interpreting the Constitution, the structural Constitution would create an *appearance* of countermajoritarian checking of majoritarian impulses that in reality would amount to nothing more than illusion.

The first section of this chapter describes the traditional conception of American constitutionalism. Traditionalism depends upon historical context to define the principle at the core of our form of constitutionalism and depends upon reverse engineering from the structural Constitution to pinpoint the apparatus fundamental to converting that idea into political philosophy. Much of the explanation of traditionalism relies on straightforward examination of the historical context within which the Constitution came into existence and the structures embedded in it. In this way, the analysis can focus on the core principle animating our constitutional regime without reliance on the type of archaeological excavation required to advance an originalist argument.[19] The traditionalist model of American constitutionalism is the common sense explanation for our structural Constitution. The system delineated by our unique written document can only be explained by the notion that the core of American constitutionalism is a skeptical optimism that balances representative governance against meaningful countermajoritarian checks designed to control that government.

The section that follows explores the two prominent modernist attacks on the traditional view of American constitutionalism. By "modernist" is meant the revisionist views of American constitutionalism proposed in recent years by a number of highly respected constitutional theorists. This section first examines constitutional realism and its argument that the entrenched, written Constitution does not comprise the totality of higher law in the United States.[20] It then proceeds to confront the modernist theories, known as "departmentalism," that question, not whether the written Constitution represents the full extent of our higher law, but rather whether American constitutionalism requires or even permits ultimate majoritarian enforcement and interpretation. The section explains why departmentalists are wrong to oppose the idea that countermajoritarian judicial supremacy is fundamental to American constitutionalism, and how popular constitutionalists err in arguing that majorities are better suited to interpret our supreme law.[21]

The third section explains the meaning of "premodern" constitutionalism. American constitutionalism is properly defined, not only by skeptical optimism and countermajoritarianism, but also by the two activating mechanisms that have come under modernist attack. The Constitution is a written document that serves descriptive and prescriptive purposes, provides for mutual checking of powers among the branches, and balances the ideals of human flourishing against the evils inherent in human nature. The written document is entrenched against the choices of temporary majorities, and the prophylactically insulated judiciary is designed to protect constitutionally guaranteed minority interests. The premodern model of constitutionalism advocated here urges a revival of traditionalism based on a critique of and reaction to the problems associated with all forms of modernism, as well as the troubling consequences that would inevitably flow from adoption of either of them.

It should be emphasized that none of this is to say that the insulated judiciary always checks majoritarian action perfectly or even effectively; indeed, the Supreme Court's actions have all too often demonstrated that it is far from infallible and may fail to protect minority interests against majority oppression.[22] But despite these lapses, the judiciary for the most part does abide by our Constitution as higher law. At the very least, unlike the executive branch, the judiciary is not a threat to impose its will through sheer military force, and unlike the legislative branch, it is not directly subject to the political pressures imposed by the whims and prejudices of the electorate. Thus, the system our Constitution deploys, through an entrenched countermajoritarian document and a prophylactically insulated judiciary empowered to interpret and enforce it, represents a structurally superior method of protecting against harmful majoritarian choices and tyranny. If there is some truth to the notion that humankind has extraordinary potential both to flourish and to oppress, then the traditionalist form of American constitutionalism—fundamentally, countermajoritarian checking of majoritarian power designed to preserve the rule of law activated through a written, supreme positive law and a prophylactically insulated judicial interpreter—is well tailored to implement it.

TRADITIONALIST CONSTITUTIONALISM REVISITED: STRUCTURAL CHOICES WITH HISTORICAL EXPLANATIONS

One of the most challenging tasks one faces in developing a premodern theory of American constitutionalism is pinpointing the traditionalism to which a return is urged. There is no rich literature devoted to defense or development of the traditionalist model. Our Constitution employs a variety of tools and structures to achieve its underlying aim of defining a balance of powers built to avoid tyranny. For years, the scholarly debate focused squarely on what those tools and structures were, what were their nature and limitations, and how those tools were to be properly utilized.[23] Formalists argued with functionalists over the best use of our constitutional regime's implementational tools, but they never argued about the underlying principles for which those tools existed in the first place.[24] Traditionalism has long been essentially a root assumption, not a logically reasoned conclusion.

For this reason, before examining the development of the two modernist views of American constitutionalism, it is necessary to explicate the traditionalist model. Traditionalist theory holds that the core of American constitutionalism is countermajoritarian checking of majoritarian power. In order to implement this vision, the proposed framework relies upon a structural written Constitution subject only to supermajoritarian modification and a prophylactically insulated judiciary, which is to act as the final arbiter of the document's meaning. This structure is uniquely suited to strike a crucial balance embodying skeptical optimism. On the one hand, our Constitution optimistically establishes representative government through the granting of a series of majoritarian powers, recognizing the continuing value of republican state governments in a federalist system, granting legislative authority to a representative Congress, and extending executive power to an elected president. Empowering majorities in this fashion grants freedom to the people to realize their potential and to flourish. On the other hand, our Constitution provides a series of countermajoritarian checks, the most important of which is the insulated Article III judiciary, designed to safeguard minority views against majoritarian overreach and ensuring that the supreme law against which the legality of all other laws is measured may be formally altered only by legal supermajoritarian action.

Put differently, the traditionalist view of American constitutionalism understands our nation's contribution to political theory as the construction of a regime that, due to its dedication to countermajoritarianism, uniquely implements its optimism that humankind can flourish if empowered. At the same time, it is determined by its skepticism that unchecked empowerment will naturally devolve into tyranny.

The Core Principle: Skeptical Optimism

Traditionalist constitutionalism consists of two fundamental elements. The first is the core principle at the heart of American constitutionalism, which can be found in the historical context from which our Constitution sprang. The second is the political apparatus effectuating that principle, which is embedded in the structural Constitution itself and is best proven by a form of reverse engineering.

First, reference to the historical context within which the Framers operated to develop our Constitution reveals the principal concerns that guided its construction. Breaking free from Britain was not merely an act of defiance of King George. It was also an act of defiance of a system of governance that was unacceptably unrepresentative of American colonists and unconcerned with protecting minority interests against majority rule.[25] Britain was a monarchy, of course, but its governmental structure made its majoritarian branch supreme. "Parliamentary sovereignty" firmly defined the British system of governance. Britain had no written constitution or formally entrenched higher law.[26] Legal change in Britain was left entirely to the discretion of Parliament, a legislative body empowered to enact ordinary legislation *and* ultimately to determine the legality and legitimacy of such legislation, for the same majority necessary to pass legislation had the power to override any judicial determination of illegality.

The Constitution thus was developed within the context of two countervailing sentiments. On the one hand, the Framing generation knew that in order to facilitate the human capacity for flourishing and to ensure that American society could achieve its potential, our new nation would need a strong, majoritarian, representative government that empowered the people. On the other hand, the Framers were well aware of both world history and their nation's own recent history. They understood that humankind is just as disposed to folly as to flourish and that concentration of power in the majority, even when representative, could easily devolve into tyranny. This "skeptical optimism" became the core driving force of American constitutionalism.

The Apparatus: Countermajoritarian Checking of Majoritarian Power

The second element of the traditionalist model is the political apparatus devised to implement the skeptical optimism at the heart of our nation's form of constitutionalism. The Framers' skeptical optimism is readily apparent in Founding Era literature and is embedded in the history of both the American Revolution and the Founding. But its political apparatus is best explicated by reverse engineering from the structural Constitution itself.

With the historical realities motivating their skeptical optimism in full view, the Framers made two crucial decisions about how the American constitutional system would be shaped. First, in a decisive break from the British tradition, America would have a written Constitution that would serve as its singular, supreme law. And second, that Constitution would, by its terms and design, establish an empowered but limited federal government.[27] The Constitution the Framers produced was a direct response to parliamentary sovereignty's potential for tyranny,[28] an affirmative statement of the new republic's constitutive law, and an effort to balance the states' interests in maintaining a degree of autonomy with the establishment of a strong enough national government to preserve national economic and political health in the global community.[29]

The structures that were chosen to implement this vision of American governance are themselves quite revealing of the principles at the heart of our constitutionalism. The Constitution was foundational, prescriptive, and aspirational, but it was primarily built to deter the accumulation of power in a single branch or system.[30] Although dedicated to preserving some level of state sovereignty, the Constitution vested executive power in an elected president and legislative authority in a full-fledged, permanent, bicameral Congress. Although it foundationally empowered each of the majoritarian branches, it sought also to guard against domination by faction and, shortly after ratification, codified a Bill of Rights affirmatively setting forth a list of negative individual rights based on the most cherished bedrock principles of our new constitutional republic. And most important of all, despite their unwavering commitment to representative democracy and political accountability, the Framers conferred the judicial power in writing to a judicial branch that would, for all practical purposes, be politically unaccountable.

Traditionalism finds its strongest support in basic logic grounded in reverse engineering: there is simply no good explanation for the momentous decision to break from the British tradition and write our Constitution down in mandatory language, proclaim the supremacy of the Constitution as positive law, make it subject to alteration only through a complex supermajoritarian process, and create a politically unaccountable judiciary charged with constitutional interpretation. Creation of one of the three branches as a prophylactically insulated body in a nation established on the promise of representationalism was no accident. The political apparatus at the core of our constitutionalism was quite clearly a system of countermajoritarian checking of majoritarian power.

There are, to be sure, a variety of ways in which constitutional regimes may practice constitutionalism, because constitutionalism is defined simply by the existence of a code of clear and identifiable foundational principles of government and social ordering, not by the means a regime uses to establish, implement, and enforce it.[31] Whether a constitution is written or unwritten, or whether it provides for pure majoritarian rule or envisions a countermajoritarian check, it can still potentially constitute a legitimate exercise of constitutionalist governance.[32]

Modernist scholars who study constitutionalism seek to celebrate general substance over particular form, holding that constitutions are the laws and norms that structure a people's relationship with its government and define how government can exercise public power.[33] John Ferejohn and Lawrence Sager have written that "constitutional practices can usefully be understood as commitment devices," methods for governments to express (to both citizens and outsiders/creditors) their commitments to protecting private property, recognizing unpopular minorities, or furthering the rule of law.[34] David Law has likewise defined constitutions "as the set of rules and practices—written or otherwise—that allocates, and structures the exercise of, public power."[35]

Structuring a nation's political powers, defining a nation's most cherished individual rights, and ensuring that the government provides a mechanism for protecting liberty are all key aspects of the process of codifying government power and limitation through constitutionalism.[36] But today's understanding of constitutionalism suggests that nations have a variety of options to do this. Ultimately, whether a regime employs a form of constitutionalism and whether a given constitutional regime is legitimate are entirely different questions. Some regimes that employ a written constitution with affirmative guarantees as to government structure and individual rights fail to live up to the promises enshrined in their constitutions.[37] Other regimes with no bill of rights or designated higher law have proven "legitimate" by constitutionalist standards because they otherwise identify the principles of law that constrain their governments and provide for the well-being of their governed.

The point to be emphasized is that despite the changing conception of what a nation must do to actually have a constitution and adhere to constitutionalism as its political dogma, American constitutionalism has always been defined by its structural design and underlying goods.[38] The two are inseparable. The American Constitution was not written simply to establish and define the relationship between the government and the governed (though it surely does that); rather, it was written primarily to effectuate a specific, very particular relationship, premised on a form of universal and mutual distrust. Other nations have chosen alternative ways to establish, implement, and enshrine their codes of bedrock principle, but this does not automatically make them any less "constitutionalist," at least on an abstract, definitional level. But the traditionalist view recognizes that American constitutionalism is, at its core, about enshrining countermajoritarianism.

To be sure, merely providing for an insulated judiciary is not necessarily the same as providing for prophylactically insulated judicial review or judicial supremacy. Scholars have puzzled over the basis of judicial review for quite some time. There is nothing written into the Constitution explicitly stating that there must be judicial enforcement of the metes and bounds of constitutional directives, either between the states and the federal government or between the federal government's coequal branches. It seems as though in order for traditionalism to have any real meaning, there must be some textual basis for judicial review.

For what it is worth, judicial review appears to have been assumed by the Framers at the time of ratification. Alexander Hamilton consciously sought to switch the textual inertia in *Federalist* No. 78, taking notice of the importance of judicial review and essentially suggesting that unless the text of our new Constitution foreswore judicial review, it should logically be inferred to be part and parcel of the exercise of judicial power under Article III.[39] But judicial review may arguably find its textual basis in the "arising under" language of Article III: by giving the judiciary the power to adjudicate "all cases, in Law and Equity, arising under this Constitution, the Laws of the United States, and Treaties made, or which shall be made, under their Authority,"[40] the Constitution empowered the judicial branch to enforce the Constitution's limits and ensure both vertical power-checking (constitutional federalism and supremacy enforcement) and horizontal power-checking (separation of powers).

Yet another conceivable textual basis for at least the bulk of judicial review is the guarantee of due process contained in the Fifth and

Fourteenth Amendments.[41] Both amendments forbid governmental deprivation of life, liberty, or property without due process of law.[42] The argument that this codifies judicial review can be framed in one of two ways. First, it could be asserted that any time individual rights to liberty, property, or life are placed at risk, a neutral, independent adjudicator is a fundamental component of the due process guarantee. This rationale works well when a right guaranteed by the Constitution is at stake. But the direct link between a structural infringement (by one branch upon another or by the federal government upon the states) and the infringement of a liberty interest protected by the Due Process Clause is, some might argue, problematically attenuated.

The other way to frame due process as the textual basis for judicial review is to argue that any litigant who satisfies Article III's standing requirement of injury in fact, or who stands to lose property by way of a damages award in a case or controversy, has a due process right to an independent adjudicator. From this perspective, due process is not triggered by the nature of the particular claim being brought, but by the fact that a property interest is at stake—regardless of the substantive basis for the litigant's claim. Alternatively, it could be argued that judicial review arises out of constitutional due process in two other, related ways: first, in disputes with or between governmental branches, adjudication must be neutral; and, second, under Chief Justice Marshall's private rights model, deciding constitutional meaning is incident to deciding cases in which constitutional issues are raised.[43]

Herbert Wechsler proposed the Supremacy Clause[44] as the textual anchor for judicial review.[45] His argument was that in textually declaring the Constitution the supreme law of the land, the Constitution itself demanded judicial review.[46] Yet this theory is problematically question begging. Yes, the Supremacy Clause dictates that the Constitution shall be the supreme law of the land, but that says nothing about which branch gets to say what that Constitution means. It can sensibly be said to imply the judiciary's role in enforcing vertical power-checking, but without acknowledgement of the logical implication that Hamilton recognized in *Federalist* No. 78,[47] the question of the judiciary's role as a means of prophylaxis against horizontal breaches remains unresolved.

In truth, the most logical explanation of judicial review is common sense, logic, and reverse engineering from the structural Constitution itself. The Constitution was the product of debate and coordination among a group of people who sought a break from the unrepresentative government of England, who feared faction,[48] and who worried about the tyranny of accumulated power. Yet despite the Founders' deep-seated belief in representative government, the Constitution provided for a federal judiciary that was insulated from majoritarian whim in three ways: the judicial branch would be staffed by unelected judges who would serve for life with salary protections, and who would only be removable on impeachment or for bad behavior. In other words, the judiciary would be structurally unaccountable. No logical explanation exists for the provision of an unaccountable judiciary except the obvious one: that the entrenched, countermajoritarian Constitution would need an insulated, prophylactic judiciary to police its structural mandate and its supremacy.[49] By defining our supreme law in a single Constitution that provides for countermajoritarian check by a prophylactically insulated judiciary, American constitutionalism is uniquely tailored to create a formal barrier against slipping into tyranny.

THE MODERNIST DEPARTURES FROM THE TRADITIONALIST POSITION

American constitutionalism is, at its core, the embodiment of skeptical optimism in a political apparatus of countermajoritarian checking of majoritarian power. This is effectuated by enshrining our highest law in an entrenched written document subject to formal revision only by means of supermajoritarian amendment, whose limitations are subject to enforcement by an insulated countermajoritarian interpreter (the judiciary). Subsequent debates about the mechanics of implementing this vision typically skip explaining or defending this first step because it is simply taken for granted.

In recent years, however, scholars have developed two forms of what can be properly called modernist theory. While acceptance of these theories in the courts is all but nonexistent, highly esteemed commentators have taken up their cause, and a wealth of literature has sprung forth advancing their arguments. Modernist scholars have engaged in an attack on the theoretical foundations located in step one, essentially challenging the nature of our constitutionalism itself. "Constitutional realists" and proponents of the "extracanonical constitution" challenge the premise that the complete American constitutional regime is set forth in the singular written document we identify as the Constitution.[50] "Departmentalists" and "popular constitutionalists," on the other hand, seem to acknowledge the value and weight of our written Constitution as the complete source of our supreme positive law, but dispute the role of the judiciary and thus our Constitution's countermajoritarian roots.[51]

Puzzlingly, scholars in each of these two camps devote virtually no attention to one another. But they are more alike than they realize, for they both misidentify the fundamental characteristic that makes our constitutionalism ours. Both of these classes of scholar are appropriately referred to as "modernists," because both mark a clear break from the traditionalist view of American constitutionalism identified here.[52] Unfortunately, both scholarly groups advocate approaches that, for reasons outlined below, must be largely rejected.

CONSTITUTIONAL REALISM AND THE EXTRACANONICAL CONSTITUTION

In the late eighteenth century, the Founders understood the Constitution to embody the sum total of American supreme law.[53] One hundred years later, as the people rejoiced in the centennial anniversary of the Constitution's ratification, commentators hailed the uniqueness of the American constitutional regime. The power of the American Constitution, they wrote with reverence, lay in its brilliant duality: a written document enacted by the people, but entrenched against change and not subject to the shifting choices of momentary majorities.[54] Use of the written format was key, "for how would it be possible to argue upon the constitutionality of any measure, when there was no constitution in existence?"[55]

The story of the American Constitution told by a number of highly regarded twentieth and twenty-first century constitutional scholars, however, is strikingly different. Starting with Karl Llewellyn, the twentieth century saw scholars adopt what they termed a "realist" view of the Constitution.[56] Llewellyn argued that the Constitution's text and the system set forth therein constitutes our government only insofar as modern practice and conventions continue to perpetuate their reign.[57] His primary argument was that the only elements of the Constitution that live on today are those to which modern Americans continue to adhere.[58] Moreover, he argued, the Constitution itself was merely an experimental first step towards creating a constitutional institution—a broad code of behavior and norms that structures the relationship between the people and their government.[59]

Recent constitutional history contributed to the scholarly shift to constitutional realism as well. This country has changed profoundly over the past one hundred and fifty years, but change has largely been effected *outside* of the constitutional amendment procedure. Article V was written to require supermajoritarian action to achieve constitutional amendment precisely because the Constitution was our supreme law.[60] Those elements of positive law that we mustered the strength to etch into stone would be emblematic of our most cherished values and would safeguard the spoils of social progress against arbitrary repeal or reversal. Yet the reality is that since the years following the Reconstruction amendments, most (though by no means all) of our greatest political and legal achievements have been implemented by ways other than resort to the amendment process of Article V.[61]

The constitutional amendment process over the past century and a half has given Congress the power to levy an income tax,[62] established direct election of the Senate by popular vote,[63] granted women the right to vote,[64] enacted[65] and discarded prohibition on the manufacture and sale of alcohol,[66] changed the date the president takes office[67] and limited the number of terms she or he could serve,[68] granted electoral college votes to the District of Columbia,[69] and established the order of presidential succession.[70] Meanwhile, the country's changing perspective on individual liberties, which were quite clearly the focus of the Bill of Rights and the Reconstruction amendments, has become the law of the land mostly by way of statutes,[71] treaties,[72] and judicial decisions.[73] And the nation has implemented major changes to the general structure of the federal government outside of the constitutional amendment process as well, most notably in the broad expansion of the administrative state during and throughout the New Deal.[74] Article V amendment simply has not been the primary mechanism by which post-Reconstruction America implements major structural change or enshrines civil liberties.[75]

That great change has taken place without constitutional amendment to facilitate it is one of the central proof points for constitutional realists: because the American people have come to understand new constraints on government power without Article V amendment, they reason, the written document and its subsequent amendments and judicial interpretations cannot possibly form the "complete" American Constitution.[76] Instead, constitutional realists assert that the complete American Constitution must consist of something more diffuse and difficult to ascertain. Realist commentators throughout the academy have thus taken to challenging the value of the written Constitution, variously claiming that American constitutionalism consists of the Founding document *and* some combination of statutes, judicial precedents, treaties, constitutional understandings, social norms, movements, and conventions.[77]

To the extent that the realists are arguing that widespread *societal* practice may effectively *repeal* provisions contained in the formal document,
their argument may well give rise to serious moral problems. By that reasoning, presumably the long-standing existence of Jim Crow laws in the
post–Civil War South would constitute a repeal—at least regionally—of
the Fourteenth Amendment's Equal Protection Clause. This form of
"repeal by adverse possession" would of course defeat the purposes of having a written constitution in the first place. To the extent the realists are
arguing, not that the written Constitution may be *reduced* by widespread
practice but rather that it may be expanded by such practice, however, the
issue becomes more complex. That the United States has a written Constitution is beyond dispute. But the issue of whether the document written
in 1787 and subsequently amended twenty-seven times comprises the complete "United States Constitution" is, remarkably, far from settled.

Modernist theorists have argued that the *complete* American constitution is broader than the written document. Todd Pettys, for example, has
described the written Constitution as a "myth" because the three chief
functions the American Constitution serves—(1) creating, empowering,
and limiting the branches of the federal government; (2) establishing basic
rights that may be asserted against government action; and (3) providing
rules of recognition—are often accomplished by statutory or other non-
constitutional means.[78]

Bruce Ackerman takes a similar "alien visitor" angle. In the latest
addition to his *We the People* collection, Ackerman begins with a fictional
account of a conversation between himself and a hypothetical Middle East-
ern scholar who is ignorant of the Constitution and the history of American social change, but is otherwise a capable constitutional interpreter.
Professor Ackerman's imaginary student walks through the Constitution,
article by article and amendment by amendment, but cannot glean from
the Constitution alone how modern Americans understand their relationship with the federal government. Ackerman rightly points out that an
alien with no knowledge of American history or custom could learn a
great deal about U.S. constitutional law by reading the original document
and Bill of Rights, but would likely give added weight and faulty historical significance to provisions that are either unimportant or misleading.[79]
Likewise, he says, so limited a reading would fail to recognize the way
major social movements since the Founding have "informally amended"
the Constitution.

Professor Ackerman's theory revolves around the idea that on occasion
popular sovereignty leads to a groundswell, from movement to party to

president, and that at the end of a five-step process of signaling, proposal, triggering, ratifying, and consolidation, the people engage in informal constitutional amendment. These "constitutional moments" change the meaning of the Constitution in some permanent way. He argues that one such moment occurred through the legislative action that took place during the brief window in time from 1935 to 1938, after which Americans accepted the New Deal and the basically limitless nature of the Commerce Clause.[80] Professor Ackerman sees signaling in the election of Roosevelt and the popular movement behind him; he sees the growth of an active federal government that can truly regulate commercial activity as the proposal; triggering in Roosevelt's first reelection; ratification in Roosevelt's second reelection (even in spite of his Supreme Court–packing plan); and consolidation when, in later years, even the Republicans simply accepted the new Rooseveltian federal government as constitutionally permissible.[81] In his latest volume, Ackerman argues that the civil rights movement and the passage of the Civil Rights Act together form another of his "constitutional moments."[82] Asserting that the same five-step process of informal amendment occurred in the 1960s, he says the Voting Rights Act, the Civil Rights Act, and the progress this country made during the civil rights revolution have been constitutionalized—even though they appear nowhere within the text of the document. "I am taking the next step," he says, "urging you to discard the residual *quasis* and other hesitations and grant *full constitutional status to the landmark statutes of the civil rights revolution*. Otherwise, our view of this great American triumph will be profoundly distorted."[83]

Ernest Young has similarly employed Llewellyn's realist logic to pinpoint what he calls "the Constitution outside the Constitution." According to Professor Young, because some statutes, treaties, conventions, and norms are "constitutive" in their form and their function, they can be said to be part of the broader American Constitution.[84] Specifically relying on Llewellyn and other early constitutional realists, Professor Young argues that "the role of ordinary law in constitutional ordering is pervasive" and thus a complete understanding of the American Constitution requires interpreters to look beyond the Constitution as formally enacted.[85] He points to a handful of statutes including the Clean Water Act of 1976 and explains that because they serve a government-ordering function and help to define our relationship with our government, they form part of the American Constitution.[86] Professor Young and other realists argue that because other statutes share traits with the Constitution—by creating government, conferring individual rights, and being (at least somewhat) entrenched against change—they can be said to be part of the broader constitutional picture in the United States.[87]

All of this amounts to self and public deception. Constitutional realists challenge the fundamental import of the Constitution's writtenness while purporting to leave intact the underlying principles at the core of the American vision. They do not deny, for example, that the judiciary is possessed of interpretive power, that the structures contained within the document serve checking purposes, or that the convention produced a document of meaningful constitutive value. Even if all of this is true, however, they argue that we have not necessarily located all of our nation's constitutive law in the written document.

The trouble with this argument is that in order to arrive at their conclusion that the written document need not embody the entirety of American constitutive law, constitutional realists necessarily disclaim skeptical optimism and countermajoritarianism as defining characteristics of American constitutionalism. Professor Pettys's three chief functions of the American Constitution are fine descriptions of some of its principal attributes, but ordinary legislation enacted by the majoritarian process of bicameralism and presentment serves those functions in a categorically different fashion. Unlike rights and dictates actually grounded in the text of the Constitution, all of these statutes, no matter how fundamental we currently deem them to be, may be repealed by the traditionally majoritarian legislative process, which requires only bicameralism and presentment. And we know this to be true—ironically—because the *real* Constitution tells us so.

The idea that much of our politically and legally transformative law has been subconstitutional is perfectly consistent with the concept of constitutional democracy. The formal amendment process was purposely made extremely difficult in order to prevent the current views of the prevailing majority from being given constitutional status, because such change binds future majorities. It is only when the alteration is truly foundational that it is to receive formal constitutional status. As a result, on most occasions when majoritarian preferences are transformed into law, they are just as easily subject to future modification due to changes in those preferences. Except for truly foundational matters that have received formal constitutional status, democracy permits nothing else.

Perhaps the modern realists are engaged in a game of semantics. Maybe they have chosen simply to equate law that is so ingrained in our nation's tradition that it is reasonably characterized as "fundamental" with law dictated by the Constitution. But while both forms of law could plausibly be characterized as "fundamental," that does not mean that the two forms of law are legally and structurally identical. The 1964 Civil Rights Act can be repealed if majorities in both houses of Congress vote to do so and the president signs that bill. The First Amendment, in stark contrast, may *not* be repealed in this manner. Rather, it may be repealed only by compliance with the extremely demanding requirements of Article V. We presume that even Professors Ackerman and Young would have to concede as much. Indeed, if they are unsure of this conclusion, a recent graduate of an eighth grade civics course could confirm it for them.[88]

Insofar as ordinary legislation limits federal governmental power or establishes basic rights that may be asserted against the government, one must ask how truly effective those limits are and how basic the rights established actually are if temporary majorities can easily erase them. To be sure, the Civil Rights Act of 1964 was a powerful piece of legislation, which undoubtedly expanded minority rights and took a dramatic step towards perfecting the vision of the Reconstruction amendments. And it is true that given current political realities, it is highly unlikely that it will be subject to repeal, at least in the foreseeable future. But American constitutionalism is premised on the idea that mere political improbability is not a sufficient safeguard against the tyranny of temporary majorities. Every trace of the prophylactic skepticism that the traditionalist view places at the heart of our constitutionalism vanishes when one ascribes constitutional weight to ordinary legislation.

Moreover, any new federal power established by majoritarian act can be nullified by the Court for noncompliance with the enumerated powers contained in the written Constitution. It is easy to say that because of its profound impact on the process of selecting the people who will serve as our representatives in the federal government and its powerful role in defining the relationship between people of color and their government, the Voting Rights Act is a piece of constitutive law.[89] But reality belies realism, as was made clear by the Court in *Shelby County v. Holder*, in which the Court held unconstitutional Congress's method of implementing a key provision of the law because it violated the structural federalism set forth in the Constitution.[90]

One might reasonably suggest that if we want to insulate legislation such as the 1964 Civil Rights Act from the choices of future majorities, we should constitutionalize it through Article V's formal amendment process. But purely as a matter of streetwise politics, it is virtually inconceivable that this would ever happen at any time in the foreseeable future. The reason, ironically, is that as presently structured, the current Congress would probably never provide the requisite majority, and if it were to do so, it is extremely doubtful that the requisite supermajority of state legislatures would concur.

Constitutional realism is not only descriptively wrong, it is also normatively undesirable, if for no other reason than that it renders ambiguous at best and incoherent at worst a constitutional regime whose simplicity at its core is one of its great virtues. If the Voting Rights Act was part of an informal process of constitutional amendment or is part of our broader American Constitution, was *Shelby County* also a judicial act of constitutional amendment? Who gets to decide when a "constitutional moment" has taken place?[91]

Moreover, the danger of ideological manipulation plagues any attempt to extend the "constitutional" label beyond the four corners of the actual document.[92] It is perhaps telling that Professor Ackerman grants constitutional significance to the New Deal and the legislation arising out of the civil rights movement, but not to the Alien and Sedition Acts, the Internal Security Act of 1950, or the PATRIOT Act—all three of which served to change the nature of the relationship between the government and the governed, all three of which had profound impacts on the exercise of federal power, and all three of which contravene liberal values. Because of its inherently vague contours, constitutional realism provides the opportunity for people to engage in all sorts of definitional subterfuge to advance their own political ideals.

What is most striking about the realist approach is, ironically, just how unrealistic it is. Realist scholars assert that some aspects of the written Constitution are borderline irrelevant because they are not significant in defining the way the government exercises public power. Likewise, they say, some extracanonical laws and norms are now to be deemed woven into the Constitution itself. But one need look no further than the *Supreme Court Reporter* to see how our Supreme Court engages in all kinds of linguistic contortionism just to stay within the boundaries set up by the written document. The very purpose of "realism" is to look past formality to acknowledge what is actually happening in the world and describe things as they are, but neither citizens nor the Court understand the statutes, movements, or social norms that supposedly comprise the American "constitution outside the Constitution" to actually function as our constitutive law in the same legally binding way the Constitution does. If the Court understood our Constitution as the realists do, there would be no reason to search for an individual right to bear arms in the Second Amendment[93] or a right of privacy in the penumbras of the Bill of Rights.[94] Nor would there have been a reason either for conservative justices to have grounded the concept of economic freedom—anomalously—in the Due Process Clause,[95] or later decisions to reject the doctrine for the very reason that it has no basis in text.[96]

All told, constitutional realism is unrealistic because it minimizes the role of our written Constitution and extends constitutional status to laws that can indisputably be altered or repealed by majoritarian action. It therefore confuses the boundary between supreme and inferior law in this country. Lawmakers, the American people, and the Supreme Court have always understood the Constitution as setting forth a dictated framework that, while subject to changing interpretation by a countermajoritarian judiciary, at its outer limits may only be changed by a difficult supermajoritarian process. The American Constitution has always been accepted as specifically removed from change by majoritarian process, and even in the context of the New Deal—the closest thing to majoritarian process changing our constitutional framework—the Court never openly ignored constitutional directives. A somewhat later example is *Griswold v. Connecticut*: even when it has recognized rights *never before found and with no textual basis in the Constitution*, the Court went out of its way to ground its decision in the written Constitution (in that case, gleaning an individual right to privacy from somewhere in the intersection of provisions of the Bill of Rights).[97]

To the realists, the divergent theories of "political" constitutionalism and "legal" constitutionalism came to be viewed as concurrently legitimate, despite their seemingly contradictory designs. Elements of each appear within the other, but the two approaches to constitutionalism are, at their roots, diametrically opposed. In her 2014 article about the British judiciary, Professor Erin Delaney identifies the fundamental difference between legal constitutionalism and political constitutionalism as located in "the institution or institutions entrusted with the responsibility for ensuring both accountability and governmental (and possibly societal) fidelity to the constitutional order," with political constitutionalists favoring nonjudicial means of doing so.[98]

It is significant that the credo of political constitutionalism is almost invariably "unwritten," or more precisely, contained in scattered sources rather than in a single comprehensive written document. In contrast, legal constitutionalism tends to look to a single source of supreme law. There are, to be sure, contrarian voices on both sides. Some scholars have argued that political constitutional regimes might have a role for courts to play and that political and social realities create a dynamic within these regimes that might expand and calcify the judicial role, and some others have offered that majoritarian influences should play a more significant role, and courts a lesser one, in legal constitutional regimes. Thus, perhaps as a general, nation-agnostic assessment of what comprises a constitution, realism makes some sense. But constitutional realism has led to what should be an impermissible logical next step: the practice of drawing lessons and importing values from nations for whom constitutionalism is not defined by the same core principles as our own.

Scholars lean on Llewellyn, Ackerman, Young and William Eskridge and John Ferejohn[99] to point out that a constitution is, above all else, the set of rules, standards, practices, and norms that compose the continuing understanding of how the government exercises power. If that is true, then the American Constitution might look a lot more like the British or Israeli constitutions than we realize, and might include a variety of ordinary laws and norms outside of our constitutional document. But as a matter of *American* constitutionalism, it seems at the very least misleading and more likely just categorically wrong to ascribe constitutional significance to extracanonical elements of our legal regime.

The word "Constitution" has traditionally possessed special meaning in the United States. It is a powerful word whose usage in political speech and legal argumentation amounts to a trump card. It is understood to be higher law, or the ground rules of the game, and it limits the scope of all other discussion of American law. A word might have a variety of definitions throughout the world, but sharing traits with the Constitution does not make these statutes part of the American Constitution. This is precisely because the United States Constitution is contained within a single document that provides for interpretation and enforcement as supreme by the insulated judiciary. That design lays the foundation for entrenchment, creation of government, and conferral of individual rights upon which politics, social movements, and legislation can build other elements of public power. By diminishing the importance of the written Constitution and ascribing constitutional significance to extraconstitutional directives, realist scholars destabilize a constitutional regime that is uniquely situated to achieve a very particular American constitutional mission. The "complete" American Constitution cannot include statutes such as the USA PATRIOT Act, the Civil Rights Act,[100] or the Clean Water Act[101] without diluting the power of our constitutional regime, especially because each of these laws can legally be displaced by simple majoritarian act.

Constitutional realists conflate the idea of constitutionalism evolving to accommodate other constitutional regimes with that of American constitutionalism evolving to include the other pieces of our code that implement our bedrock principles. But they fail to recognize that our form of constitutionalism does not allow for acknowledgment of bedrock principles in non–higher law statutes. This is because our method of promulgating a code that includes our bedrock principles and determining how we would like to create, implement, enforce, and protect that code is by means of a single comprehensive document that establishes a checking branch. Including other forms of law under the constitutional heading minimizes the uniqueness of our contribution to political theory, threatens to dilute the force of the *real* Constitution, and at best gives rise to enormous confusion and at worst, to cynical political manipulation.

Given the traditional American understanding of the term "Constitution," the concern is more than semantic, for to attribute constitutional weight to noncountermajoritarian elements of our legal and governmental system, regardless of the phrasing one uses, is downright deceptive. To the extent that the words "constitutional" and "constitution" retain their long-accepted American meaning, the realists are simply wrong. American constitutionalism is, at its very core, the practice of codifying countermajoritarian limits on majoritarian government. So long as those laws and norms that realists deem part of the "extracanonical constitution" are subject to modification by majoritarian processes, realists cannot be describing the "Constitution" in the American sense of the word. And we know the elements of the extracanonical constitution are subject to majoritarian change, ironically, because the Constitution itself authorizes majoritarian processes to bring about such change.

DEPARTMENTALISM AND POPULAR CONSTITUTIONALISM

Constitutional realists adopt the modernist view that the use of a singular written document to set forth the totality of our supreme constitutive law need not be viewed as a core characteristic of American constitutionalism. But these scholars do not purport to challenge the root principle or political apparatus embedded in the Constitution. It is unlikely that many of these scholars would deny that the document we call our Constitution contains a system of countermajoritarian checks on majority power (though, as noted earlier, if one took literally the idealists' identification of constitutionalism with accepted practice, this would not be true). Instead, they focus their energy primarily on arguing that the written Constitution is an incomplete capsule of our supreme law, both because some aspects of it are unimportant or defunct and because various laws and movements outside the document are politically entrenched and serve to define the relationship between the government and the governed.[102]

In contrast, another group of modernist scholars claims to understand and accept the countermajoritarian design of our Constitution and the value of such an apparatus, but proposes that another of the key methods of activating this countermajoritarian apparatus should not be considered central to our constitutionalism and should thus be abandoned. Rather than challenging whether the written Constitution is the sole source of our nation's supreme law (as the realists do), these scholars challenge the validity and worth of judicial review and supremacy. These scholars may generally be sorted into two subcategories: "departmentalists" and "popular constitutionalists." Departmentalists are those scholars who suggest that the Constitution neither commands nor permits judicial supremacy. They argue for equal measures of interpretive authority across all three branches of the government (and particularly emphasizing the role of the executive in constitutional interpretation).[103] Popular constitutionalists, on the other hand, do not argue that judicial supremacy is unconstitutional, but rather that it is normatively undesirable, and that because judicial review is not explicitly provided for in the Constitution's textual directives, constitutional interpretive authority can and should be transferred from the unrepresentative judiciary back to "the People."[104]

Both theories should be viewed with skepticism and concern. The pro-phylactically insulated judiciary is both an essential complement to and a logical outgrowth of the explicit textual commitment to the precept of countermajoritarianism. This nation was born of a revolution fought for political accountability but chose to completely insulate one of the three branches of its fledgling national government from public accountability, recognizing that a democratic republic could be protected from itself only in this way. Democracy embodies a belief in human flourishing, that the people can control their own destiny by participating and believing in their representative government. But by establishing a federal government featuring a politically unaccountable, coequal judicial branch, the Framers effectively acknowledged that unchecked majoritarian government would allow temporary majorities to stifle unpopular opinions and oppress minorities. Concerned primarily with thwarting the threat of tyranny in any form, the Framers constructed a Constitution that enshrined as supreme law our uniquely American skeptical optimism. Including a judiciary both entirely insulated from political influence and equipped with interpretive authority was the keystone to the achievement of the

Constitution's devised ends. Without a countermajoritarian judiciary armed with the power of judicial review, the entire design of our national government would be meaningless. Unfortunately, neither the departmentalists nor the popular constitutionalists recognize this foundational insight.

Departmentalism: A Historical and Doctrinal Argument Against Judicial Supremacy

Departmentalism, in its various forms, denies judicial supremacy in saying "what the law is,"[105] instead asserting that each department—legislative, executive, and judicial—has equal authority to engage in constitutional interpretation in fulfilling its respective constitutional role and performing its assigned duties. This theory is based on the idea of "coordinacy": our system, they argue, is primarily designed to achieve the independent, coordinate status of coequal branches. Accordingly, the three coordinate branches were intended to serve as checks on one another, and no single one was meant to reign over the other two. At its core, departmentalism is focused on undermining the role of the judiciary as the ultimate arbiter of constitutional meaning, and on locating much of the final interpretive authority in the executive branch.

Departmentalism's most vocal and extreme proponent, Michael Stokes Paulsen, begins by arguing that the president has a large degree of interpretive power. He contends that the rationales for executive review are the same as the rationales for judicial review set forth in *Marbury v. Madison* and *Federalist* No. 78.[106] Those rationales, he argues, explain why executive review is equally as valid in the context of vetoes and pardons as it is in faithful execution of the law and the enforcement of judicial final judgments.[107] Paulsen then asserts that because the rationale for executive review is the same as the rationale for judicial review, any counterarguments against executive review are equally applicable to judicial review. One cannot believe in one without believing in the other, he reasons, and the ultimate power of judicial review cannot be "supreme" over the power of executive review without undermining the argument for judicial review in the first place.[108] Thus, because the judiciary lacks the authority to execute its own final judgments, it is the *executive* that holds the ultimate power of interpretation. According to Professor Paulsen, this should logically mean that the president can defy judicial rulings without upsetting the constitutional balance of powers.

This view problematically understands coordinacy to require that the executive branch possesses the same *type* of power as the judiciary, when in fact coordinacy requires only that the branches possess the same *quantum* of constitutional authority. In other words, the mere fact that the branches are designed to possess equal *levels* of power in no way necessarily implies that they possess *identical* power. Indeed, no one suggests that the judiciary has power to assert the executive power vested by Article II in the president. There is, then, no reason to assume that the executive logically must possess the exact equivalent of the judiciary's authority. The concept of "coordinacy" was discussed in *The Federalist*, but it was discussed as a means to the structural end that became our Constitution.[109] It is folly to suggest that separation of powers and the system of checks and balances that the Framers built to advance the goal of coordinacy allows the executive to control the entirety of our legal process, empowering it to (1) choose whether or not to execute the law as promulgated by Congress; (2) execute that law; and (3) ignore an Article III court's judgment as to that law's constitutionality.[110] This seems to be the very definition of "a tyrannical concentration of all the powers of government in the same hands"[111]—which James Madison viewed as the primary evil against which our Constitution would need to guard.[112]

Interestingly, it is Madison's own written expressions of commitment to the notion of coequal authority that, Paulsen argues, demonstrate the validity of departmentalism. Paulsen acknowledges that Madison eventually conceded that judicial interpretation would typically constitute the "final" resolution of constitutional issues because "the judiciary generally would be the *last* branch to act on a particular question by virtue of the order in which the branches' respective powers would be exercised."[113] Yet Paulsen insists that Madison adopted this position reluctantly, while remaining committed to the concept of coordinacy, and that just because the judiciary would often interpret last did not necessarily require that its interpretation should bind.[114] Empowering the judiciary with the authority to bind other branches by its interpretation, Paulsen contends, would contravene the opinion of *Federalist* No. 49 that no branch should have "an exclusive or superior right of settling the boundaries between their respective powers."[115] Ultimately, "[t]o hold that one branch's interpretation controls another is to bestow a 'practical and real omnipotence' on the controlling branch. . . . [T]o grant the *courts* interpretive supremacy would be to give *them* a 'practical and real omnipotence.'"[116]

Departmentalists such as Paulsen fail to understand that the whole point of coordinacy, especially as it is implemented through our

Constitution, is countermajoritarianism.[117] The structural allocation of power set forth in the Constitution, the series of checks and balances it provides, and the salary and tenure protections it grants the judiciary all exist to ensure that both the document and the courts serve countermajoritarian roles. It makes eminent sense for the sole branch that is insulated from majoritarian pressures to render final and binding interpretive judgments of the foundational countermajoritarian document. If the very majoritarian bodies that the Constitution limits may have final say as to the meaning of those limits, the Constitution is no limit at all.[118] It would make no sense for checked branches to have the final say as to what the checks on them mean.[119] The judiciary *is* "the least dangerous branch,"[120] insofar as it has been given no power to execute or legislate. It therefore makes sense, structurally, to give final interpretive authority of the Constitution to the branch least capable of compulsion or coercion, and to insulate that branch from the evils of temporary political movement. This is what makes the branches coordinate. Put another way, without judicial supremacy, coordinacy would be impossible. Without the authority to exercise its countermajoritarian power and definitively determine "what the law is," the judiciary would not merely be the least dangerous branch; it would arguably be no branch at all. At the very least, it would be impossible to call it a "coordinate" branch.

It is no coincidence that the judiciary is the last branch to analyze the constitutionality of legislation. Departmentalists seem to view it as a happy accident that the judiciary gets the final word because it happens typically to decide constitutional questions last in time. But none of this is coincidental. The Framers created a republic with a legislative branch whose job it is to promulgate legislation that both complies with the Constitution and serves majoritarian interests. To avoid placing too much power in one single branch of the government, the Constitution denied the legislative branch the power to execute those laws, placing the executive power in the hands of the executive branch. And if the legislature passed a law and the president executed it, the third branch would be empowered to rule on its legality.

Professor Paulsen diverges from other critics of judicial supremacy by drawing a distinction between judicial *supremacy* and judicial *review*. He does not argue against judicial review. In fact, he pledges a degree of allegiance to the idea, explicating *Marbury v. Madison*'s logic and explaining why it supports his theory as well. He calls his analytical method "Euclidean."[121] *Marbury*, he says, rests on (1) the major premise that when ordinary law conflicts with the Constitution, the Constitution prevails; and

(2) the minor premise that the judiciary has the authority to interpret the rule of law in the course of applying the rule of law. Instead of arguing against judicial review, he asserts that both the major and minor premises of *Marbury* support his theory that the judiciary is not the *exclusive* arbiter of constitutional interpretation. After all, the president and Congress take an oath just as the judiciary does to protect and defend the Constitution; they are in just as good a position to interpret the law as is the judiciary. And in taking care to faithfully execute the laws of the United States, the executive, too, might be viewed as competent to interpret the laws it applies.

Paulsen's proof is anything but Euclidean. First, to say that the coordinate branches are equally equipped to interpret the Constitution and "say what the law is" by virtue of the ubiquity of oaths of office completely ignores the structural reality that gave rise to judicial review in the first place. Yes, the president and Congress also take an oath to protect and defend the Constitution, and should act within its bounds at all times. In a vacuum, the very idea of coordinacy would suggest that all three branches should have the exact same power to determine what those bounds are. But that is in a vacuum, and the vacuum ignores the harsh political realities of our system. The president and Congress are not only accountable to the Constitution; they are, by design, accountable as well to their constituents. The judiciary, in contrast, was *uniquely and purposefully* insulated from political influence. Its commitment is to the Constitution *alone*, not to the people and their constantly evolving majoritarian choices. The Framers' choice reveals a commitment to judicial review, and judicial review requires judicial supremacy. The simple and inescapable fact is that vesting final say as to the meaning of the Constitution in either the president or Congress effectively undermines—if, indeed, it does not completely destroy—the countermajoritarianism that is so fundamental to our form of constitutionalism.

In his quest to demonstrate the validity and worth of executive interpretation in our constitutional regime, Paulsen urges that the Constitution should be understood not only to permit the president to interpret the Constitution when he takes care to faithfully execute the laws Congress promulgates, but also to refuse to enforce particular judicial decrees.[122] Paulsen's analysis suffers from a fatal circularity. Of course, he is right that a court's decision that is counter to the Constitution is invalid, because the Constitution is our supreme law and trumps any action of a subordinate that the Constitution has itself empowered. But to assume that the court's decision is incorrect is to beg the question. How are we to know *ex ante* that it is the president's interpretation that is correct and the court's interpretation incorrect? Moreover, we are left asking the same initial question: how does the Constitution indicate that the president should be empowered to determine whether the judiciary has given a "contradictory" rule to the Constitution? When the judiciary interprets the Constitution differently from the way the political branches believe it should, the judiciary is not "acting unconstitutionally," much as a president who vetoes a bill because he does not think it is constitutional (even though Congress or the Supreme Court might think so) is not "acting unconstitutionally."

There exists an even more fundamental problem with departmentalist analysis: it ignores Lord Coke's famed warning that, for obvious reasons, no man can be a judge in his own case.[123] The idea that a branch of government may have final say as to the constitutionality of its own actions effectively guts any notion of limited power, ignores the mutual mistrust that serves as the foundation for the Constitution, and renders wholly illusory the concept of interbranch checking.[124]

Departmentalism can be framed slightly differently in order to avoid some of the most direct criticisms, but such framing ultimately leads to similar results. In a way, departmentalism describes nothing more than the political-question doctrine, pursuant to which the Court occasionally refuses to rule on constitutional challenges, instead deferring to the branch whose actions have been challenged. Paulsen notes that the political-question doctrine makes sense insofar as there are some things that should evade judicial review and be left entirely to the executive to determine. From there, he observes that scholars have rightly pointed out how difficult it is to confine the political-question doctrine to a certain, clearly delimited collection of areas that fall exclusively within the executive's purview of interpretation. Instead of viewing the blurred limits of the doctrine's scope as indicative of its fragility, he posits that there are no clear limits, because executive interpretive authority cannot be readily confined in a principled fashion, and it should thus be functionally limitless.

Contrary to the political-question doctrine's logic and holding that it must allow for majoritarian control over the interpretation of our counter-majoritarian Constitution (the precise opposite of the document's structural vision), it is the judiciary that is best fitted to police the boundaries *actually contained within the Constitution* or necessary to achieve its structural aims. True, the political-question doctrine is problematic, because it claims that some constitutional provisions do not lend themselves to clear and measurable standards, but makes no principled distinction between those provisions that can be distilled down to standards and tests and those that cannot.[125] A more legitimate form of the "political question" doctrine asks only whether the text of the Constitution explicitly places the action or decision in question within the cognizance of the judiciary, or is instead agnostic as to the manner in which a particular constitutionally granted power is exercised. For example, a court may consider whether the executive has complied with the Constitution's directive that the president may block legislation by veto, for in saying what the Constitution means the Court will be forced to determine the meaning of the term "veto" in Article II.[126] But Article II is agnostic as to permissible rationales for exercising the veto power. Nowhere does that provision indicate that a validly effectuated veto may be issued only for good cause, or that a president must reasonably believe the statute is unconstitutional, or any criteria whatsoever.[127]

The Constitution does not provide that the president may veto bills only when those bills defy the Constitution; instead, it simply empowers the president to veto bills, presumably for whatever reason she or he deems appropriate.[128] The Constitution requires that the president actually veto those bills in order to block their passage, so it seems logical for the courts to pass on whether the president's method of effectuating his veto constitutes a "veto" according to the text of the Constitution. But it is the Constitution's unambiguous provision of the veto power unconditionally to the president that removes the question of the legitimacy of motivating force from the Supreme Court's purview.

When the political branches exceed their constitutional authority, they pose a great risk to the people and to our constitutional regime. Our structural Constitution seems to understand this by ordaining a judiciary branch as the final arbiter of the constitutionality of government action. But the judicial branch is completely insulated from majoritarian impulses and political pressure, and it has authority over neither purse nor sword. It is unlikely to breach its constitutional duty because—at least for the most part—political pressures (the winds that may blow the political branches towards ultra vires action) do not exist for judicial officers in our government.[129] And even if the courts do breach their duties, such breach carries with it relatively limited risk to our institutional structure, because the judiciary is so strapped for power. This is why, for example, the courts are in the appropriate position to define the bounds of their own jurisdiction, while Congress is not in the appropriate position to define the bounds of its own power. Frankly, necessity requires that *someone* define the contours of these powers. But our structural Constitution understands that the judiciary is less positioned to undermine the system than are the political branches.

Does this mean that there exists absolutely no danger of judicial excess? Surely it would be wrong to make such an assumption. The era of the Supreme Court's specious economic substantive due process during the early twentieth century certainly stands as evidence to the contrary. But at least in a relative sense, this danger is far less likely to lead to embedded tyranny than are excesses by one or both of the political branches. Whatever the Court does or does not hold, the majoritarian branches invariably will possess far more power. Moreover, eventually the makeup of the Court will change to reflect the views of current majorities. At the very least, unlike the political branches (particularly the executive), it is all but inconceivable that the judiciary will seize power and impose tyrannical rule through the exercise of brute force.

Paulsen insists that as long as the president has complete power to veto or pardon based on her or his interpretation of the Constitution, it must be true that the president has interpretive (and thus discretionary) authority as to execution of statutes, abidance by judicial precedent, and enforcement of judicial decrees in specific cases. He argues that there is no principled distinction warranting interpretation of the Constitution to accord absolute authority to the executive regarding vetoes and pardons while denying such authority elsewhere, and that executive defiance of judicial interpretation in the context of a veto is just as nefarious as in the context of legislation or court decree. "If Supreme Court precedents are otherwise 'supreme' in the sense of being binding law for the other branches," he writes, "then the President's refusal to adhere to such law simply because the courts cannot (or will not) review his actions does not make those actions lawful and legitimate, but rather the cynical actions of a Holmesian bad man."[130] But once again, his reasoning is faulty.

It makes sense that the president possesses complete control over a veto or pardon, so long as it is done by constitutionally valid means. The Constitution gives the president "the Power to Grant Reprieves and Pardons for Offences against the United States, except in Cases of Impeachment,"[131] and empowers the president to consider bills approved by both houses of Congress—"If he approve he shall sign it, but if not he shall return it, with his Objections to that House in which it shall have originated."[132] Neither of these provisions affixes a legal obligation to the president's discretion; if he so chooses, he may pardon an offender against the United States based on that offender's hair color, and he may veto legislation for using verbiage he finds irritating (even in spite of the law's likely efficacy, social utility, and obvious compliance with constitutional law).[133] However, the president lacks similar discretion in deciding whether or not to execute the law. The president is obligated to "take Care that the Laws be faithfully executed."[134] Read in conjunction with the Supremacy Clause,[135] it is sensible to conclude that this constitutional dictate requires that the president execute the law of the land unless higher law requires otherwise. If the president can justifiably assert that the ordinary federal law she refuses to execute is unconstitutional, then the president is faithfully executing the law (by adhering to the Constitution). But if a court empowered to interpret and enforce the Constitution decrees in the adjudication of a case or controversy that the law in question is in fact constitutional, the president may no longer rely on her position that the law is unconstitutional as a justification for her refusal to enforce it. To allow the president to continue in her refusal would provide an easy subterfuge for any president who is politically disinclined to enforce a particular statute.

Departmentalism's entire foundation—that the theory of coordinacy empowers the executive to ignore the judiciary's interpretation of the Constitution in favor of its own—thus sprouts from poisoned roots. When the president interprets the Constitution in the course of vetoing or pardoning, she does so in the context of a process of constitutionally delegated decision making that, according to the document, requires no lawful motive or explanation. By contrast, when the president executes ordinary legislation, she does so in the process of taking care that the laws—all of them, including especially and supremely the Constitution—are faithfully executed. Contrary to Paulsen's argument, whether the president may refuse to execute a statute has nothing to do with how important or valuable certain constitutional grounds might be.[136]

This also explains why judicial review resulting in a declaration of unconstitutionality must bind the executive. In the exercise of its authority to adjudicate cases and controversies, the judiciary is necessarily tasked with the final round of interpretation and declaration of what the law is. The judiciary exists as a check upon the legislative and executive branches, for if they are so consumed by popular sentiment or momentary majoritarian interests that they promulgate inferior law that is noncompliant with the Constitution, the judiciary can protect minority and countermajoritarian interests by declaring the inferior law invalid. If the executive can defy this pronouncement, the judiciary is rendered functionally irrelevant; it becomes a mere instrument of the executive designed to offer advisory opinions that the president may acknowledge or ignore. Thus, the established implications of Article III's "case-or-controversy" requirement inescapably dictate that the president—like everyone else—must comply with a court's order that is the product of an adverse adjudication, based on that court's interpretation of the Constitution. Otherwise, the speculative nature of the president's response fatally denies that decision the element of "redressability" that is deemed an essential element of the judiciary's authority to act pursuant to Article III's "case-or-controversy" requirement.[137] Where the Court declares a law constitutional, the president might have the opportunity in future cases to refuse to execute that law on the grounds that an as-applied challenge would succeed. In other words, the executive may continue, in a way, to check the judiciary where the judiciary *permits* legislative and executive action. But where the judiciary *rejects* legislative and executive action as unconstitutional—that is, *serves its countermajoritarian purpose*—providing for an executive override completely contravenes the Constitution's structural design.

If the Supreme Court rules a particular presidential action unconstitutional, is the president constitutionally bound not to take the identical action against a distinct private party under parallel circumstances? Assuming the two situations are, in fact, legally identical, it is probably accurate to conclude that the president is bound in this manner, on ethical and moral levels.[138] As a constitutional matter, however, it is probable that technically the president is not bound in case 2 to refrain from even identical behavior found unconstitutional in case 1. Using Justice Oliver Wendell Holmes's "bad man" theory, perhaps the president can play hardball by complying only with a direct order of the court. But at worst, such presidential behavior would require the private challenger to pursue case 2 to resolution, which would of course lead to the same conclusion as in case 1. Alternatively, the president could be subjected to an equitable class action,[139] thereby subjecting the president to a formal court order controlling her behavior as a general matter. But it is important to recognize that even were the president permitted to play the law so close to the line, in the end she is still subject to judicial directive, and judicial supremacy is still maintained.

Not everyone who sympathizes with Paulsen's theory of executive interpretive power is prepared to reject judicial supremacy while granting the value or correctness of judicial review itself. Professor Steven Calabresi, for example, has applauded Professor Paulsen for making clear that the president has just as much a right and obligation to interpret the Constitution as do the courts, but emphatically rejects the notion that the executive can simply offer its own interpretation and ignore the judiciary once a court issues judgment in a case.[140] It is correct to conclude that Paulsen's argument is plainly wrong, and that, as Professor John McGinnis has also pointed out, such a design would render the judiciary meaningless and place it in a position of merely offering advisory opinions,[141] which is known to be contrary to the judiciary's constitutionally ordained mission and purpose.[142] But given a proper understanding of the term, it is inaccurate to characterize scholars like Calabresi or McGinnis as true "departmentalists." Far and away the most controversial element of the theory is Paulsen's assertion that, because the executive and the judiciary are to be deemed equal as constitutional interpreters, the president may ignore judicial decisions interpreting the Constitution when she disagrees. Because both Calabresi and McGinnis understand and accept the authority of a court to bind the president to its constitutional interpretation, their approach does not differ substantially from the foundational elements of the traditionalist model.

Popular Constitutionalism: A Normative Attack on Judicial Supremacy

Other opponents of judicial supremacy make a different argument. They contend that regardless of whether the Constitution can be read to provide for judicial review, judicial supremacy does not protect the virtues we think it does or should, and entrusting either the people or their chosen representatives—the executive or Congress—with interpretive authority would be preferable. This is because such a practice aligns more closely with our first principles, grounded in precepts of representative democracy.[143] Pioneered and championed most vocally and consistently by Larry Kramer, popular constitutionalism (again, in various forms) struggles to combat the descriptive truths of the structural Constitution by devoting little energy to description and focusing almost exclusively on observational and normative argument. Kramer argues that the notion of judicial supremacy is highly antagonistic to the democratic values that are core to the American vision supported only by "aristocrats"[144] who have "deep seated misgivings about ordinary citizens"[145] and view "democratic politics as scary and threatening."[146] Accordingly, he urges that final interpretive authority be given to "the people themselves," who should have "active and ongoing control over the interpretation and enforcement of constitutional law."[147] Comparison of Kramer's approach to the true foundations of our form of constitutional democracy readily demonstrates the serious flaws in his analysis.

The very notion of a countermajoritarian Constitution refutes Kramer's normative claim. Conceding unchecked power to branches of government that are electorally responsive to majority impulses is inherently dangerous, for those branches cannot be limited by a constitutional document whose limitations they can freely interpret without consequence.[148] Transferring interpretive authority to the diffuse and unidentifiable mass that is "the people" (a concept left consistently vague in Kramer's analysis) carries with it similar definitional dangers, while also being virtually impossible to implement or confine. One need look no further than the several states with elected judiciaries to observe how troubling the juxtaposition of tasking politically accountable judges with neutral adjudication and constitutional interpretation is.[149]

The argument Kramer and others advance is not only normatively unpersuasive, it is also logically untenable in light of the structural Constitution and the basic premises of American constitutionalism. The traditionalist view understands the value of countermajoritarian checking as a political mechanism for enshrining skeptical optimism, which can be readily deduced from the Constitution's structural design.[150] Our constitutionalism is thus principally concerned with facilitating democracy while promoting rule-of-law values and protecting minorities.[151] The reality is that any argument that temporary majorities (or those directly accountable to those majorities) are either more capable or more suitable arbiters of constitutional meaning ignores the careful framework for promoting these values that was etched into our supreme law at the Constitutional Convention. Our proclaimed unflagging commitment to due process of law, the existence of a supreme document ratified by supermajoritarian movement and subject to formal alteration only through a supermajoritarian process, and our provision of a politically insulated judiciary are all brightly flashing signals that our system understands the importance of speed bumps designed to slow majorities down. Popular constitutionalism seems to forget—or intentionally ignore—all of this.[152]

FASHIONING THE THEORY OF PREMODERN CONSTITUTIONALISM

Prior to the rise of modernist theories of American constitutionalism, the traditionalist view went largely unexplained and undefended. As explained previously, the best defense of the traditionalist understanding (without reference to or reliance upon later competing theories) is through a focus on historical context and a process of reverse engineering.[153] The traditionalist view defines the core of American constitutionalism as consisting of two fundamental elements: the foundational principle of skeptical optimism (revealed through examination of the historical context within which our constitutional democracy was established) and its implementer, the political apparatus of countermajoritarian checking of majoritarian powers (revealed through reverse engineering from the structural Constitution). Historical context suggests that the Constitution was born out of skeptical optimism. The Founders were optimistic that humankind, when empowered and encouraged to work together and form movements, had great potential to flourish. At the same time, they doubted that majoritarian movements, if left unchecked, could avoid devolving into chaos or tyranny. Reverse engineering from the structures created in our Constitution, then, revealed the essence of American constitutionalism to be countermajoritarian checking of majoritarian governmental action. After all, there is no other reasonable explanation for pledging commitment to representative government, creating powerful majoritarian legislative and executive branches, and then establishing a judiciary that is insulated from political pressure.

The traditionalist view of American constitutionalism understands the import of both our written Constitution and prophylactically insulated judicial review, because those methods of activating our form of constitutional governance logically connect to the principle and actuate the political apparatus. But without the benefit of modernism as a foil, traditionalism's descriptive power can only go so far in placing at the core of American constitutionalism the principle and the apparatus. Standing on its own, the traditionalist view is equipped only to observe the value, both normative and structural, of each of the two methods of activation that the two camps of modernists seek to undermine. Nothing inherent in the traditionalist approach requires, as a descriptive matter, that these mechanisms be deemed a part of the core of American constitutionalism.

The premodern approach to understanding the fundamental characteristics of American constitutionalism, on the other hand, is both descriptive and analytical at every level. It recognizes the tripartite core of our constitutionalism as consisting of principle, political apparatus, *and* activating mechanisms. Historical context reveals American skeptical optimism as the guiding principle. Structural reverse engineering demonstrates that this skeptical optimism inexorably leads to countermajoritarian checking of majoritarian power as the political apparatus at the heart of American constitutionalism. Understanding the inherent fallacies that plague the modernist analysis further demonstrates that the underlying principle and apparatus are not the only aspects of American constitutionalism that are inextricably tied to it. In fact, so, too, are the two particular characteristics of the Constitution through which the principle and apparatus are manifest: the Constitution's writtenness and the provision of judicial review by a prophylactically insulated judiciary. By responding to the various modernist alternatives, premodernism necessarily articulates the rationale for the formation of the traditionalist model, while simultaneously pointing out the serious flaws in models that have sought to displace it.

The historical and contextual evidence strongly favors the traditionalist view of American constitutionalism. But the virtue of premodern constitutionalism is that in addition to relying on strong historical and contextual evidence, it draws strength from consideration and rejection of competing modernist theories. In this sense, those of us who believe in the notion of constitutional text as the countermajoritarian supreme law that is to be definitively interpreted and enforced by a prophylactically insulated judiciary owe a backhanded thanks to the modernist theorists criticized in this chapter. In the classic Millian sense in which true ideas become sharper and more persuasive when contrasted to false ideas, understanding the fundamental flaws of modernist theories sharpens our understanding of the force of the logic underlying the traditionalist model. While its conclusion is largely identical to that of the traditionalist model, it has considerably strengthened that model in its careful and detailed response to the dangerous fallacies of the modernists.

Ultimately, premodern constitutionalism recognizes that structure is imbued with inherent meaning. Perhaps the American Constitution could have been fashioned in unwritten form, and not structured as it was. *But it was,* and for good reason. Fear of tyranny in Founding Era America permeates the document. Shortly after winning a war begun to free the colonies from Britain's insufficiently representative rule, our fledgling nation enacted a singular, written Constitution that provided for a republican form of government with majoritarian, representative branches structured to impose a system of mutual checking and a prophylactically independent judiciary. The legislature would promulgate legislation, the executive would execute it, and the judiciary was built to check the danger that the majoritarian branches might tend towards tyranny. To be sure, this judiciary itself was not built to be totally trusted—hence the structural choice to withhold all lawmaking and executive authority from the judicial branch and to provide the accountable branches with some level of control of judicial jurisdiction. But the foundational assumption was that *none* of the branches could be fully trusted, and judicial review was the best available option as one element in the intricate checking process to which the Constitution gave rise.

CONCLUSION

It has been suggested that America has no ideology whatsoever, and that pragmatism is this country's guiding principle.[154] When Madison was chastised for refusing to design a federal government whose branches were completely separated as Montesquieu had advised, his response was pragmatic: a system of checks and balances was more important than maintaining complete separation. But this rolled-up sleeves American pragmatism is appropriately viewed as an ideology in itself. It represents first, the cold, hard, "streetwise" recognition of the danger of accumulated and unchecked power, and second, a belief in the power of a written, entrenched document to both empower the majority and protect it from itself. Constitutionalism—*American* constitutionalism—is this country's great contribution to political thought, born not out of the postulates of theorists but out of the depths of necessity, the mother of invention. We risk modifying or reshaping it—particularly in the ways suggested by the modernists—at our peril.

A Taxonomy of Judicial Independence

INTRODUCTION

Since the nation's beginning, the concept of federal judicial independence has been almost as confusing to political and constitutional theorists as it is fundamental to the successful operation of our form of constitutional democracy.[1] On the one hand, the Constitution's Framers consciously chose to insulate members of the federal judiciary from at least the most acute forms of potential political pressure by expressly providing for the protection of their salaries and tenure.[2] On the other hand, the Framers simultaneously provided the groundwork to facilitate the exercise of seemingly substantial congressional control of the jurisdiction of the federal courts, thereby potentially undermining the very independence expressly provided to the judges of those courts.[3] While this apparent theoretical contradiction is largely consistent with the pragmatic balances found throughout the Constitution, it has often given rise to both theoretical[4] and doctrinal uncertainty.[5]

Additional questions might be raised concerning the extent to which constitutionally guaranteed judicial independence conflicts with congressional efforts either to exert control over the procedural operation of the federal courts[6] or significantly to curb the discretion of federal judges in imposing criminal sentences.[7] Further inquiry has been made concerning the extent of any constitutional obligation of Congress not to reduce the nonsalary support services that have already been supplied to the federal judiciary.[8] Therefore, the time now appears ripe for a wide-ranging reconsideration of the constitutional and political scope of federal judicial independence.[9]

Such a reexamination reveals that much of the present theoretical and doctrinal confusion results from the general failure to recognize that the concept of federal judicial independence can itself be subdivided into five conceivable categories: "institutional" independence, "lawmaking" independence, "countermajoritarian" independence, "decisional" independence, and "judgmental" independence.[10] Institutional independence refers to the non-case-specific protections of salary and tenure explicitly provided in Article III of the United States Constitution. They are described as "non-case-specific" because they concern the generally applicable independence protections of the federal judiciary as an institution, untied to the adjudication of a specific case, group of cases, or substantive issue. Thus, a federal statute seeking to reduce the salaries of federal judges could presumably be held unconstitutional on its face, even though the reduction was not tied to the prospective adjudication of particular cases.[11] Lawmaking independence refers to the ability of the federal courts to create either controlling subconstitutional substantive legal principles or governing general rules of procedure in the course of individual adjudications, free from interference by the other branches of the federal government.[12] Countermajoritarian independence describes the ability of the federal courts to interpret applicable provisions of the Constitution in the course of individual adjudications, free from direction or interference by the political branches.[13] Decisional independence concerns the ability of the federal courts to *interpret* and *apply*, rather than *create* substantive legal principles in the specific context of an individual adjudication, free from control or interference by the purely political branches of the federal government.[14] Finally, "judgmental" independence refers to the prohibition on congressional authority reopening final judgments of the federal courts.[15]

While the scope and meaning of institutional independence may be ascertained largely by resort to traditional methods of interpreting constitutional text,[16] one is forced to resort to alternative methodologies to ascertain the proper scope of the other subcategories of judicial independence. Ultimately, examination of constitutional text alone proves unsatisfactory in performance of this task. Instead, one must guide interpretation of that ambiguous text with a proper understanding of underlying principles of constitutional and political theory. Although decisional and countermajoritarian independence are essential as matters of both American political theory and constitutional directive,[17] the same cannot, at least for the most part, be said of lawmaking independence in either its substantive or procedural manifestations.[18] Indeed, recognition of this form of judicial independence would in many instances undermine the essence of American democratic theory, which places the primary power to fashion subconstitutional public policy in the hands of those who are representative of and accountable to the electorate.[19] Finally, "judgmental" independence, while not in any way as misguided as "lawmaking" independence, appears not to flow inexorably from a commitment to the dictates of constitutionalism, as long as the requirements imposed by the other forms of judicial independence have been satisfied.[20]

The first section of this chapter explores the text, purposes, and conceivable interpretive models of the textually dictated guarantee of institutional independence, as well as the most significant doctrinal questions to which that provision gives rise. The second section contrasts the concepts of countermajoritarian, decisional and lawmaking independence from the perspectives of both constitutional analysis and American political theory. The chapter then considers the implications of that analysis for congressional efforts to constrict judicial decision making authority on both substantive and procedural fronts.

INSTITUTIONAL INDEPENDENCE: THE PROPER SCOPE OF
THE SALARY AND TENURE PROTECTIONS

Although the Constitution gives Congress discretion not to create lower federal courts, it mandates the presence of certain attributes if inferior federal courts are created: "The Judges, both of the supreme and inferior Courts, shall hold their Offices during good Behaviour, and shall, at stated Times, receive for their Services a Compensation, which shall not be diminished during their Continuance in Office."[21] While controversy existed at the time of the Constitution's framing over whether a system of lower federal courts should be created, there was apparently no significant disagreement that if inferior federal courts were created, they should be made independent of the other branches of the federal government. The Framers sought to protect this independence by the constitutional guarantee of salary and tenure.

At first glance, at least as to the issue of judicial salary, the Compensation Clause appears as straightforward as virtually any constitutional provision. Closer examination reveals, however, that interpretation of the clause is fraught with potential confusion. For example, does the protection against salary reduction extend to auxiliary services the government provides, such as law clerks and secretaries? If not, does it prohibit congressional reductions in these services when such reductions are unambiguously imposed as retribution for a decision or series of decisions made by the federal courts? Does the clause require salary raises during periods of inflation, so that the judges' real income is not diminished? Does it authorize the imposition of newly created general nondiscriminatory taxes on judges that are applied to all citizens, or at least to all federal employees?

In answering these questions, it is important to ascertain both the likely purposes sought to be attained by insertion of the salary and tenure protections and the particular methodology chosen to attain those goals. The former may well be considerably more obvious than the latter. The drafters of Article III sought to insulate the federal judiciary from potential pressures, from either the representative branches of the federal government or the public, that might skew the decision-making process or compromise the integrity or legitimacy of federal court decisions. In light of this reasoning, one might assume that any congressional action that has the effect of threatening, or at least is intended to threaten, federal judicial independence should be deemed a violation of Article III. This conclusion is undermined, however, by recognition of the particular methodology utilized to accomplish their purpose. Basically, two conceivable modes of implementation were available, both of which may be analogized to the alternative methods for determining whether a suit is untimely when filed: a "statute of limitations" approach and a "laches" approach. Under a laches approach, as with the equitable doctrine of the same name, a court examines each case individually to determine whether, under the circumstances, the concerns that gave rise to the limitation are present.[22] Thus, in deciding whether a suit is untimely under a laches approach, a court would decide whether, in light of all the relevant circumstances, it would be unfair or unreasonable to allow the plaintiff to proceed.[23] By analogy, a court employing a case-by-case method to ensure judicial independence would invalidate any congressional action that, under all of the relevant circumstances, presented a real threat to that independence.

By its terms, however, Article III appears to reject use of a case-by-case methodology, and with good reason. Both the difficulties in determining whether judicial independence has in fact been compromised in the individual instance and the political friction that could result from such an inquiry by the judiciary could be devastating. Instead, Article III clearly employs a statute of limitations approach, whereby a rigid "line in the sand" is drawn and applied, regardless of the special needs of the individual situation. In enforcing a statute of limitations, a court is not permitted, in an individual case, to conclude either that suit would be unfair even though filed a day before the expiration of the statutory period, or that suit would be fair despite the fact that it was filed a day after expiration. Therefore, in determining the timeliness of a lawsuit, a statute-of-limitations approach is employed for the very purpose of avoiding the uncertainty inherent in use of a case-by-case approach. Analogously, Article III appears to impose a rigid line, disallowing reduction of federal judicial compensation, regardless of the underlying congressional motivation for the reduction. However, other than its guarantee against salary reduction, Article III imposes no further limitations on congressional authority to regulate judicial benefits. Thus, as long as Congress has not reduced judicial salaries, the Compensation Clause is neutral on congressional action, even when that action may actually have the effect of undermining judicial independence.

Under this analysis, a reduction in judicial support services, such as law clerks and secretaries, would be unconstitutional only if we may properly define the constitutional term "salary" to encompass such services. If one were to employ an originalist approach to the definitional question,[24] the answer would almost certainly be no. There is no reason to believe that the Framers ever contemplated the concept of support services within the concept of "salary." Even under a modern definitional model,[25] it is highly unlikely that such support services could properly be squeezed into the concept of "salary." Surely the Internal Revenue Service today does not consider an employer's provision of secretaries or assistants to be part of an employee's taxable income.

It might be responded that such a narrow and formalistic definitional approach to the interpretation of constitutional provisions is unduly grudging in light of the well-established flexible interpretive standards the Supreme Court of the United States traditionally employs in analysis of constitutional text. Pursuant to this argument, if the political and social purposes served by a particular constitutional provision are fostered by an extension of its reach to distinct but analogous areas, such an extension would be proper. How one resolves this interpretive debate turns on issues of constitutional theory that go well beyond the narrow issue of the Compensation Clause's construction. However, unless, at some outer boundary, language imposes at least some constraints, the Constitution effectively becomes meaningless (in the literal sense of that term).[26] In any event, it is important to keep in mind that if one were willing to construe the Compensation Clause to extend to the provision of support services, the resulting limit on congressional power could not be confined to selective retaliatory cuts in support services. This is because of the methodological choice inherent in the structure of that clause: Violations are determined exclusively in a manner that disclaims any inquiry into individualized social or political consequences. Thus, if the clause were construed to protect against cuts in nonsalary benefits, it would have to extend as well to any such cut, regardless of Congress's purpose or motivation for imposing that cut.

If, on the other hand, one concludes (as I do) that by its terms the Compensation Clause does not extend to nonsalary support services under any circumstances, one would also have to conclude that the clause fails to prohibit even cuts in support services that are unambiguously designed as retaliation for a specific decision or series of decisions in the federal courts. As instinctively troubling as this conclusion may seem, it flows inexorably from the choice, inherent in Article III, in favor of an easily applied, unbending statute-of-limitations-like approach to judicial independence. In fashioning the Compensation Clause, the Framers avoided reliance on a case-by-case inquiry into the effect of congressional actions on judicial independence in favor of an easily applied bright-line standard. As already noted, they did so probably in an attempt to avoid the very uncertainty and political friction that would plague an inquiry into the retributive nature of specific congressional action. Thus, congressional retaliation that does not actually reduce judicial salaries should not be deemed to violate Article III.

Theoretically, though highly unlikely as a practical matter, Congress could so drastically reduce judicial support services so as to render impossible the courts' performance of the judicial function. Determining at exactly what point that level is reached for the most part involves a factual question that would have to be answered in each individual situation. It should be noted, however, that once such a point is reached, the congressional action would be unconstitutional only to the extent that the Constitution requires *federal* judicial action. Because, under accepted constitutional standards, state courts may constitutionally be vested with final authority to resolve virtually all matters reached by the federal judicial power, the category of matters that actually require Article III federal judicial action is likely to be relatively small—if it exists at all.

One might respond that while Congress may have the power to exclude Article III federal court jurisdiction completely, as long as Congress continues to vest jurisdiction in the federal courts it has a constitutional obligation, under inherent principles of separation of powers, to enable federal courts to perform at a minimal level of effectiveness. Hence, Congress is more likely to exercise its generally accepted authority to curb federal court jurisdiction than it is to reduce federal judicial support services below minimally operative levels. It is conceivable, however, that such congressional retributive action could be found to violate due process in an individual litigation. That constitutionally grounded concept requires a hearing in front of a neutral and independent adjudicator before either property or liberty may be taken away.[27] If judges are aware that Congress has denied them benefits or privileges specifically because they have decided particular cases in a particular manner, it is arguable that they are rendered incapable of the requisite adjudicatory independence in future similarly situated cases. But because Congress's retributive action would presumably have no effect on the outcome of the specific case to which Congress was reacting, the litigants in that case would have neither the requisite practical interest nor legal standing to challenge the congressional retributive action. Moreover, because such congressional action would not violate Article III, it is doubtful that Congress's action could be successfully challenged on its face. However, to the extent that one could establish that (a) Congress's reduction in nonsalary judicial benefits or privileges was in fact designed as retribution for past judicial decisions, and (b) the litigant in a subsequent case stands in an identical position to the successful litigants in the case or cases to which Congress was negatively reacting, the subsequent litigant could conceivably raise a successful due process challenge, not directly to the congressional action, but rather to adjudication of his case by a federal judge in light of that prior congressional action. If state court adjudication were feasible under the circumstances, however, presumably a transfer to that forum could satisfy due process, at least in light of how that constitutional dictate is currently construed.[28]

Pursuant to this reasoning, a congressional refusal to raise judicial salaries, even a refusal motivated by retaliatory concerns, does not violate Article III. It is true that during periods of inflation, if judges' salaries are not increased, their real incomes decline. By inaction, Congress could effectively reduce real income, posing a potentially serious constitutional problem, especially if the salaries of other federal officials are increased during the inflationary period.[29] Despite substantial inflation, the salaries of federal judges and a few other federal officials were not substantially increased between 1969 and 1975.[30] While the judiciary has wisely held that congressional attempts to revoke vested cost-of-living increases for Article III judges violate the Compensation Clause,[31] Congress's simple failure to raise salaries to keep pace with inflation should not be deemed unconstitutional. The history of the enactment of the Compensation Clause indicates that the Framers were well acquainted with the problems of inflation and the need to make periodic increases in the judges' salaries.[32] A proposal to provide that judges' salaries could not be increased during their term of office was defeated by arguments that such increases might be necessary to maintain the attractiveness of judicial service in light of changing economic conditions and judicial workloads.[33] The Constitution, however, seems to leave to Congress's discretion the determination of the need for such increases.

Acceptance of the bright-line statute-of-limitations analogy as the governing interpretive model for the Compensation Clause has interesting implications for several other potential permutations. If one concludes that even *retaliatory* measures that do not formally reduce judicial salaries are permissible under such a model, it would seem reasonable to conclude correspondingly that even *nonretaliatory* congressional actions are unconstitutional when they do, in fact, reduce judicial salaries. After all, if the reason for adopting a bright-line approach is presumably to avoid the difficulty, uncertainty, and political friction inherent in a case-by-case inquiry into congressional purpose, motive, and effect, one should be unwilling to allow Congress to purify salary reductions by the assertion of nonretaliatory purposes. A bright line is, after all, a bright line.

This conclusion would apply to any legislative reduction aimed exclusively at judicial salaries.[34] It is, no doubt, equally true of a reduction imposed indirectly, as through a tax imposed exclusively on judicial salaries. More uncertain, both theoretically and doctrinally, is the constitutionality of nondiscriminatory reductions imposed on all federal employees when Article III judges are included. The issue first arose when Congress sought to apply the federal income tax to sitting federal judges.[35] After initially ruling that the tax could not be imposed even on judges appointed after the income tax was enacted,[36] the Supreme Court reversed itself and held that a general nondiscriminatory tax could be applied to federal judges appointed after the enactment of the tax.[37] The decision emphasized that the tax did not discriminate against judges and that judges, like all citizens, had a responsibility to pay their fair share of the cost of government.[38] The decision seems to be based on the view that the purpose of the Compensation Clause is to protect federal judges from legislative attempts to impinge on judicial independence.[39] A general income tax, applied to all wage earners, poses little risk of such interference. Yet use of the bright-line interpretive model would logically seem to effectively preclude reliance on such reasoning.[40]

How one resolves the constitutionality of general salary reductions applied to judicial incomes depends on whether or not one adopts what could be described as the "antidiscrimination" interpretation of the

Compensation Clause. One could interpret Article III, much as the Free Exercise Clause is currently construed,[41] to insulate the protected activity merely from discriminatory treatment. When this approach is combined with the bright-line model, the result is that if Congress singles out judicial salaries for reduction, that reduction is incapable of justification, regardless of the reason.[42] However, if Congress reduces judicial salaries as part of a broader reduction in the salaries of all federal employees, the inclusion of judicial salaries within that reduction would, pursuant to this antidiscrimination approach, be constitutional.

While the antidiscrimination model appears difficult to reconcile with the seemingly absolute terms of the Compensation Clause, it might be defended as a relatively easily applied compromise that fulfills the core independence concerns underlying the clause. This model accomplishes this without either invoking a troublesome case-by-case approach or significantly undermining legitimate efforts at fiscal restraint. Whichever way one resolves this debate, it is important to note that the conclusion reached should control both direct and indirect salary reductions, for there exists no logical or practical basis on which to distinguish between the two.[43] Given this fact, practical considerations might well push a reasonable observer into acceptance of the antidiscrimination principle. Otherwise, one would be logically forced to reach the arguably impractical conclusion that Congress may not constitutionally apply general increases in the income tax to sitting federal judges.

COUNTERMAJORITARIAN, DECISIONAL, AND LAWMAKING INDEPENDENCE CONTRASTED

Defining Terms

When one moves analysis from the textually based guarantees of institutional independence to more substantive aspects of judicial independence, the nature of the inquiry shifts its focus from the words of the Constitution to the theoretical framework underlying the relevant constitutional provisions. Before exploring that framework, however, it is necessary to understand the subtle but significant differences in the types of substantive judicial independence.

The concept of *decisional* independence refers to the ability of the judge in an individual case to ascertain, interpret, and apply the governing legal principles to the facts of the case before her as she deems appropriate, free from external or extraneous influences and pressures that might reasonably be thought to affect her decision. The concept of *lawmaking* independence, on the other hand, concerns a judge's ability to fashion general substantive rules of decision or rules of procedure that are designed to govern, not only the case before her, but future similarly situated cases as well. Admittedly, this distinction is not one of day and night. It is, however, a distinction of fundamental importance. Examination of both established constitutional principles and fundamental precepts of American political theory demonstrates that decisional independence is the *sine qua non* of the federal judiciary's operation. Lawmaking independence, on the other hand, is not centrally important to performance of the judicial function and would often undermine the principles of democratic theory that underlie the American political system.

In certain ways, *countermajoritarian* independence bears greater similarities to lawmaking independence than it does to decisional independence. Like lawmaking independence and unlike decisional independence, countermajoritarian independence includes the power to fashion generally applicable law—in other words, legal principles that extend beyond the narrow confines of an individual case. The key difference between countermajoritarian and lawmaking independence, however, is that the former flows logically from the initial commitment to institutional independence for the judiciary while the latter is wholly inconsistent with the judiciary's formal insulation from the dictates of representation and accountability inherently associated with democracy.

The Federal Judiciary's Role in American Constitutional Theory

As the prior chapter made clear, that the judiciary possesses the independent and final authority to interpret the Constitution is established by the simple fact that the entire point of the Constitution is to impose a countermajoritarian restraint on majoritarian government.[44] As Chief Justice Marshall wrote famously in *Marbury v. Madison*,[45] "a legislative act contrary to the constitution is not law." Otherwise, "written constitutions are absurd attempts, on the part of the people, to limit a power in its own nature illimitable."[46] Common sense tells us that to leave the final say as to the constitutionality of a majoritarian branch's actions in the hands of that branch effectively destroys the inherently countermajoritarian nature of the Constitution. There is, then, an important reason that the Framers, who had only recently fought the American Revolution over the principle of no taxation without representation, nevertheless chose to formally insulate one of the three branches of government from the democratic process. Without a countermajoritarian branch of government to have the final say as to the meaning and enforcement of the countermajoritarian Constitution, the document is rendered worse than meaningless, for it would then amount to a sham designed to defraud the populace into believing that the majoritarian branches are checked when in reality the check would be illusory.

At the same time, because of their insulation from majoritarian pressure and the resultant threat to the workings of the democratic process, the federal judiciary has been denied purely legislative or executive power, and expressly confined to the exercise of the traditional judicial function of case adjudication.[47] Unless limited in this manner, the largely unrepresentative and unaccountable federal judiciary could threaten the fundamental principle of representationalism by usurping the policy-making power which the legislative and executive branches traditionally exercise.

To be sure, there exists a long Anglo-American tradition of substantive common law development by the judiciary. In the U.S. federal judicial system, however, the tradition is largely to the contrary. Since the early years of the nation's existence, Congress has, in the Rules of Decision Act,[48] prohibited the federal courts from fashioning common law rules of decision.[49] Although the Supreme Court has on occasion recognized judge-made exceptions to this seemingly total statutory bar, the Court has always emphasized the narrow and limited nature of those exceptions.[50] In any event, even in those cases in which courts are authorized to fashion subconstitutional rules of decision, no one could seriously doubt that a legislature has the authority to supersede common law rules by appropriate legislative action. Thus, lawmaking independence—at least to the extent that it would include the authority to trump inconsistent legislative action—is not part of the independence that the Constitution guarantees to the federal judiciary. Any other conclusion would turn the foundations of representative democracy on their head.

Constitutional Sources of Federal Decisional Independence

Two constitutional principles provide the legal foundation for the concept of the federal courts' decisional independence: due process and separation of powers.

Due Process. The argument from due process postulates that "[n]one of the core values of due process . . . can be fulfilled without the participation of an independent adjudicator."[51] The point, in other words, is that the procedural safeguards of notice, hearing, counsel, transcript, and the ability to call or cross-examine witnesses, all methods of assuring decisional accuracy and essential elements of fair procedure, are of little value if the decision maker bases his finding on factors other than his neutral and wholly objective assessment of the evidence.

The absence of a neutral adjudicator contravenes both the instrumental and noninstrumental values thought to underlie the constitutional guarantee of procedural due process. To the extent that a court's decision is based on factors other than fair assessment of the evidence, the instrumental goal of accurate decision making is of course undermined. To the extent one places a value on considerations that affect a litigant's individual self-worth and faith in and respect for the adjudicatory system, the absence of a neutral adjudicator is also a matter of grave concern.[52] At the very least, adjudicatory independence is therefore a necessary condition of truly fair procedure, which in turn, is the essence of procedural due process.

Due process is of only limited value as a protector of decisional independence, however, for two reasons. First, by its terms, the Fifth Amendment's Due Process Clause is triggered only when a cognizable life, liberty, or property interest is at stake,[53] concepts that have received appropriately limited construction.[54] Second, even when the clause is invoked, determination of exactly what constitutes an unconstitutional encroachment of decisional independence remains in a state of doctrinal uncertainty.[55]

Separation of Powers—Formalism. There exist several textual sources for the separation-of-powers' protections of federal decisional independence. First, Article III expressly vests "the judicial power" in the judicial branch,[56] and this directive, however ultimately defined, may be violated by attempts by other branches to usurp the judiciary's decisional authority. Under a so-called formalist model of separation of powers,[57] no branch may exercise authority not delegated to it by the Constitution. The key element of the formalist model is its rejection of any form of pragmatic or functionalist balancing test that could conceivably authorize exceptions to the Constitution's tripartite distribution of power when social circumstances are found to warrant.[58] Beyond that point, however, the submodels of formalism differ in their definitional approach to branch power. What could be called classic formalism employs an originalist[59] and/or rigidly syllogistic[60] approach to the definition of branch power. In this manifestation, formalism has been the subject of severe criticism by legal theorists.[61] However, formalism may also be utilized in a more pragmatic fashion, leading to what I have previously referred to as the "pragmatic formalist" model.[62] This version of formalism posits that "in fashioning its definitions of branch power, the Court should look to a combination of policy, tradition, precedent, and linguistic analysis."[63]

Under a formalist model, Congress may, pursuant to Article I, exercise only the legislative power; pursuant to Article II, the president may exercise only the executive power; and pursuant to Article III, the judiciary exercises the judicial power. While other provisions of the Constitution on occasion delegate narrowly framed supplemental powers to the branches,[64] for the most part, according to the formalist model, branch authority is confined by the definitional scope of the authority granted to it in one of the first three articles.

Under the formalist approach, the judiciary's power is protected by the simple fact that the judicial power has been delegated solely to the judicial branch. However, it does not necessarily follow that the respective branch powers are hermetically insulated from each other. To the extent that the powers of the other two branches might reasonably be defined to include activities that could also be appropriately characterized as judicial, a strict formalist model may not fully protect the judiciary's exercise of the judicial power. One might therefore have to supplement a strict formalist model with a form of functionalism to deal with situations in which, even though the definitional approach of formalism is satisfied by a particular exercise of branch power, a significant threat to the values of branch integrity nevertheless results. A supplemental functionalist model therefore posits that while the definition of branch power provides a floor for separation of powers, even when a branch acts within the scope of its delegated powers, such action may be unconstitutional if it nevertheless is found to unduly interfere with the proper operation of another branch. And there can be little doubt that directing the decision of a specific case by a court disrupts the judiciary's performances of its constitutionally designated function.

Separation of Powers—Functionalism. The primary theoretical alternative to the formalist model of separation of powers is the functionalist model. Use of a purely functionalist model could conceivably allow what are admittedly invasions of the judicial province by the other branches under certain circumstances. The unifying philosophy that underlies all of the variants of the functionalist model is a willingness to ignore definitional or conceptual constraints on branch power in light of the needs of the applicable social and political context.[65] Beyond that, the variants differ in the contextual factors they deem relevant. Under one submodel, which could appropriately be labeled the *internal functionalist* approach, even when a branch's actions do not fall within the scope of its constitutionally authorized powers "the reviewing court invalidates branch usurpation only if it is found to reach some unspecified quantitative level of intensity—in other words, if it is found to undermine another branch's performance of its essential function or to accrete 'too much' power to the usurping branch."[66] This submodel's focus is thus on the internal effect of the usurpation on the operation of branch power. Under a second submodel, which could be described either as an *external functionalist* or *ad hoc balancing* approach, "branch usurpation may be justified by a sufficiently strong competing social interest."[67] While the first submodel is satisfied as long as no branch either gains or loses "too much" power, the second submodel contrasts the intensity of the asserted social justification for the usurpation of one branch's power by another branch against the harmful effects thought to derive from that usurpation. Under a functionalist model, it is conceivable that Congress could openly usurp the judicial power with impunity as long as a reviewing court concluded either that the judiciary's province had not been invaded unduly or that a competing social interest justified such usurpation. Because of the inherently subjective and unpredictable nature of all variants of the functionalist model, it is simply impossible to predict a decision on the constitutionality of particular legislative or executive invasions of the judicial province when employing a functionalist standard.

Although some form of functionalism appears to dominate much recent Supreme Court separation-of-powers precedent,[68] both of these submodels are subject to strong criticism, because they either "ultimately degenerate into little more than the statement of a wholly subjective conclusion"[69] or "undermine the key structural assumption of separation of powers theory—that it will be impossible (at least until it is too late) to determine whether or not a particular breach of branch separation will seriously threaten the core political values of accountability, diversity, and checking."[70]

CONGRESSIONAL LIMITATION OF FEDERAL COURT POWER TO PRESCRIBE SUBSTANTIVE RULES OF DECISION

The Decisional / Lawmaking / Countermajoritarian Triumvirate from the Perspectives of Constitutional and Political Theory

Application of accepted principles of American constitutional and political theory to the decisional-lawmaking-countermajoritarian distinction gives rise to four basic conclusions: (1) Congress may adopt constitutionally valid generalized rules of both decision and process, and require the federal courts to enforce them; (2) Congress may not dictate to the federal courts how to interpret the Constitution; (3) Congress may not constitutionally adopt a particular rule of decision yet indirectly require the federal courts to enforce a different or contrary rule of decision; (4) Congress may not directly dictate the result of an individual litigation.

Although by considerations of tradition, constitutional text, and political theory, Congress possesses substantial power to control the jurisdiction of the federal courts,[71] separation of powers principles may nevertheless limit the scope of that power. Congress may often exclude completely the Article III courts from the adjudicatory process, as long as the due process requirement of an independent adjudicator is satisfied through alternative means.[72] However, strict limits exist on Congress's power to employ the Article III courts for interpretation or enforcement, yet simultaneously restrict the scope of their decisional authority. Congress seriously threatens the concept of decisional independence by allowing the federal courts to adjudicate cases within their proper jurisdiction while simultaneously excluding from the scope of the judicial inquiry constitutional or legal issues that may arise in the course of the litigation, or by directing how part or all of a particular case is to be decided.

It is generally accepted that Congress has constitutional power completely to exclude the lower federal courts from adjudication of a particular category of cases, as long as the only consequence is to have the matters adjudicated in the state courts.[73] State courts have traditionally been deemed competent adjudicators and enforcers of federal rights[74] and bound by the Supremacy Clause[75] to give effect to controlling federal law.[76] However, when Congress does vest adjudicatory authority in the federal courts, separation-of-powers principles impose certain limits on congressional authority to control the outcome of the case, either by directing decision or excluding judicial power to resolve particular legal or factual questions that arise in the case.

The source and contours of this separation-of-powers limitation are somewhat murky, especially in light of the well-established principle that, within constitutional bounds, Congress may provide the substantive rule of decision for a case falling within the federal court's federal question jurisdiction.[77] Surely, no one could doubt that the federal courts lack authority either to ignore or overrule congressionally dictated substantive rules of decision, as long as those rules are found to be constitutionally valid.[78] Thus, one might question the basis for invalidating congressional attempts to limit federal judicial power to resolve the substantive outcome of individual cases.

Drawing a Constitutional/Subconstitutional Distinction: The Centrality of Countermajoritarian Independence

To understand the role of separation of powers in this area, one must view the issue from the perspective of well-established American political theory. First, one must distinguish between congressional attempts to prescribe constitutional rules of decision, on the one hand, and subconstitutional rules of decision, on the other. In vesting the federal courts with power to adjudicate a case, Congress may conceivably seek either to exclude judicial power to inquire into the constitutionality of the law that Congress is enforcing or to prescribe a particular outcome of the constitutional inquiry. These congressional attempts are unconstitutional, because they undermine the essence of the countermajoritarian principle that underlies American political theory. That principle posits that the very majoritarian bodies intended to be limited by the countermajoritarian Constitution may not sit as the final arbiters of the constitutionality of their own actions, lest the Constitution be effectively rendered a dead letter.[79] This conclusion, in short, describes the concept of countermajoritarian independence.

The fact that Congress presumably has power under Article III to exclude federal jurisdiction completely does not alter this conclusion. The postulate that "the greater includes the lesser" is inapplicable in this context, because the congressional power to exclude federal adjudicatory power proceeds on the assumption that in such an event the state courts will be in a position to exercise the full judicial power.[80] When Congress leaves enforcement power in a federal court but denies to that court the power to review the constitutionality of the law it is enforcing, the hypothetical availability of the state courts fails to provide a safety valve, even though those courts could themselves have constitutionally been vested with full adjudicatory power. This type of congressional action undermines the quid pro quo philosophy implicit in the structure of Article III. If Congress wishes to enlist the special legitimacy traditionally associated with the decision of an Article III court, Congress must allow that court to decide the case freely. The textual basis of this principle of separation of powers derives from the precept that an inherent element of the judicial power textually described in Article III is the power of the court to assure that its actions are consistent with the Constitution that the judges are sworn to enforce.

When the issue concerns the power of Congress to limit federal judicial power to find subconstitutional rules of decision, however, the attacks on congressional authority become considerably more problematic. The democratically elected Congress has power under Article I to adopt laws that provide substantive rules of decision in the federal courts. The unrepresentative, unaccountable federal judiciary has no authority to ignore or supplant these rules of decision, short of a finding of unconstitutionality.

Procedural Limitations on Judicial Power to Apply Substantive Law

The preceding reasoning supports the conclusion that the federal courts are denied *lawmaking* independence, at least to the extent that Congress dictates otherwise. The principle of *decisional* independence, however, places important limitations on congressional power to restrict judicial authority. One of those limitations occurs in situations in which Congress has provided a general rule of decision but has simultaneously imposed procedural or evidentiary rules that effectively prohibit the federal courts from accurately applying that rule of decision in a particular situation. In this context, one should note the important distinction between congressional power to create general exceptions to a generalized substantive rule of decision, on the one hand, and congressional power to prohibit the federal courts from finding that the standards of a general rule of decision have been either met or violated in an individual case, on the other. In the former situation, Congress is simply exercising its legislative power to establish general rules of behavior, and, assuming no equal protection problems, the creation of such exceptions should pass constitutional muster. In the latter context, Congress is interfering with the proper performance of the judicial function by effectively conscripting the judiciary as an unwilling co-conspirator in what amounts to the imposition of a legislative fraud on the public.

From the perspective of American political theory, such congressional behavior is unacceptable. For example, in formally adopting "standard A" as a general rule of decision, while simultaneously requiring the federal courts to reach decisions that effectively amount to adoption of "standard B" or "standard 'not A,'" Congress has substantially subverted the representational democratic process. It has done so by undermining the ability of the electorate to judge members of Congress through those members' votes on legislation embodying particular normative social policy choices.[81]

This congressional action is invalid, even if one assumes that Congress could constitutionally have chosen to adopt either "standard B" or "standard 'not A'" as the controlling substantive rule of decision in the first place. Under separation-of-powers principles, this congressional action is constitutionally defective, because it effectively enlists the federal judiciary in a scheme to bring about voter confusion.

Under certain circumstances, such legislative action could also violate the procedural due process rights of a litigant to a full and fair adjudication of his claim. Though Congress may have power to prescribe a different or even contradictory rule of decision, unless and until it does so, a litigant has a right to be fairly heard on his claim that the standard of the existing rule of decision has been met in his individual case (at least to the extent that liberty or property interests are sufficiently implicated to trigger the due process requirement).

For these reasons, Justice Antonin Scalia was incorrect in rejecting a procedural due process challenge in *Michael H. v. Gerald D.*[82] The case (which primarily concerned questions over the scope of substantive due process rights) involved a constitutional challenge to the denial of parental rights of a man claiming to be the biological father of a married woman's child. His procedural due process objection concerned section 621 of the California Evidence Code,[83] which provides that a child born to a married woman living with her husband, who is neither impotent nor sterile, is presumed to be a child of the marriage.[84] The presumption may be rebutted only by the husband or wife, and even then only in limited circumstances.[85]

Justice Scalia, speaking for a majority of the Court, rejected the challenge, because

> This claim derives from a fundamental misconception of the nature of the California statute. While section 621 is phrased in terms of a presumption, that rule of evidence is the implementation of a substantive rule of law. California declares it to be, except in limited circumstances, irrelevant for paternity purposes whether a child conceived during, and born into, an existing marriage was begotten by someone other than the husband . . .
>
> Of course the conclusive presumption not only expresses the State's substantive policy but also furthers it, excluding inquiries into the child's paternity that would be destructive of family integrity and privacy.[86]

Justice Scalia conceded that "[a] conclusive presumption does, of course, foreclose the person against whom it is invoked from demonstrating, in a particularized proceeding, that applying the presumption to him will in fact not further the lawful governmental policy the presumption is designed to effectuate."[87] He responded, however, that "the same can be said of any legal rule that establishes general classifications, whether framed in terms of a presumption or not."[88] In this reasoning, Justice Scalia missed the key point underlying the concept of decisional independence.

To be sure, assuming no violation of relevant substantive constitutional rights, California may adopt the rule that a biological father has no rights in his child when the mother is married to another man. But California did not adopt such a rule. Instead, it adopted a law that purports to have rights turn on the factual issue of who the natural father is, yet, through evidentiary manipulation indirectly effects a very different public policy.[89] If government wishes to attain a particular public policy, our constitutional democratic theory dictates that government do so openly, to assure that the choice is subject to the scrutiny, and ultimate judgment, of the electorate.

For reasons of both separation of powers and due process, then, the deceptively simple logical principle that "the greater includes the lesser"[90] does not work in this context. The mere fact that a legislature constitutionally *could* have chosen a particular substantive legal standard should not be taken to imply that it constitutionally may purport to establish a different substantive standard yet effectively create an alternative standard for controlling substantive law by resort to procedural and evidentiary manipulation. One may draw an analogy to an aspect of modern public choice theory: an interpreting court should not construe a legislative enactment framed in terms of public purposes to achieve some surreptitious private-regarding purpose, even if the interpreting court is convinced that such a private purpose actually does underlie the statute.[91] If the legislature wishes to attain its private-regarding purpose, it should be required to so provide explicitly, lest public policies effectively be developed in disguise.

Legislative or Executive Resolution of Individual Litigation

A second limitation on congressional authority that the principle of decisional independence imposes is that Congress may not, through legislation, dictate the resolution of an individual litigation. Of course, Congress may, through enactment of generally applicable substantive legislation, *effectively* dictate the result in individual cases, because the federal courts are bound to apply constitutionally valid congressional legislation in the course of individual litigations. But if the principle of separation of powers dictated by the Constitution's allocation of distinct authority to the several branches means anything, it must mean that one branch may not totally usurp another branch's function.[92] When Congress does nothing more than dictate resolution of an individual litigation, much as when it enacts a constitutionally prohibited bill of attainder,[93] it exceeds its constitutional authority.

CONGRESSIONAL REOPENING OF FINAL JUDGMENTS:
THE SCOPE AND RATIONALE OF JUDGMENTAL
INDEPENDENCE

One conceivable application of decisional independence concerns the constitutionality of congressional efforts simultaneously to alter substantive law and reopen final judgments of the federal courts in order to revise them in accordance with those substantive alterations. The Supreme Court dealt with this issue in its decision in *Plaut v. Spendthrift Farm, Inc.*[94] The case concerned the constitutionality of Section 27A(b) of the Securities and Exchange Act of 1934,[95] a provision added to the Act by amendment in 1991. The amendment came in response to a Supreme Court decision construing the 1934 Act to establish a uniform rule that " litigation instituted pursuant to section 10(b) . . . must be commenced within one year after the discovery of the facts constituting the violation and within three years after such violation."[96] In a separate decision made the same day, the Court held that this statute of limitations was to be applied to pending claims brought under section 10(b).[97] As a result, various district courts dismissed pending suits. In response, Congress enacted section 27A, which provided:

> (a) Effect on Pending Causes of Action—The limitation period for any private civil action implied under section 78j (b) of this title that was commenced on or before June 19, 1991, shall be the limitation period provided by the laws applicable in the jurisdiction, including principles of retro-activity, as such laws existed on June 19, 1991.
> (b) Effect on Dismissed Causes of Action—Any private civil action implied under section 78j (b) of this title that was commenced on or before June 19, 1991 -
> (1) which was dismissed as time barred subsequent to June 19, 1991, and
> (2) which would have been timely filed under the limitation period provided by the laws applicable in the jurisdiction, including principles of retroactivity, as such laws existed on June 19, 1991. shall be reinstated on motion by the plaintiff not later than 60 days after December 19, 1991.[98]

In *Pacific Mutual Life Insurance Co. v. First Republicbank Corp.*,[99] a decision subsequently affirmed by an equally divided Supreme Court, the United States Court of Appeals for the Fifth Circuit rejected a challenge to section 27A(b) as a violation of Article III.[100] The Fifth Circuit reasoned that section 27A(b) respects the principle that Congress may not resolve individual cases, because the provision actually changed the governing generally applicable substantive law.[101] The *Pacific Mutual* Court assured that " if we understood a statute's purpose to be the reversal of results in particular controversies between private individuals, we would strike the statute as violative of our authority to decide cases."[102]

While most courts of appeals to have considered the issue reached a similar conclusion,[103] the United States Court of Appeals for the Sixth Circuit in *Plaut*[104] found section 27A(b) to be an unconstitutional interference with the performance of the judicial function.[105] Relying on the early Supreme Court decision in *Hayburn's Case*,[106] the Sixth Circuit concluded that "the Supreme Court has from the beginning maintained the rule that Congress may not retroactively disturb final judgments of the Federal courts."[107] The court's reliance on *Hayburn's Case*, however, was misplaced. Indeed, by contrasting the situation in *Plaut* with that in *Hayburn's Case*, we can better understand the limits of the concept of decisional independence. In *Hayburn* the Court invalidated, on separation-of-powers grounds, a congressional directive authorizing the secretary of war to review decisions of the federal courts accepting or rejecting applications by Revolutionary War veterans for disability pensions.[108] The secretary could deny pensions where he suspected imposition or mistake.[109]

The Sixth Circuit cited *Hayburn* "to illustrate that the Supreme Court has from the beginning maintained the rule that Congress may not retroactively disturb final judgments of the Federal courts."[110] But *Hayburn* really establishes no such thing. Instead, it rightly establishes that Congress may not authorize an executive officer to review and reverse *specific, individual federal court decisions*. Section 27(A), in contrast, alters *the general governing law* of the statute of limitations in securities fraud cases and directs that the new law be imposed with total retroactivity, even to the point of reopening previously final judgments. Assuming no controlling due process rights of litigants in those judgments,[111] such legislative action constitutes no breach of constitutionally protected judicial independence. Decisional independence prohibits review and reversal by the legislative or executive branches of the result of a particular litigation; decisional independence does not, however, prohibit congressional alteration of controlling substantive law that has the effect of altering a class of federal court decisions.

Despite the fact that Section 27 (A) was wholly consistent with the dictates of decisional independence, the Supreme Court held the provision to be an unconstitutional interference with judicial independence. While Justice Scalia, writing for the majority, acknowledged that the provision was consistent with traditional forms of decisional independence, he nevertheless concluded that "§27 A (b) offends a postulate of Article III just as deeply rooted in our law as [other forms of judicial independence]."[112]

Justice Scalia noted that "the Framers crafted [Article III] with an expressed understanding that it gives the Federal Judiciary the Power, not merely to rule on cases, but to *decide* them, subject to review only by superior courts in the Article III hierarchy—with an understanding, in short, that 'a judgment conclusively resolves the case' in short, because 'a' judicial power is one to render dispositive judgments.'"[113]

There appears to be a fatal flaw in Justice Scalia's logic. While no one would likely dispute any of his statements as an abstract matter, the challenged provision was in no way inconsistent with any of them. Nothing in the provision revoked the federal judiciary's authority ultimately to decide the case. Nor did the statute *reverse* any federal court judgments. It merely required those federal courts to open up prior judgments in order to resolve them in accordance with altered (or what Congress would probably have called corrected) controlling substantive law. Absent any issue with retroactivity—and nothing in the Court's opinion focused on that issue—the challenged statute does not in any way interfere with the independent authority of the federal judiciary ultimately to decide an individual case.

The fact remains, of course, that *Plaut* continues to be good law. At least as a descriptive doctrinal matter, then, this category of "judgmental" independence must be included as a category in the modern taxonomy of judicial independence. However, in terms of the manner and degree in which legislative interference threatens the precepts of American constitutionalism, threats to judgmental independence pale in comparison to similar threats to either decisional or countermajoritarian independence.

IMPLICATIONS OF THE DECISIONAL-LAWMAKING DISTINCTION: CONGRESS'S POWER TO PRESCRIBE PROCEDURAL RULES FOR THE FEDERAL COURTS

Deciding whether congressional prescription of procedural rules for the federal courts violates the constitutional protection of separation of powers necessarily requires one to recall the various models of separation-of-powers theory.[114] From a formalist perspective, the constitutional inquiry is limited to the questions of whether such action falls within the concept of legislative power, and if so whether the action falls within the scope of the powers the Constitution provides to Congress. As to the first question, the definitional requirements of the exercise of legislative power have been met as long as the rules prescribed are of general applicability and affect the behavior of citizens. As to the second inquiry, the Supreme Court made clear in *Hanna v. Plumer*[115] that Congress's enumerated power to create inferior federal courts,[116] combined with its auxiliary power under the Necessary and Proper Clause,[117] provides Congress with the authority to prescribe procedural rules for the federal courts.[118]

If one were to shift the focus to functionalism,[119] one would inquire whether an otherwise legitimate exercise of the legislative power should be invalidated because it unduly invades the province of a coordinate branch. The only way this question could be answered in the affirmative is by concluding that the task of promulgating rules of procedure is so intimately bound up in the performance of the judicial function that the courts could not effectively exercise the judicial power without retaining exclusive authority over procedural rulemaking. But reaching this conclusion appears difficult in light of the long established history of congressional involvement in the rulemaking process. Indeed, the Supreme Court's power to promulgate procedural rules has traditionally been rationalized as a congressional delegation of *legislative* power to the Court.[120] At the very least, Congress has always retained ultimate authority under the Rules Enabling Act to overrule specific rules promulgated by the Court. This power would, of course, have to be deemed unacceptable if the judicial power over rulemaking were thought to be exclusive.

On a comparative basis, the power to promulgate generally applicable rules of procedure—at least untied to adjudication of a live case or controversy—is in some senses easier to conceptualize as a legislative action than as a judicial one. Exercise of the judicial power is inherently characterized by the adjudication of individualized live disputes.[121] Promulgation of free-standing rules of general applicability does not fit within this model, even when those rules deal with matters that are intimately intertwined with performance of the adjudicatory function.

Even if one were to conclude that procedural rulemaking does fall within the judicial province,[122] that judicial authority over rulemaking is exclusive does not automatically follow. From a purely functionalist perspective, Congress retains a legitimate and significant interest in the procedures and operations of the federal courts for a number of reasons. First, the success of the substantive federal legislative programs enforced in the federal courts is inescapably intertwined with the procedural efficiency of those courts. Second, the federal budget is invariably affected by the procedural efficiency levels achieved in the federal courts. Thus, on the basis of a type of functionalist interest analysis, the level of Congress's legitimate interest in the choice of procedural rules that govern federal court operation is virtually as intense as that of the federal courts themselves.

The fact that congressional prescription of procedural rules is not, as an abstract matter, invalid does not necessarily imply that all rules that Congress could potentially adopt would pass constitutional muster under a separation-of-powers standard. Conceivably, for example, a specific procedural rule could so interfere with the courts' performance of the judicial function—the full and fair performance of the adjudicatory process of finding facts[123] and/or interpreting applicable law and applying it to the facts[124]—as to invade the courts' "judicial power" under Article III. However, this conclusion could be reached only in the context of a consideration of challenges to particular rules.

CONCLUSION

Although Congress possesses broad constitutional authority to regulate federal court jurisdiction, it would be both inaccurate and dangerous to believe that the federal courts possess no meaningful independence from the representative branches of the federal government. The institutional independence guarantees expressly provided for in the Compensation Clause of Article III provide a basic prophylactic floor of independence. Moreover, the established constitutional principles of due process and separation of powers, embodying fundamental principles of American constitutional and political theory, guarantee to the federal courts, or at least to the judiciary as a whole,[125] both countermajoritarian and decisional independence. These guarantees ensure judicial authorities the power to interpret the Constitution and apply the law to individual cases free from pressure or control of the representative branches.

An equally unwise assertion, however, would be that the constitutional principle of judicial independence somehow corrupts the democratic integrity of our governmental system by authorizing the federal courts to promulgate generalized rules of decision or procedure that are insulated from alteration or preemption by the representative branches, at least absent a grounding in the Due Process Clause. Like most aspects of the American political system, judicial independence reflects a delicate balance of both democratic theory, concerned with principles of representationalism and accountability, and republican precepts, focused upon the need to curb democratic excesses. Such a balancing process may be properly performed only by recognition of the subtle variations in the framework of federal judicial independence.

Judicial Impeachment, Judicial Discipline, and American Constitutionalism

INTRODUCTION

Both the American Revolution and the nation that grew out of it adopted as their guiding political philosophy the principles of representationalism and accountability:[1] decisions of governing political and social policy are to be made, for the most part, by citizens who are both representative of and accountable to the populace.[2] This, in a nutshell, describes the *sine qua non* of a democratic society. To be sure, those who framed our Constitution never contemplated either a direct or an unlimited form of democracy, and although ultimate accountability to the people—if only indirectly—was a fundamental premise of U.S. government, decision making by officials was limited by the constitutional separation of powers.[3]

At first glance, the Framers' choice to provide the members of one of the three branches of government with constitutional guarantees of both salary and tenure thus seems puzzlingly inconsistent with their overall theoretical plan. Such insulation from the populace naturally raises the possibility that fundamental decisions affecting the lives of the citizenry will be made by officials who have not been chosen by the populace and will never have to account for their decisions at the polls. However, as the prior chapters have established, the Framers were quite clear that they deemed such insulation essential to the maintenance of the judiciary's independence from the political branches of government. This independence, in turn, was deemed essential to maintain both the integrity of the judicial process and the vitality of constitutional government.

In part, such independence is necessary to preserve the effectiveness of the judicial review process. As Chief Justice Marshall persuasively argued in *Marbury v. Madison*,[4] if the majoritarian branches of government are to sit as final arbiters of the meaning of the countermajoritarian constitutional limits on their power, those constitutional limits are effectively rendered meaningless. But they are rendered equally meaningless if the final arbiters are individuals who are subject to the direct control of those majoritarian branches.

The salary and tenure protections of Article III, however, are not confined to judges who decide cases arising under the Constitution. Rather, they apply to all judges of Article III federal courts, regardless of the nature of the cases they adjudicate. Thus, the decision to provide these judges with protections of salary and tenure must have been designed to accomplish more than merely the preservation of meaningful judicial review and adherence to constitutional constraints. Instead, the concern must also have extended to the need to preserve the integrity of the judicial process in all its applications.

While the Constitution's protection of judicial independence obviously gives rise to important systemic benefits, in what is predominantly a democratic society there are also costs that must be incurred. As already noted, judicial independence means that judges may decide cases in a manner that will prove to be unpopular with the polity without fear of professional retribution. Moreover, the life tenure given to judges to preserve their decisional independence may cause significant problems when judges, for whatever reason, become unwilling or unable to perform their function in an honest and effective manner. In other words, either through disability or personal choice, judges may on occasion abuse their office. If the life tenure they have been afforded were to provide for no safety valves, the seemingly salutary constitutional assurance of life tenure would effectively deprive society of any practical means of controlling such renegade or dysfunctional judges. Not only would such a result undermine the democratic principles of accountability and representationalism that are essential to American political theory, it would also undermine the very judicial integrity that the protections of judicial independence were designed to ensure.

On the other hand, if the structure of judicial independence were modified to enable society to remove and/or punish judges who fall within this description, the obvious danger would arise that those in power could employ such avenues as a subterfuge to intimidate the judiciary or influence their decision making. This would, of course, render the carefully structured protections of judicial independence largely meaningless.

That the Framers themselves may not have fully reckoned with this democratic dilemma is evidenced by the fact that at one point in *The Federalist*, Alexander Hamilton writes eloquently of the necessity of judicial independence as an element of limited democratic government,[5] while at another insists that it will be possible to remove insane judges from office.[6] At no point does he acknowledge the possibility that the assumed power of government to remove judges whom it chooses to characterize as insane could be easily manipulated to circumvent judicial independence.

Though they are, thankfully, relatively few and far between, one need not search very far to find examples of political attempts to circumvent the constitutional protections of judicial independence in order to intimidate or improperly influence federal judges' decision making. Early in the nation's history, the Republicans' impeachment of the controversial federalist Supreme Court Justice Samuel Chase constituted an instance of just such a political attempt.[7] To point to a more modern example, in the 1980s, widespread negative political reaction to the decision of Federal District Court Judge Harold Baer to exclude evidence in a criminal trial on the grounds that it had been obtained unconstitutionally led to numerous calls by powerful governmental leaders for Judge Baer's impeachment.[8] Subsequently, Judge Baer reversed his own decision.[9]

This chapter is intended to explore the competing societal concerns of judicial independence and judicial responsibility from the perspective of constitutional analysis. In so doing, it will attempt to view these issues as a matter of both textual and structural interpretation. By this I mean that I will seek to develop coherent constructions of the various constitutional provisions that deal with either judicial independence, judicial removal or judicial discipline. I consider these questions in the first instance by seeking rational constructions of the words that appear in the Constitution concerning federal judicial removal. However, because both ambiguities in individual provisions and tension, or even conflicts among different provisions, often exist, I also recognize the need to employ an analysis designed to weave the various relevant constitutional provisions into a viable, coherent integrated textual structure, grounded in the foundational principles of American constitutionalism. It is only by means of such an attempt to link seemingly unrelated portions of text, I believe, that one can effectively understand the Constitution's often intricate structural web of judicial protections and judicial limitations.

The initial textual and structural inquiries are, quite naturally, into the Constitution's network of judicial independence protections.[10] Once the structure of judicial independence is explored, I turn to an analysis of the

Constitution's authorization of judicial discipline, consider the conceivable means by which government may constitutionally remove or discipline federal judges, and measure those options against the constitutional guarantees of judicial independence.

The Constitution itself appears to provide two potential avenues of removal: the impeachment power of Article II[11] and the "good Behaviour" qualification of the life-tenure guarantee of Article III.[12] Although respected scholars have argued that the Good Behavior Clause is properly construed to create an alternative and supplemental constitutional means of disciplining federal judges,[13] I will demonstrate in the section that follows that such an argument is unjustified as a matter of policy, text, and history. The *only* constitutionally authorized means of judicial removal is through resort to the formal impeachment process. The Good Behavior Clause is properly construed as nothing more than a textual cross-reference to the impeachment power, designed to avoid the confusion that might otherwise have resulted from the seeming contradiction between the unqualified life-tenure protection of Article III and the impeachment provision of Article II. The textual role played by the Good Behavior Clause, then, is merely to make clear that the Impeachment Clause modifies the Tenure Clause, rather than the other way around.[14] Left unresolved, however, is the question of exactly how the Impeachment and Tenure Clauses interact. Although it is clear that the latter does not wholly supersede the former, it would be wrong to assume that the Impeachment Clause can be properly construed without reference to the purposes, goals, and explicit directive of the Tenure Clause.

The conclusion reached here is that whenever either salary or tenure of Articles III judges may be negatively affected, the constitutionally available methods of judicial discipline must be narrowly circumscribed. The only conceivable method of discipline implemented by the other branches under such circumstances is through resort to the impeachment process, and the availability of even that process is to be narrowly confined to situations in which the judge has engaged in criminal behavior that threatens the integrity of the judicial role. Under no circumstances may a federal judge be impeached for a decision he or she has reached in the course of an adjudication. Moreover, I conclude that the political-question doctrine should have absolutely no applicability as a bar to judicial review of the legislative determination that the challenged judicial behavior does, in fact, constitute an impeachable offense under the Constitution. Rather, the judiciary should be deemed to have full authority to review a congressional determination that an Article III judge has committed an impeachable offense.

The necessary implication of my conclusion about the exclusivity of the impeachment remedy is that no form of judicially self-imposed discipline affecting either salary or tenure may constitutionally be employed.[15] I reach these conclusions, because I believe that any more expansive constructions of the disciplinary power would indirectly but inescapably contravene Article III's salary and tenure protections, effectively rendering those prophylactic protections of judicial independence all but meaningless.

The first part of this chapter explores the intersection of the Impeachment and Good Behavior Clauses. The second part explains why the constitutional standards for and limitations on the impeachment power must be unique when applied to federal judges, as opposed to other federal officers.[16] The third part seeks to reconcile the impeachment power with core notions of judicial independence expressly provided for in the Constitution's text. The final part of the chapter explores the extent to which judicial review of congressional impeachment decisions is appropriate. I conclude there that a certain level of judicial review of congressional invocation of the impeachment power against Article III judges is necessary to effective implementation of the prophylactic reach of Article III's Tenure Clause.[17]

RECONCILING THE GOOD BEHAVIOR CLAUSE WITH THE IMPEACHMENT POWER

Two constitutional provisions on their face concern the possible removal from office of a federal judge protected by Article III, section 1's life-tenure clause. One provision is the impeachment power of Article II,[18] which permits removal of federal officers in accord with the procedure laid out in Article I.[19] The second provision is the "good Behaviour" Clause of Article III, section 1, which makes judicial life tenure conditional on compliance with the dictates of "good Behaviour."[20] While the circumstances triggering the impeachment power are expressly confined to a finding of "high crimes or misdemeanors," the phrase, "good Behaviour" remains cryptically vague, on two levels. First, it is unclear whether the clause represents nothing more than a cross-reference to the impeachment power, or instead establishes an alternative, additional basis on which to remove a federal judge from office. Second, if the latter construction is adopted, it is unclear exactly what the requirements of "good Behaviour" are, who gets to decide that issue, and by what processes that decision is to be reached.

Up to this point, purely as a doctrinal matter, the Good Behavior Clause has played no independent role in the removal of federal judges.

Rather, all efforts to remove federal judges from office have been confined to the impeachment power. However, in recent years Professors Si Prakash and Steven Smith have argued that the Good Behavior Clause is constitutionally capable of playing a far greater role in policing federal judges than it has played up to now. They contend that the traditionally accepted view that impeachment is the exclusive constitutionally recognized means of removing federal judges from office is "unpersuasive and ahistorical."[21] The "better reading," they suggest, is that under the Good Behavior Clause "officers with good-behavior tenure forfeited their offices upon a finding of misbehavior in the ordinary course."[22] They see the clause as providing a means, in addition to the impeachment power recognized in Article II, Section 4, for the political branches to regulate the federal judiciary.

Moreover, they argue, the standard of improper judicial conduct that justifies invocation of the Good Behavior Clause—while concededly quite murky—is distinctly lower than that set by the "high Crimes and Misdemeanors" language of the Impeachment Clause.[23] The upshot of acceptance of their proposal, then, would be the recognition of a potentially dramatic expansion in the ability of the political branches to remove federal judges, protected by the qualified life tenure and salary guarantees of Article III, from office.[24]

The Prakash-Smith proposal represents the strongest possible compilation of arguments to support so sweeping and radical a doctrinal alteration in the constitutionally authorized means of removing federal judges. Close analysis, however, reveals that their historical arguments by no means inexorably lead to the constitutional conclusion they reach. To the contrary, a detailed critical review of their arguments shows them to be counterintuitive, incomplete, or inconsistent with unambiguous historical evidence. Prakash and Smith fail to meet their burden of historical proof to show that those who drafted and ratified the Constitution intended, by use of the "good Behaviour" language, to incorporate the preconstitutional historical practice wholesale.

Far more problematic, however, is the deeper flaw in their argument: their failure to deal adequately with the broad—and troubling—theoretical implications of their suggested construction of the Good Behavior Clause for foundational notions of American constitutionalism. Because their examination of the "trees" of historical practice is so detailed,[25] it is all too easy to ignore the "forest"—the extremely problematic effect that their proposed interpretation would have on the vital role that federal judicial independence necessarily plays in preserving the foundations of the nation's political and constitutional structure. Put bluntly, by substantially expanding the ability of the political branches to remove, and therefore threaten and intimidate, members of the federal judiciary, the Prakash-Smith proposal to recognize the Good Behavior Clause as an independent means of judicial removal seriously endangers the ability of the independent federal courts to police the constitutional excesses of the political branches and to protect individual rights from majoritarian incursion. By threatening the meaningful exercise of judicial review as a check on the majoritarian branches—and make no mistake, that is undoubtedly the result to which the Prakash-Smith proposal would lead[26]—their suggested construction of the Good Behavior Clause would dangerously upset the delicate balance of checks and balances the Framers so wisely developed.

As a textualist,[27] I would be forced to accept their proposal were I convinced that it represented the only reasonable construction of the applicable constitutional text, regardless of how dangerous I believed it to be to the foundations of American constitutionalism. But even Prakash and Smith readily concede that their approach is not the only plausible construction of the text. To the contrary, they acknowledge that, as a purely textual matter, one might conclude that the Good Behavior Clause can be read to be nothing more than a cross-reference to the standard for impeachment described in Article II, Section 4.[28] So viewed, the language would be designed simply to prevent possible confusion and conflict between the otherwise unlimited judicial tenure dictated by Article III and the directive of Article II subjecting federal judges to removal from office through exercise of the impeachment power.[29]

When a textualist is faced with more than one linguistically plausible option, the text can of course no longer exclusively control the ultimate interpretive choice. Thus, in making that interpretive choice in this case, it is necessary for the interpreter to attempt to determine what effect each of the alternative constructions would have on both the textual framework of judicial independence and the role that judicial independence is properly deemed to play within the broader framework of American constitutional and political theory. This Prakash and Smith have failed to do, or at least do adequately.[30] Instead, they have employed a form of "constitutional isolationism," in which each provision is interpreted largely in a textual and political vacuum, without any meaningful examination of how the chosen interpretation fits within this broader and more holistic constitutional structure.[31]

CONSTITUTIONAL HISTORY AND THE
GOOD BEHAVIOR CLAUSE

The Prakash-Smith Argument

Professors Prakash and Smith make an elegantly simple argument to support their position that the Good Behavior Clause provides a distinct means, above and beyond the impeachment power, by which the political branches may remove federal judges from office. They meticulously demonstrate that, under established preconstitutional practice (on both sides of the Atlantic), "Good Behaviour" was a term of art, employed as a basis for judicially removing a wide variety of both public and private officeholders from office.[32] Apparently, this practice had no clear relationship to the wholly distinct process of impeachment. Thus, it would be "ahistorical," Prakash and Smith believe, to construe the "good Behaviour" language the Framers inserted as the qualifying standard on the otherwise unlimited tenure of federal judges in Article III, as simply a cross-reference to the "high Crimes and Misdemeanors" standard for impeachment set out in Article II, section 4, to which federal judges are also subject.[33]

Although Prakash and Smith are certain that, as a historical matter, "good Behaviour" represented a distinct, self-contained means for removing officeholders above and beyond the impeachment power, they are far less certain "about what constituted misbehavior."[34] They do suggest—without a great deal of explanation—that the "'good Behaviour' provision . . . seems more general and less severe" in its standard for removal than does the "high Crimes and Misdemeanors" language of the Impeachment Clause.[35] In defining the "good Behaviour" standard in preconstitutional historical practice, they occasionally refer to "[t]hose who did not exhibit good behavior—i.e., those who misbehaved."[36] This circular explication, however, is far from helpful. Although they acknowledge that what constitutes constitutionally recognized "misbehavior" under preconstitutional practice is "murky," they point to Lord Coke's description of "three grounds for forfeiture: abuse of office, nonuse of office, and refusal to exercise an office."[37] But at no point do they describe what, historically, counted as an "abuse of office." More important, they fail to explain how the historical understanding of "abuse of office" would translate into the nation's modern political and constitutional structure. Could the phrase today possibly apply to judicial interpretation of the Constitution in a manner found offensive, inaccurate, or politically unacceptable by members of Congress or the president? On this issue, even if one were able to unearth it, preconstitutional historical practice could not possibly provide meaningful assistance, because the inquiry would be anachronistic. The American version of strong judicial review, clearly contemplated by those who crafted the Constitution and long accepted in U.S. practice,[38] simply did not exist at that point in time, particularly in England, where, Prakash and Smith tell us, the concept of good-behavior tenure emerged.

Nor is their examination of history, as detailed as it is, particularly helpful in explaining exactly how, under the U.S. constitutional system, the Good Behavior Clause of Article III is to be implemented procedurally. Prakash and Smith suggest that Congress may invoke its authority under the Necessary and Proper Clause of Article I[39] to enact statutes providing for judicial removal on grounds of misbehavior.[40] However, the Necessary and Proper Clause is not a freestanding grant of power. Rather, both by its express terms and venerable judicial doctrine,[41] that clause is purely catalytic and facilitative of other, preexisting powers granted to Congress in Article I, section 8. Prakash and Smith fail to tell us exactly which preexisting power of Congress or another branch of the federal government the statutes would facilitate or implement.[42]

Acceptance of the Prakash-Smith proposal would mean the following: "good Behaviour" provides a distinct method, above and beyond impeachment, for removing federal judges from office, at a standard of misbehavior somewhat lower than that required under impeachment (though exactly how much lower remains unclear). However, we know virtually nothing about how "good Behaviour" is to be defined, who gets to define it either generally or in the individual case, or from where Congress derives the constitutional authority to provide a statutory mechanism by which to enforce the Good Behavior Clause.

I have no basis on which to question the detailed preconstitutional historical description provided by Prakash and Smith concerning the use of the "good Behaviour" standard for unseating both public and private officers.[43] Even assuming the accuracy of their historical portrayal, however, there are a number of significant gaps or flaws in their attempted linkage of that history with modern constitutional interpretation of Article III's Good Behavior Clause that renders their historical inquiry of no modern relevance.

The Implications of Historical Practice for Interpretation of Article III

The history described in such detail by Prakash and Smith clearly demonstrates that the good-behavior requirement evolved in preconstitutional

English practice, not as a means of *controlling* officeholders, but rather as a means of actually *protecting* their tenure. According to the Prakash-Smith historical assessment, absent insertion of the good-behavior requirement, the king would have been able to remove judges or other officeholders at his pleasure. With the requirement that judges could be removed only upon a showing of the absence of good behavior, however, the officeholder must have been found, through resort to the judicial process, to have "misbehaved" before the king could remove him.[44] The good-behavior requirement developed, then, not as a means of increasing political control over judicial tenure, but rather as a means of expanding judicial officeholder independence.[45] Yet both the purpose and impact of the Prakash-Smith approach to good behavior in Article III are to achieve the diametrically opposite result—namely, to undermine and reduce the independence of judicial officeholders. In contrast, when the "good Behaviour" language is viewed as merely a cross-reference to the procedurally and substantively protective impeachment standard, it serves much the same purpose that it was universally intended to serve (at least in the case of public officeholders) in its preconstitutional historical context—that is, to protect the officeholder from unduly invasive and capricious treatment by those in power in a manner that might compromise performance of the officeholder's task. Indeed, Hamilton's relatively brief references to the Good Behavior Clause in *Federalist* No. 78 quite clearly demonstrate that he intended it to *protect* federal judges from intimidation, not to serve as an additional means of controlling judicial behavior.[46]

Did the Framers clearly contemplate that good behavior in Article III was to be a mirror image of the standard for impeachment in Article II? It appears likely that they failed to focus sufficiently on the issue to have any defined perspective on the point.[47] But what *is* clear is that they deemed an independent judiciary to be an essential element of the American constitutional system.[48] It is also clear that the only references in *The Federalist* to the control of judicial excesses concern the impeachment power, without any reliance on the Good Behavior Clause as an alternative method of policing judicial misbehavior.[49] Indeed, the only references in *The Federalist* to the Good Behavior Clause—and there are relatively few—are to the protective purposes the clause serves in preserving judicial independence. When *The Federalist* refers to the need to check the actions of federal judges, it refers explicitly only to the impeachment power.[50]

The Jeffersonian attempt after ratification to impeach the federalist Supreme Court Justice Samuel Chase is consistent with the view that the impeachment power was intended to be the sole means of regulating judicial excess.[51] The Republican effort to satisfy the high standards for conviction in the Senate failed, following impeachment in the House of Representatives.[52] If, as Prakash and Smith assert, the Good Behavior Clause of Article III was generally understood at the time of framing both to provide an alternative means of judicial removal and to impose substantively and procedurally lower standards for judicial removal than does the Impeachment Clause, it is very puzzling that the Republicans did not even attempt to resort to that constitutional strategy, especially after their impeachment strategy failed.[53]

With Professor Steven Calabresi, Professor Prakash has previously argued that post-ratification practice should be considered in assessing Framers' intent only as a last resort.[54] But that argument makes sense only for the purpose of excluding *strategically self-serving* post-ratification practice—for example, the president's assumption of additional power above and beyond that seemingly granted by the text of Article II. Such self-serving practices are necessarily colored by considerations of strategic political gain and therefore demonstrate little, if anything, about the Framers' understanding at the time of ratification. However, when the post-ratification practice is strategically self-restrictive, as was the case in the Republican failure to consider possible resort to the Good Behavior Clause in the effort to remove Justice Chase from office, the practice is appropriately deemed strongly probative of Framers' understandings. This is especially true when—as in the case of the Chase impeachment—the practice occurs at a point so temporally close to the Constitution's drafting and ratification. Indeed, of greatest significance is that apparently at the time of the Chase impeachment absolutely no one even suggested resort to the Good Behavior Clause as an alternative means of judicial removal. Thus, while Prakash and Smith attempt to summarily dismiss the incident's relevance,[55] the simple fact remains: if those who drafted and ratified the document understood that the Good Behavior Clause was intended to create an alternative means of judicial removal, above and beyond the impeachment power, there is no reason why the Republicans would have failed to resort to the supposedly more flexible good-behavior alternative once their impeachment efforts had failed.

Ultimately, the Prakash-Smith historical argument fails because of a simple lack of supporting evidence. While they seem to be capable of providing a historical basis on which to establish some abstract preconstitutional understanding of the good-behavior concept in England or colonial America, Prakash and Smith totally fail to demonstrate widespread contemporaneous consensus as to how those words were meant to be understood when placed in the complex textual and political setting of the United States Constitution. The two contexts are by no means identical. Nor are Prakash and Smith capable of establishing that either the Framers or post-ratification Congresses understood that by inclusion of the "good Behaviour" language, Article III was intended to employ the clause as a supplemental, freestanding, less demanding means of removing federal judges, above and beyond impeachment. This is true, even though there certainly were situations in which use of such a procedure would have been strategically very helpful to those seeking to intimidate sitting judges. Prakash and Smith have therefore failed to satisfy even the most minimal burden of historical proof that logically rests on their shoulders, even if one assumes the validity of originalist analysis.

GOOD BEHAVIOR AND AMERICAN CONSTITUTIONALISM

The gaps and flaws in the historical case made by Professors Prakash and Smith are, unfortunately for them, the least of the problems with their proposal. Whatever one thinks about the implications of all of the arcane eighteenth-century British statues to which they point or any other pre-constitutional practice on which they rely, their proposal would severely undermine a number of fundamental elements of U.S. political and constitutional theory. Thus, when the dust settles, the historical practice concerning use of the phrase "good Behaviour" in the years prior to its insertion in Article III should make absolutely no difference; acceptance of the Prakash-Smith proposal would contravene the foundations of American constitutionalism, to which meaningful judicial independence is central. Acceptance of the Prakash-Smith suggested interpretation of the Good Behavior Clause would, to put it bluntly, gut any meaningful level of judicial independence.

Defining American Constitutionalism

The concept of American constitutionalism, as used throughout this book, links two distinct, albeit intertwined, levels of theoretical analysis. One is appropriately described as "macro" and the other as "micro." Both represent essential elements of American political and constitutional theory.[56]

On the "macro" level, the phrase refers to the basic notion of limited government, confined not solely by the will of a simple majority or the decisions of the majoritarian branches of government, but also by a binding, written constitutional structure, subject to revision, repeal, or amendment only by an intentionally demanding supermajoritarian process. While this is surely not the only form of democratic government a society could select, there can be little question that, at some basic level, this is exactly the system our nation chose. First, the nation chose to have our Constitution embodied in a written constitutive document, rather than remaining unwritten. Second, by its express and unambiguous terms, the document's directives are framed as commands, rather than as suggestions, recommendations, or pleas. Third, also by its express terms, the document is subject to alteration only by a cumbersome supermajoritarian process.[57] Fourth, if the words of the document were for some reason deemed insufficient, the unambiguous history of the framing of the document clearly demonstrates that the understanding of those who drafted it was to provide for a limited form of government in which the growth of tyranny would be rendered virtually impossible and minority rights were protected from the whims of majorities.[58] The only way these goals could even conceivably be achieved was through imposition of a binding, written, countermajoritarian constitutional structure.

On a "micro" level, to maintain their legitimacy, all democratic governments must adhere to some form of social contract with their individual constituents. The implicit understanding between them necessarily posits that government will not employ its power in an arbitrary, invidious, or irrational manner against the individuals to whom it is accountable. No truly representative government could appropriately treat its citizens in any other manner. Presumably for this reason, the Constitution (in its Bill of Rights) assures its citizens that government may not deprive them of life, liberty, or property without "due process of law." As an outgrowth of this commitment to due process, the nation further committed itself to two fundamental postulates. First, our judicial system must comply, not only with the demands of procedural justice, but also with "the appearance of justice."[59] Second, no person can serve as a judge in her own case.[60] Without assuring that both of these demands are satisfied, our system cannot comply with the dictates of due process that are imposed on us positively by the terms of the Fifth and Fourteenth Amendments and normatively by the very notion of legitimate democratic government.

The Role of Judicial Independence in Satisfying the Demands of American Constitutionalism

There can be little question that neither the macro nor the micro demands of American constitutionalism can be satisfied when the very majoritarian government body whose actions have been constitutionally challenged is the final judge of the legitimacy of those actions. No more satisfactory would be the vesting of the final power to resolve such disputes in the hands of those who are subject to the direct control of that government body. As a practical matter, such decisions would differ little from having decisions made by the government body itself. At the very least, under such circumstances, even if one were (with questionable accuracy) to assume the workings of actual justice, one most definitely could not be assured of the *appearance* of justice.

On the macro level, recognition of the basic precept of judicial review goes back to Hamilton in *Federalist* No. 78[61] and Chief Justice Marshall's famed opinion in *Marbury v. Madison*.[62] Both recognized that the practice of independent judicial review was necessary to prevent "giving to the legislature a practical and real omnipotence, with the same breath which professes to restrict their powers within narrow limits. It is prescribing limits, and declaring that these limits may be passed at pleasure."[63] Acceptance of such an argument, Marshall concluded, "reduces to nothing what we have deemed the greatest improvement on political institutions—a written constitution."[64]

On the micro level, the Supreme Court has long recognized that decisions involving the potential loss of life, liberty, or property do not comply with the requirements of procedural due process when the adjudicator stands to gain or lose financially on the basis of her decision.[65] This is so, even absent any concrete showing that the potential financial interest actually influenced the adjudicator's decision.[66] The obvious reason for so strict a constitutional standard is the reasonable apprehension that otherwise the adjudicator's decision would be deprived of all legitimacy in the eyes of the litigants. This concern is intensified when the government is on one side of the case and the adjudicator is subject to the government's financial control. Presumably, similar concerns led the Framers to impose an unwavering prohibition on reductions in the salaries of Article III judges.[67]

Implications of the Prakash-Smith Proposal for Judicial Independence

Absent acceptance of the Prakash-Smith proposed interpretation of the Good Behavior Clause, the nation's structure of judicial independence looks roughly like this: Once appointed and confirmed, Article III judges sit for life, and their salaries cannot be reduced. However, for the commission of "high Crimes and Misdemeanors," they (like other civil officers) can be subjected to a supermajoritarian two-House process of impeachment and removal.[68] The reference in Article III to judicial tenure during "good Behaviour," in the non-Prakash-Smith world, is construed as nothing more than a textual cross-reference to the impeachment power set out in Article II, section 4. The language was included in Article III presumably to avoid a confusing conflict between the seemingly unlimited tenure guaranteed in Article III and the simultaneous existence of the impeachment power.

When one inserts the Prakash-Smith proposal into this framework, we are left with the following structure of judicial independence: Much of the previously described scenario concerning the role of impeachment would continue to exist; however, some nebulous power in Congress to legislatively establish an as-yet undefined judicial procedure by which Article III federal judges could be removed, absent either the protections of the substantively demanding "high Crimes and Misdemeanors" standard or the procedurally demanding two-House supermajority process set out by Article I's impeachment method, would also be recognized. We would have no clear concept of what activity on the part of federal judges actually constitutes the absence of "good Behaviour," other than that it is some form of "misbehavior"[69] or "abuse of office."[70] Moreover, whether Congress would possess unreviewable power to define the concept or only be permitted to set up the process, with the enforcing courts construing it, would remain unclear. Indeed, whether Congress's legislatively established definition of the phrase would constitute an unreviewable "political question," effectively excluding the courts from involvement in the definitional process, also remains unclear.[71]

The impact of this proposal on the judicial independence necessary for the success of both branches of American constitutionalism would be devastating. At present, federal judges know that they may be removed only by resort to an extremely difficult process and that as long as they stay in office, their salaries cannot be reduced for any reason. That removal process exists simply as a safety valve in extreme cases.[72] Under the Prakash-Smith proposal, in contrast, judges would know that not only their financial interests[73] but their very employment might well rest on the extent to which their decisions—interpreting both constitutional and subconstitutional federal law—offend those in political power.[74] This would be true even if it were the enforcing judges, rather than Congress, who were to exercise final say on the meaning of "good Behaviour." Judges appointed by the current administration could then use that power as a means of intimidating or removing judges appointed by prior administrations that held political viewpoints in conflict with those of the current administration.

Whether recognition of the political power under the Good Behavior Clause advocated by Prakash and Smith would, in fact, be employed retributively is, of course, largely beside the point. It is the impact of the fear that it might be so employed on federal judicial decision making, and the concern on the part of the citizenry that judges might be affected in their decision making, that could so dramatically disrupt the notion of American constitutionalism and the social contract between democratic government and private citizens that underlies that concept.

Prakash and Smith argue that while judicial independence is, of course, important, it cannot be unlimited.[75] They therefore conclude that acceptance of their proposed dramatic expansion of the political control of federal judicial tenure is "the better" approach.[76] What they fail to recognize, however, is that their proposal does not merely reduce judicial independence by some limited amount. Rather, it effectively guts it by failing to place any outer limits on the reach of the powerful club they are putting in the hands of the political branches to be held over the heads of the members of the judicial branch.

More important is the fact that other than their contention that pre-constitutional historical practice somehow inexorably leads to acceptance of their interpretation of the Good Behavior Clause, they never make any serious attempt to explain why their approach is "better" than the generally accepted structure, under which federal judges have life tenure, subject in extreme cases only to the complex and demanding supermajoritarian process of impeachment. Presumably, to establish that their practice is "better," they would need to demonstrate that there is some invidious judicial practice currently taking place that the impeachment process is incapable of remedying, or at least has failed to remedy to this point. But I am aware of no such practice, and they point to none.[77]

I am able to come up with only two conceivable reasons to support the Prakash and Smith approach, one hermeneutical and the other politically normative. The first is the originalist argument that we must adopt their interpretation of good behavior for the simple reason that that is what the phrase meant at the time of drafting and ratification. But for reasons I have discussed elsewhere,[78] their historical arguments are far less than persuasive. To the contrary, they are counterintuitive, given the broader theoretical context in which the "good Behaviour" concept was unambiguously employed by the Framers. In any event, for reasons I have discussed in detail elsewhere,[79] such rigid originalism should play no role in modern constitutional interpretation. The second conceivable reason is that it is necessary to empower the political branches in this manner to enable them to intimidate federal judges into confining their constitutional interpretations to those that comport with the political and constitutional views of the majoritarian branches themselves. But such a rationale directly undermines the very purpose of inserting the constitutional protections of judicial independence in the first place.

JUDICIAL INDEPENDENCE VERSUS THE IMPEACHMENT POWER: RESOLVING THE SEEMING CONSTITUTIONAL INCONSISTENCY

Delimiting the Scope of Impeachable Offenses: Application of Textual and Structural Analysis

To this point, the chapter has established that the Good Behavior Clause is not properly construed as a supplemental source of judicial removal. Instead, its most appropriate construction is as nothing more than a cross-reference to the impeachment power, which is properly viewed as the sole method of removing federal judges. The next task, then, is to determine the most appropriate construction of the constitutional standard for impeachment—in other words, the meaning of the phrase, "high crimes and misdemeanors," as applied to Article III judges. The first question in delimiting the scope of the concept of impeachable offenses is the extent to which that scope should be deemed to vary based on the type of federal officer sought to be impeached. To be sure, by its terms, the provision authorizing the impeachment power draws no such distinction.[80] To the contrary, Article IV refers generically to the impeachment of "officers." On that basis, one might at first assume that a textualist would be forced to conclude that the scope of impeachable offenses must be constant, varying not at all on the basis of the nature of the officer to be impeached. However, an important conceptual distinction must be drawn between a textualist and a literalist. While a literalist interprets only the actual words of a provision, viewed in a vacuum, a textualist (or what might more accurately be described as a "purposive textualist") takes a more holistic interpretive approach, viewing each provision as part of an integrated, purposefully directed structured whole, presumed to be designed to achieve a coherent and consistent set of constitutional goals. In short, while the literalist views the linguistic trees, the purposive textualist views the linguistic forest. Hence, in interpreting a particular constitutional text, the purposive textualist will, where necessary, attempt to synthesize related and possibly conflicting provisions in order to discern a coherent textual structure.[81]

Once it is decided that the Good Behavior Clause acts as nothing more than a cross-reference to the Impeachment Clause,[82] the next step is to determine the scope and limits of the impeachment power as applied to judges protected by Article III's salary and tenure guarantees. Such an effort is intended to achieve two interpretive goals: (1) Wherever possible, to avoid construing the Constitution in a manner that results in including diametrically opposing provisions within the same document, and (2) under any circumstances, to avoid a construction of one provision that renders another provision or set of provisions effectively either nugatory or virtually meaningless. The former goal is framed in a contingent manner, while the latter is not. This is because although it is at least conceivable that a coherently crafted and structured document could be fashioned in such a manner as to contain provisions that simultaneously point in opposite directions, it is wholly inconceivable that such a document would contain one provision whose inherent and inescapable effect would be to eradicate another provision (unless, of course, that end is achieved through a process of subsequent amendment). Although this interpretive analysis may not be dispositive of the issue of the unitary nature of the impeachment standard, it most certainly appears at least to have some relevance in answering that question.

A purposive textualist would appropriately construe the Impeachment Clause in a manner that takes account of the unique position of the federal judiciary within the nation's political system, as unambiguously manifested in Article III's protections of judicial salary and tenure. As previously mentioned, Article III on its face distinguishes members of the federal judiciary from members of the other branches by expressly insulating them from key pressures and influences of the political process. The salutary political purposes served by such insulation in the American form of constitutionalism are obvious. Absent an independent judiciary free from most political pressures and influences, individual rights intended to be insulated from majoritarian interference would be threatened, as would the supremacy of the countermajoritarian Constitution as a whole. No officer of the executive branch serves these functions. It is only the judicial branch whose members are both given life tenure and vested with authority to adjudicate and enforce the countermajoritarian dictates of the Constitution. A broad construction of the scope of impeachable offenses could easily undermine the vitally important functions manifestly served by Article III's protections of salary and tenure by giving rise to the very danger of external political influences on the judicial process that those protections were clearly intended to prevent. Thus, to ensure that the

salary and tenure protections are allowed to perform the valuable functions which they obviously serve, it is necessary to employ special care in
construing the category of impeachable offenses when a member of the
federal judiciary is subjected to the impeachment process.

It might be argued that even under a broader construction of the scope
of the Impeachment Clause, the salary and tenure protections of Article
III still perform an important function because conviction on impeachment can be obtained only by means of a supermajoritarian vote of the
Senate. Thus, the argument proceeds, even under a broad construction
of the Impeachment Clause, the salary and tenure protections would still
assure federal judges of more sweeping guarantees of their position than
elected or other appointed federal officials. But while this argument has a
superficial appeal, it ignores the key purpose sought to be served by the
salary and tenure protections—that is, to remove, or at least significantly
reduce, the possibility of external political intimidation designed to offset
or undermine the judicial decision-making process. A broad reading of the
scope of the impeachment power may well give rise to the possibility of
such intimidation, aimed at the very heart of the interests protected by
Article III. By relying on the supermajoritarian conviction requirement,
this argument has the dubious advantage of confining the susceptibil-
ity of federal judges to political intimidation to those cases in which an
extremely large portion of the public or government has been angered by
their decisions.

Although leading scholars appear to agree that a unique impeachment
standard is appropriate for members of the federal judiciary, they often
tend to go in the completely opposite direction from the interpretation I
have suggested. Professor Michael Gerhardt, for example, has argued that
because of the unique need to preserve judicial integrity, members of the
federal judiciary should actually be held to a *higher* behavioral standard
than are executive officers.[83] For example, he notes that a federal judge
might be subject to impeachment for publishing a "particularly controversial" law review article, while executive officers should not be deemed
subject to impeachment for similar behavior.[84]

On one level, perhaps, it may be possible to sympathize with Gerhardt's
concern for preserving judicial integrity. For the very reason that federal
judges are, in fact, insulated from most forms of external political pressure,
it is necessary to maintain the judiciary's high status in the mind of the
public. But such an expansive conception of impeachable offenses on the
part of the judiciary must nevertheless be rejected, because it would inescapably invite far-reaching and even crude political attempts to intimidate

members of the judiciary in their decision making—again, the very result sought to be avoided by the creation of the salary and tenure protections in the first place.

Before one can conclusively reject Gerhardt's suggested examples of specific impeachable judicial behavior, however, it is first necessary to adopt an overarching doctrinal model of impeachable offenses, and then apply that model to those examples. In fashioning such a model, the task at hand is to glean a coherent textual structure from an interpretive synthesis of what on their face appear to be provisions potentially in tension, namely, the impeachment power of Article II and the salary and tenure protections of Article III. Such a synthesis should seek to reconcile the need to insulate federal judges from political pressures caused by threats to their tenure with the need to provide the political branches with a necessary safety valve to preserve judicial integrity.

Any analysis of a constitutional provision must begin (though usually not end) with the words of the provision. By its terms, the Impeachment Clause authorizes impeachment for treason, bribery, or "other high Crimes or Misdemeanors." When viewed apart from any historical context, these words appear solely to describe criminal behavior. For one thing, the words "crimes" and "misdemeanors" refer exclusively to criminal acts—at least when viewed outside of the specific context of the Impeachment Clause. Moreover, the fact that the provision initially refers to specific criminal acts and then expressly includes "other" similar acts tends to establish, at least as a textual matter, that the category of impeachable behavior is confined to acts in some way criminal. Moreover, under such a narrowly circumscribed definition of impeachable offenses, there would be no basis on which to confine the construction to members of the judiciary.

When one adds an analysis of broader constitutional structure to this narrow textualist analysis, one should be able to understand the argument in favor of confining the scope of impeachable offenses to such objectively characterizable criminal behavior solely to members of the federal judiciary. Simply put, that argument is that Article III's special protections of salary and tenure underscore the unique and vital role in our constitutional democratic system played by federal judges in enforcing the countermajoritarian Constitution against the political branches and to preserve the rule of law in what is otherwise a nakedly political system. Article III's provision of life tenure is quite obviously intended to insulate federal judges from undue external political pressures on their decision making, which would undermine and possibly preclude effective performance of the federal judiciary's checking function in our system. Yet if the scope of impeachable offenses is not confined in some meaningful and largely objective manner, the possibility of impeachment would threaten to eviscerate the salutary impact of the life-tenure protection.[85] In effect, under this construction, the impeachment power would effectively consume the tenure protection of Article III.

If a plausible construction of a constitutional provision is available that does not have such a destructive impact on attainment of the purposes served by a separate, but presumably equal, provision, a proper structural analysis of constitutional text—if not simple common sense—dictates that such a construction be adopted. Therefore, as applied exclusively to Article III judges, a construction of the Impeachment Clause confined to objectively definable criminal behavior should be adopted. This is so because such a construction would dramatically reduce the ability of Congress to employ its impeachment power as a tool of intimidation to influence future judicial decision making or penalize past judicial decision making. In this manner, the two provisions are interpreted in a manner that preserves the legal and political vitality of both.

This argument, premised on an understanding of normative constitutional policy gleaned from a structural analysis of constitutional text, is logically limited to issues involving the impeachment of members of the federal judiciary. No other category of federal officer possesses the same express constitutional guarantees of his tenure, nor does any other federal officer possess the need for countermajoritarian protection the way Article III judges do. Hence, there is no reason to extend this narrow construction of the scope of the impeachment power to the impeachment of federal officials in the executive branch.

It is easy to anticipate the nature of the attacks that can be made against this structural analysis. Such criticisms can be grouped under four broad headings: historical, theoretical, pragmatic, and textual. Although these critiques may seem superficially appealing, closer examination reveals that they fail to undermine the compelling logic underlying my suggested holistic structural interpretation of the impeachment power as applied to Article III judges.

The Historical Attack on the Holistic Structural Interpretation of the Impeachment Power

The scope of impeachable offenses viewed from a purely historical perspective offers a very different picture from the one dictated by the holistic structural interpretation put forward here. According to respected scholars, under well-established preconstitutional English precedent, both impeachment practice and the concept of "high Crimes and Misdemeanors" extended well beyond behavior that was technically criminal.[86] I am readily willing to stipulate—if only for purposes of argument—to the accuracy of these scholarly assertions. Even assuming the accuracy of this historical perspective, however, it is by no means clear that history dictates a parallel modern construction of the Impeachment Clause.

Initially, even if we assume that modern constitutional interpretation should for some reason be constrained by the modern perception of the Framers' understanding (an issue far from resolved),[87] it does not automatically follow that their understanding was necessarily designed to incorporate by reference all prerevolutionary English practice. Indeed, while our constitutional structure obviously borrowed much from English political theory, it is also true that much of the political system established in the American Constitution was designed specifically to depart from English practice. What is missing from this historical analysis is evidence definitively establishing that the Framers intended to incorporate this English practice, without qualification or modification, into American constitutional practice.[88] Indeed, there is much evidence that those who led the Revolution widely regarded the English judiciary's lack of judicial independence as one of the most offensive aspects of its treatment.[89]

There is, however, a more fundamental problem with the argument grounded in preconstitutional practice. It is puzzling that scholars who devote their attention to the Impeachment Clause appear almost uniformly to have assumed—apparently without the slightest discussion or explanation of their overarching theory of constitutional interpretation—that historical practice is somehow dispositive of modern constitutional doctrine. The only issue, then, would involve the task of determining exactly what that practice was.[90] Yet in most areas of modern constitutional doctrine, the Supreme Court has never deemed itself bound by a narrow understanding of practice either before or after ratification, or the Framers' understandings of it.[91] It is at very least arguable that when the Framers drafted both the impeachment power and Article III's protections of salary and tenure, they simply failed to recognize the potential tension between the two. Constitutional interpretation has, throughout our history, involved an evolutionary process in which modern generations learn from the mistakes of their predecessors. Where, as is so often the case, the text is sufficiently broadly framed as to be susceptible to more than one linguistically plausible interpretation, there is no reason why we should not recognize compelling reasons for adopting one of those plausible interpretations, construing potentially conflicting provisions of the Constitution in a harmonious, holistic fashion.

If the Impeachment Clause is more deserving of rigid historicism in its interpretation than any other constitutional provision, the scholars who have employed such an approach have failed to explain the reason. Nothing in the text of the provision directs use of such a restrictive historical mode of interpretation, any more than virtually any other provision does. Indeed, even where the text of a constitutional provision arguably does appear expressly to direct such a historical inquiry, as does the Seventh Amendment's directive that the right to jury trial in civil cases "at common law" be "preserved,"[92] the Court has often modified modern interpretation in order to take into account the impact of modern practices and conditions on the traditional legal/equitable dichotomy.[93] Thus, even conclusive evidence of historical practice should not be deemed dispositive in modern constitutional interpretation. Hence, even were we to assume unambiguous and consistent historical extension of the scope of impeachable offenses for judges beyond the category of criminal behavior in both England and the United States, it does not necessarily follow that modern constitutional interpretation must or should be bound by that practice. If it is recognized today that the constitutional goal of attaining and prophylactically preserving judicial independence as embodied in Article III cannot be effectively achieved absent a narrower construction of the category of impeachable offenses for federal judges, then that category must properly be confined to criminal behavior. This is so, whether or not those who drafted or ratified the Constitution fully grasped that necessity at the time.

What the Framers enacted, what they passed on to subsequent generations, was not their own subjective perceptions and assumptions, but rather the text itself. If, because of either subsequent developments or simply the luxury of a broader, more carefully reasoned social, legal, or political perspective, we today can appreciate difficulties or problems that the Framers apparently did not—namely, that their own understanding of one constitutional provision in reality has a dangerously destructive impact on the unambiguous purposes sought to be served by a separate constitutional provision—there is no reason that we must make the same mistakes that they did. Unless the Framers tied the hands of subsequent interpreting generations by use of linguistically narrow and unambiguously restrictive wording, there is no reason that we should not be able to benefit from structural and interpretive insights that the Framers were either unable or unwilling to see (or, perhaps, to foresee).

The Theoretical Attack on the Holistic Structural Interpretation:
The Argument From Judicial Accountability

Even if one were to accept my response to the historical critique, it is necessary also to deal with the possible contention that the interpretive analysis advocated here fails to perceive the important role that the availability of impeachment plays in assuring the ultimate accountability of the judiciary within our democratic system. Absent the availability of such a majoritarian check, the argument proceeds, the unaccountable judiciary would be able to exceed its intended limited role through what amounts to lawless decision making. Pursuant to this reasoning, confining the scope of impeachable offenses to criminal conduct would undermine the important political checking function that the availability of impeachment for Article III judges is intended to perform.

Note that this argument turns not at all on assumptions about either historical practice or the Framers' understanding of the scope of impeachable offenses. It turns, rather, exclusively on the application of considerations of normative political theory. The primary problem with this approach, however, is that in seeking to prevent the unaccountable judiciary from usurping political authority, it for all practical purposes removes the judiciary as a countermajoritarian check on the political branches, in contravention of both the foundational premises of American constitutionalism in general and the implementational device of Article III's salary and tenure protections in particular. If one assumes that a federal judge may be impeached because of nothing more than the perceived incorrectness of his constitutional decisions, then a judge will always be potentially subject to external political pressure in his constitutional decision making, in direct contravention of the unambiguous purpose designed to be served by the prophylactic protections of Article III's tenure protection. To construe the impeachment power to enable Congress to penalize or threaten federal judges because of nothing more than congressional disagreement with their substantive decisions would thus dangerously upset the balance of branch power inherent in American constitutionalism.

One might respond that, at most, this reasoning supports a view of impeachable offenses that excludes impeachment grounded in nothing more than disagreement with a judge's decision in a suit. In other words, perhaps impeachment of a federal judge should not be permitted because of a particularly unpopular judicial decision that Congress deems incorrect, but it does not necessarily follow that judicial impeachment must be confined to criminal behavior. Under this modified alternative approach, Congress would be able to impeach a member of the federal judiciary because of noncriminal behavior, but not because of the alleged inaccuracy, ideology, or impropriety of a particular decision or series of decisions made by the judge in question.

There can be no doubt that from the holistic structural perspective advocated here, a standard that excludes overtly decision-based grounds of judicial impeachment is far preferable to a standard with no limits whatsoever. The problem with this suggested alternative, however, is that it fails to provide sufficient breathing room to the needs of judicial independence. This is because, absent restriction to a relatively objective standard such as one confined to criminal behavior, impeachment will always present a threat of covert and indirect decision-based penalization. Of course, even a standard of purely criminal behavior could be employed selectively against only those judges whose decisions are found to be wrong or offensive. But the prerequisite that the judge's behavior be objectively characterizable as criminal at least provides a built-in limitation on the power of congressional manipulation that does not exist when the standard is merely one that excludes overtly decision-based impeachment.

The Pragmatic Attack on the Holistic Structural Interpretation of the Impeachment Power

A critic of the holistic structural interpretation advocated here might contend that confining the scope of impeachable offenses to criminal behavior would give rise, purely as a practical matter of judicial administration, to what are preposterous results. Such a standard, the argument proceeds, would necessarily preclude Congress from removing from office judges who engaged in public drunkenness, sexual harassment, or behavior suggesting insanity, to the extent that such behavior could not be characterized as criminal. This result might arguably undermine public respect for the federal judiciary and lead to pragmatically untenable situations.

In considering the force of this argument, it is interesting to note that no real-life federal judge in recent memory has been impeached on noncriminal grounds. Thus, no practical difficulties would have resulted even if the scope of impeachment had in the past been confined to criminal behavior.[94] Moreover, it should be emphasized that the unavailability of impeachment does not necessarily imply that government lacks means to deal with extreme, albeit noncriminal, judicial behavior. Judges who are truly incapable of continuing to perform their judicial function due to infirmity may presumably have their caseloads transferred to other judges for the period during which they are incapacitated. Because such a remedy is appropriately viewed as administrative, rather than punitive, impeachment is not involved. Finally, there is presumably nothing in the Article III independence protections that precludes private civil suits, where legally appropriate, against members of the federal judiciary.

It cannot be denied that a narrow construction of the scope of impeachable offenses leaves open the possibility, at least as a theoretical matter, that extremely questionable judicial behavior will fail to lead to removal of the judge from office. But surely those who drafted or ratified Article III's protections of salary and tenure must have understood that those protections might have a cost. If they did not, they should have. Life tenure will naturally mean that judges may remain in office long after the public or the government no longer wants them there. Indeed, that is the very point of the protections: The decision was made to risk this lack of accountability in order prophylactically to ensure judicial independence. Any argument that impeachment must be shaped to allow government to remove judges from office at any time that their behavior is deemed unacceptable by society effectively ignores the initial constitutional choice inherent in the creation of the salary and tenure protections to protect federal judges from external political influences through threats to their tenure in office. The point, simply, is that while my suggested holistic structural interpretation may certainly give rise to problematic situations, it is nevertheless far preferable to the alternative.[95]

The Textual Attack on the Holistic Structural Interpretation

Much of the holistic structural approach here is grounded in a baseline form of textualism. Where text cannot plausibly be construed to reach a particular result, that result must be deemed unacceptable as a matter of constitutional interpretation. It might be suggested that the duality in impeachment standards advocated here fails this test. After all, nothing in the text of Article II, section 4 in any way authorizes a distinction in impeachment standard on the basis of the nature of the officer being impeached.

While this is true when the text is myopically viewed narrowly and in a vacuum, when one takes a more structurally holistic approach to constitutional interpretation a ready textual basis for the duality of my approach becomes evident. For one cannot properly construe the Impeachment Clause without taking into account both the directive and purposes of Article III's Salary and Tenure Clause. As already shown, the purposes sought to be achieved by that clause—ensuring judicial independence— would be seriously threatened by permitting judges to be impeached for no reason other than political or ideological disagreement with their decisions. No other government officers subject to the Impeachment Clause have been given such prophylactic protections of their independence. Thus, it is Article III's clear dichotomy between judges and other government officers, not the Impeachment Clause, that textually dictates a distinction. As the name of my approach suggests, constitutional text must be construed as a whole, and when that is done, it is clear that, read together, the two clauses dictate a special position for judges of Article III courts in the context of impeachment.

Contrasting Criminal Prosecution and Impeachment

If, as I conclude, impeachment is the sole means of judicial removal, one must ask whether judges who have not been subjected to the impeachment process may nevertheless be subjected to criminal prosecution, at least when the result of that prosecution is imprisonment. As a practical matter, imprisonment precludes a judge from performing the functions of her office. Yet it is widely assumed that federal judges may be subjected to criminal prosecution, even when they have not previously been impeached.[96] The rationale appears to be that even while imprisoned, federal judges remain "in office." Although unable to handle a caseload, of course, they can still presumably be paid their salaries while in prison.[97]

Obvious questions can be raised about this reasoning, because imprisonment may easily be viewed as a form of constructive removal. Perhaps the answer is that criminal prosecution should be deemed appropriate as long as the criminal law that has been violated does not subject federal judges to uniquely negative treatment. For example, if Congress were to enact a law making it a crime for federal judges alone to engage in specified behavior, then the imposition of criminal punishment could appropriately be viewed as an impermissible form of constructive removal that circumvents the impeachment process. However, if a federal judge is prosecuted for behavior that would also be a crime when committed by those other than federal judges, then imprisonment should not be viewed as an impermissible removal from office.

In support of this suggested distinction, one might argue that the imposition of neutrally fashioned and applied criminal law to federal judges in no way threatens the judicial independence that the restrictions on the availability of impeachment are designed to avoid. In this sense, criminal prosecutions could properly be analogized to the impact of a generally imposed tax increase on federal judges in light of Article III's guarantee against salary reduction. The Supreme Court has found such tax increases to be constitutional, even though in a certain sense they will inevitably have the effect of reducing judicial salaries.[98] Yet if Congress were to impose a special tax solely on federal judges, such a law would no doubt be held to constitute an unconstitutional reduction in judicial salaries. Consistent with this mode of thinking, application of generally applicable criminal law to federal judges does not present the threat to judicial independence that both Article III's guarantee of tenure and the restrictions imposed on the impeachment process were clearly designed to prevent.[99]

It is true that this rationale is not free from interpretive problems. It should be recalled that the tenure protection is not framed in contextual or conditional terms. A judge's tenure is protected regardless of whether the threat to tenure is motivated by or has the effect of undermining judicial independence in a particular situation, presumably because it is often impossible to determine in an individual case whether such threats actually exist. Yet the rationale premised on the selective nature of the criminal penalty seems to turn entirely on an attempt to distinguish between situations in which constructive removal does present a threat to judicial independence from those in which it does not.

One possible response to this criticism is that the judge-based focus of the criminal penalty does not require use of a case-by-case inquiry into the specific motivations and harm to judicial independence. Instead, it establishes a priori rules: criminal prosecutions based on laws that single out federal judges are unconstitutional, whereas prosecutions of federal judges for violation of generally imposed prohibitions are constitutional.[100] Ultimately, one may have to accept this arguable departure from the exclusivity of the impeachment device simply in order to establish that federal judges are not above the law. However, if it were at some point held that imprisonment does violate the tenure protection of Article III, Congress could possibly avoid the untenable conclusion that federal judges are above the criminal law simply by resorting to impeachment preliminary to ultimate criminal prosecution. The drawback of such an approach, however, is that it would require Congress to determine whether the judge engaged in criminal behavior, whereas in the case of impeachment after conviction of a crime, Congress could simply employ the judicial finding of criminality as collateral estoppel.

THE CONSTITUTIONALITY OF JUDICIAL DISCIPLINE
NOT AFFECTING SALARY OR TENURE

My proposed holistic structural interpretation of constitutional text may give rise to a very different scenario when judicial discipline directly affects neither salary nor tenure.[101] In such situations, the salary and tenure protections of Article III play no role whatsoever in preventing invasions of judicial independence. Because the salary and tenure protections are structured in narrow, noncontextual terms, they cannot properly be construed to protect against all conceivable threats to judicial independence. Thus, unless one of the other constitutional protections of judicial independence—including the Due Process Clause and the Vestiture Clause of Article III[102]—is triggered, even those disciplinary measures that could be deemed to present real threats to judicial independence would have to be considered constitutional, as unwise as they might seem purely as a matter of policy.

One can posit numerous hypothetical disciplinary measures that cannot, as a literal matter, be deemed to violate the salary and tenure protections, yet which also give rise to consequences that are troubling, if not truly frightening, from the perspective of judicial independence. One vivid example is a law providing that federal judges who decide a constitutional issue in a specified manner will be deprived of their law clerks or their secretaries. As long as law clerks and secretaries are not deemed to be part of a judge's salary—and surely, the Internal Revenue Service does not consider them to be such—then their removal cannot possibly be construed to violate the salary protection of Article III. Yet it is certainly conceivable that such a threatened deprivation could improperly influence judicial decision making.

In any event, one could also hypothesize a congressional statute that openly grants a salary increase only to those federal judges who have decided a constitutional issue in the manner desired by Congress. Because nothing in Article III's protection against salary reduction prohibits a total congressional refusal to award judicial salary increases or the award of a decision-based selective salary increase, that Article III protection must be deemed irrelevant to the constitutionality of the hypothetical legislation. But this does not necessarily mean that such legislation should ultimately be held constitutional. If it is to be held unconstitutional, however, it must be attributable to a violation of an alternative protection of judicial independence provided for in the Constitution's text. It cannot be merely because we find that such legislation contravenes some abstract political conceptualization of judicial independence.

Whether this legislation would in fact, violate some other constitutional guarantee of judicial independence is not entirely clear. It likely would violate procedural due process in *future* federal litigation presenting a parallel issue, because in such cases the judges could not be considered the neutral adjudicators required by the Due Process Clause.[103] This would be true, even of federal judges who had not been directly affected by the legislation. Once such legislation has been enacted, the possibility of undue external influence on the judicial decision-making process is considerably more than abstract, hypothetical, or potential. Rather, the danger that the judge will be influenced by factors other than her assessment of the merits of the case is as real, as in cases such as *Tumey v. Ohio*[104] and *Aetna Life Insurance Co. v. LaVoie*,[105] where the judge stood to gain personally from a decision one way more so than the other.

To be sure, one cannot be certain that, in each case, the judge will be improperly influenced. But due process has never been construed to require such a showing in an individual case. Instead, for due process to be violated, it suffices merely for a temptation that would affect a reasonable decision maker to exist. No one could reasonably doubt that this standard would have been satisfied had Congress enacted a statute selectively revoking nonsalary judicial benefits on the basis of disagreement with substantive decisions of the federal courts.

It is by no means certain, however, that due process would serve the exact same function that the salary and tenure protections would serve had they been applicable. For one thing, while presumably the judges themselves would have standing to immediately challenge the constitutionality of a congressional statute under the salary and tenure protections, that would not necessarily be the case where the Due Process Clause, rather than the salary and tenure protections, provides the constitutional source of the protection of judicial independence. The due process right is that of the future litigants, not of the judges themselves. Thus, it may well be that when the Due Process Clause triggers the protection, the determination of constitutionality will have to await a future suit raising the very same issue on which Congress premised its selective reduction in nonsalary benefits.[106]

A second potential difficulty caused by reliance on the Due Process Clause is the clause's prerequisite that either liberty, property, or life be at stake. While the Supreme Court has often defined property interests broadly to include statutory entitlements,[107] this has traditionally been considered a controversial position on the Court,[108] and possibly subject to future doctrinal revision. Thus, due process may provide a somewhat limited check on congressional threats to judicial independence that do not involve either salary or tenure.

It is also arguable that a selective reduction in nonsalary benefits would be considered a violation of the Vestiture Clause of Article III. The vesting of the judicial power in the federal judiciary has already been construed to prohibit either executive or legislative reversal of particular decisions by the federal courts.[109] Applied in the present context, the argument would be that congressional retaliatory action based on specific decisions of the federal courts so interferes with the individual judge's resolution of the same issue in future parallel litigation that such legislative action effectively removes judicial power from the federal judge, or at least significantly undermines the court's authority to exercise it.

The success of this argument is uncertain. In previous situations in which the Court has invalidated legislative or executive control of judicial decision making, either Congress or an executive official was found to have reviewed and reversed specific decisions of the federal courts. Here, in contrast, the interference is not nearly as direct. To be sure, one could fashion a reasonable argument that the exercise of the judicial power requires that the decision maker not be influenced by extraneous forms of intimidation, and that the concrete fear of decision-specific retaliation by Congress constitutes just such extraneous intimidation. However, at least as a doctrinal matter, it remains at best unclear whether such indirect interferences would be held to constitute a violation of the Vestiture Clause. Moreover, as a conceptual matter, one might readily distinguish situations in which another branch has retained power actually to reverse a judicial holding from those in which the other branch has merely sought to influence the holding. In the former case, in no meaningful or even technical sense does the actual final decision making power remain in the hands of the judge, whereas in the latter case, the judge still retains ultimate power to decide the case. Thus, this area of the law of judicial independence remains in a state of virtually total uncertainty.

CONCLUSION

There has been a great deal of scholarship on the issues of judicial independence, judicial impeachment, and judicial discipline. To this point, however, very little of it has sought to consider the constitutional implications of those issues primarily from the broader perspective of constitutional interpretation. For example, some of it has implicitly assumed historical practice and the Framers' intent to be dispositive without ever seeking to explain why, as a matter of interpretive theory, this should be the case.

Moreover, this scholarship has rarely sought to view the relevant provisions of the Constitution from a holistic perspective that views each distinct provision as part of a coherent, organic synthesis of all of the distinct but related provisions. Use of such an interpretive approach would give rise to a number of interesting conclusions about the reconciliation of judicial independence with the need for appropriate legislative power to impose judicial discipline. Described in a summary manner, the holistic analysis of constitutional text and textual structure advocated here establishes that where judicial discipline threatens either judicial salary or tenure, impeachment provides the sole constitutionally valid mechanism of judicial discipline. Additionally, the scope of the category of impeachable offenses must be narrowly confined, lest the threat of impeachment effectively consume the decision-making independence that Article III's protections of salary and tenure were so clearly designed to preserve. At very least, the impeachment power must be construed to exclude overtly decision-based retaliation, and a strong argument can be fashioned to support a view that confines the impeachment power's reach to behavior that is objectively criminal. Concededly, historical practice appears never to have been confined in such a manner. But purely as a textual matter, the Impeachment Clause easily lends itself to such a construction and, if it is ultimately found that such a construction is necessary to avoid significantly undermining the scope of constitutionally dictated judicial independence, then, pursuant to the holistic textual-structural interpretation that I have advocated here, the provision may be so interpreted.

When the inquiry turns to the constitutionality of judicial disciplinary measures that do not affect salary or tenure, the holistic textual-structural interpretation advocated here dictates a very different set of conclusions. In such cases, the salary and tenure protections are rendered irrelevant by their very nature. Article III does not impose an overarching protection of judicial independence against all conceivable threats. Instead, the provision selects specific methods of potential invasion of judicial independence for absolute prohibition so as to preserve the broader goal of judicial independence in general. When such methods are employed by other branches, the protection forms an impenetrable shield. However, when judicial independence is threatened by other means, this selective instrumentalism model is of no help. At that point, other constitutional protections of judicial independence—for example, the Due Process Clause of the Fifth Amendment or the Vestiture Clause of Article III—may come into play. Both forms of independence protection, however, suffer from restrictions or limitations that may reduce their effectiveness in protecting against retaliatory or intimidating action by Congress.[110]

It is certainly conceivable that if we were today writing on an entirely clean slate, we would choose methods of guaranteeing judicial independence that differ from those of our Constitution. But this is a choice denied to us as long as the Constitution remains the law of the land and without further amendment. However, as long as an interpreter is willing to view the different portions of the Constitution that concern both judicial independence and judicial discipline as parts of an integrated whole, the tools with which our Constitution has provided us should prove to be sufficient to ensure that federal judiciary plays its proper role in the system of American constitutionalism.[111]

State Courts, Due Process, and the Dangers of Popular Constitutionalism

INTRODUCTION

In *Caperton v. A. T. Massey Coal Co.*,[1] the Supreme Court found for the first time that conduct related to a judicial election campaign could violate a litigant's due process rights.[2] A "serious risk of actual bias" that was "too high to be constitutionally tolerable" had resulted, the Court held, when a recently elected West Virginia Supreme Court of Appeals Justice, Brent Benjamin, adjudicated an appeal involving Massey's CEO, Don Blankenship, his biggest campaign contributor.[3] Blankenship had spent millions to support Benjamin's successful bid for the high court, knowing his case would come before the court shortly after the election.[4]

The due process danger that the *Caperton* Court identified rests on a fear of retrospective gratitude—that is, the fear that Justice Benjamin might be so grateful for the generous campaign support that he would decide Blankenship's case differently from the manner in which he otherwise might have done. Although that was undoubtedly within the realm of possibility, as a constitutional matter the logic of the Court's rationale may well prove far more than the Court intended to prove. The idea that Justice Benjamin might feel obligated to decide in favor of someone who had "a significant and disproportionate influence in placing" him on the court[5] appears indistinguishable from a variety of well-accepted forms of backward-looking gratitude that judges may encounter on the bench, short of a finding of quid pro quo bribery. For example, an Article III judge would presumably be continually grateful to the president responsible for her lifetime appointment. Yet it has always been understood that the Constitution somehow tolerates that risk: federal judges are not constitutionally barred from hearing cases involving the president who appointed them. Indeed, any other conclusion might well lead to chaotic results.

This exclusive focus on retrospective electoral gratitude as a threat to independent adjudication renders *Caperton* simultaneously overinclusive and underinclusive. It is overinclusive because it encompasses judicial conduct and relationships that, as a general matter, have never been thought to violate due process. Despite attempts to confine the decision to "extreme facts," Justice Kennedy's majority opinion offers an amorphous and potentially expansive basis for finding due process violations.[6] This leaves unclear exactly how much spending on a judge's behalf is sufficient to violate due process if that judge later hears a campaign supporter's case (either as litigant or attorney).

Yet in another sense *Caperton* is simultaneously underinclusive, because it focuses on election-related retrospective gratitude, while simultaneously ignoring the far greater *prospective* constitutional threats inherent in existing methods of state judicial selection.[7] For the most part, the constitutional problem with state judicial selection is not the *initial* selection process. Every state judicial position has to be filled somehow. Whether it is by gubernatorial appointment, election, or some form of so-called "merit" selection process, judges owe their appointment to someone or some group. Moreover, even in the federal system we have long accepted the influence of some form of majoritarian interests on the initial selection process. After all, both the president who appointed the judge and the senators who confirm the appointment are themselves the product of majoritarian selection processes. Thus, whatever one thinks of the comparative merits of the various selection alternatives purely as a policy matter, foundational constitutional interests are, for the most part,[8] unaffected by the ultimate choice of selection methodology.

Of far greater constitutional concern on a number of levels is the method of deciding upon judicial *retention*—the method by which the judge's continuation in office is determined. It is here that all of the constitutional concerns about judicial independence converge, because it is here that the very real threat exists that deciding a particular case a certain way may have seriously negative consequences on the adjudicator's continued employment. This threat may well influence the judge to decide the case in a manner different from her preferred resolution of the matter, purely on the case's merits. For example, where a judge fears that her preferred resolution of a case will be substantially unpopular with the electorate, use of an electoral method for determining retention seriously threatens the fair and neutral determination of that case. Moreover, in cases involving the assertion of constitutional rights, a judicial concern with electoral accountability effectively turns foundational precepts of American constitutionalism, which is firmly grounded in notions of countermajoritarianism, on their heads. Similarly, if retention rests in the hands of an elected official or group of officials, the fear that the judge's preferred resolution will offend or annoy those officials could have the same skewing effect on the judge's decision-making process.

No doubt, numerous cases will arise in which neither the electorate nor elected officials will have the slightest interest in the outcome. But there is no simple way *ex ante* to distinguish such cases from those that will trigger electoral backlash. In any event, there is no way to insulate the adjudicator's independence solely in those cases where such fears are found to be realistic. As long as a judge knows that the voting public, legislature, or executive holds the power to remove her as a result of her decisions on the bench, the very real possibility exists that she will—if only subconsciously—shape those decisions in a manner designed to win their favor, or at least to avoid offending them. That danger, far more than the possibility of gratitude, presents a threat to due process "too high to be constitutionally tolerable." Yet the Supreme Court has never even seriously considered the possibility that popularly based methods for determining state judicial retention are constitutionally suspect. This hesitancy appears to spring, in varying degrees, from a misguided, question-begging federalism concern,[9] a desire to avoid impugning the integrity of state court judges, and reluctance to upset the inertia of long-established judicial selection systems.[10]

Perhaps more ominously, the judicial unwillingness to explore the serious constitutional flaws in popularly grounded methods of state judicial retention may flow from a sorely misguided belief in what several scholars have described as "popular constitutionalism"—an ill-defined notion, as described earlier in this book, that the Constitution belongs to "the people" and that judicial review by judges insulated from the electoral process is therefore undemocratic and illegitimate.[11] None of these rationales even comes close to justifying the constitutionality of majoritarian-based retention methods. While scholarly advocates of this theory are frustratingly short on details as to exactly how constitutional interpretation is to be exercised by "the people,"[12] it is certainly plausible to view constitutional interpretation by judges chosen by the electorate as the closest feasible alternative. As the carefully structured system of federal judicial independence clearly demonstrates, however, democratically grounded judicial review is diametrically opposed to the inherently countermajoritarian nature of our constitutional system and core precepts of American constitutionalism. Article V of the Constitution imposes a complex and demanding method of supermajoritarian alteration.[13] Moreover, Article III, the judicial article, expressly insulates federal judges whose power extends to cases arising under the Constitution of the United States from majoritarian accountability.[14] This was not an accident. If only as a historical or descriptive matter, then, it is simply incorrect to suggest that our system is committed to some notion of democratically accountable judicial review. Even purely as a matter of common sense, however, the concept of democratically accountable judicial review is a puzzling one. The countermajoritarian Constitution is designed to serve as a check on democratically grounded government.[15] Giving popularly accountable judges the final say as to the Constitution's meaning is thus contrary to its intended role. The fundamental flaw in the theory of popular constitutionalism is as simple as that.

Equally important is the dangerous skewing impact that external influence caused by popular accountability will often have on the neutral adjudication required by due process. For a judge to be forced to focus on the possible impact of her decision on her future employment seriously threatens the rights of the litigants to fair procedure and a judgment based exclusively on a neutral judicial assessment of both facts and law, in accordance with long-established requirements of due process.

Although the Court's willingness in *Caperton* at least to acknowledge a possible constitutional problem related to the popular electoral check on state judiciaries unfortunately has left a potential doctrinal mess in its wake, the Court's failure to deal with the issue of popularly retained state judges does not make the practice any less of a real problem. To guarantee due process and avoid a confusing patchwork of decisions going forward, the Court needs to examine state judicial selection through a new lens. This chapter aims to provide exactly that—by focusing on how judges are retained, not how they take the bench in the first place. The inquiry draws by analogy on Article III's appointment and life-tenure provisions, which signal that how a judge gains his or her office is nowhere nearly as important as how he or she can lose it.[16]

While characterized by a wide consensus that judicial elections are undesirable, much of the voluminous, long-running debate on judicial selection[17] also accepts that such elections are not going away and therefore focuses on ways to improve them, such as through campaign finance and recusal reform.[18] However, such efforts, though no doubt well intentioned, either ignore or give short shrift to the foundational constitutional problem. Retention elections present a far greater threat to due process than does any existing method of initial electoral selection, and until this insight is recognized, the serious constitutional problem will remain unchanged.

Unlike legislative and executive officials, the very nature of what a judge does requires that she make decisions independent of popular sentiment.[19] This is true in every case, since litigants are constitutionally guaranteed a neutral adjudication on the basis of the facts and law of their individual cases. But as previously noted, it is especially important when countermajoritarian constitutional rights are at stake. Core precepts of American constitutionalism depend on it. Yet popularly based judicial retention inherently makes the exact opposite result a very real possibility. Indeed, democratic accountability is the most common justification for requiring methods to determine judicial retention in the first place.[20] Moreover because retention gives voters the power to remove a judge for any reason, it has unique, forward-looking power to influence a judge's decisions once on the bench. In this respect, what judges do to stay on the bench matters more than what they might do to get there, at least from the constitutional perspective of judicial independence.

To be sure, initial campaigns for judicial office may on occasion give rise to legitimate due process concerns, such as those tied to campaign donations and the possibility of candidates pre-committing themselves on issues. But judges must always be selected by somebody and will quite naturally feel some sense of gratitude to those responsible for placing them on the bench, no matter who that may be. Thus, though some type of gratitude tied to initial selection might be undesirable, it is also unavoidable. By contrast, future electoral pressure exists purely out of choice and tradition, not necessity.

This distinction matters because more than anything else, procedural due process requires a neutral adjudicator.[21] A decision maker who bases her findings on factors outside of the evidence before her renders all other procedural safeguards—including notice and the opportunity to be heard, principles at the core of the Supreme Court's procedural due process holdings—basically meaningless.[22] A non-independent decision maker impedes the search for the truth and thereby delegitimizes the adjudicatory system.

Yet every day in thousands of state courts, judges weigh life, liberty, and property under the often very real threat of loss of employment if they make a decision sufficiently unpopular to provoke voters, or those who control or influence voters, in the next election. This threat looms in states that use judicial reelection and retention elections, but also in those that rely on any form of majoritarian branch reappointment—either legislative or gubernatorial—to determine whether judges remain on the bench.

The consequences are not merely theoretical. The bulk of citizens' interactions with courts occur on the state level. Article III's guarantee of life tenure, intended to ensure independence, currently encompasses 874 federal judgeships.[23] By contrast, there are at least 10,000 state court judges nationwide, and roughly 90 percent of them must stand for retention or reelection to keep their jobs.[24] These judges decide everything from traffic infractions to death penalty cases, often including constitutional questions, and are likely the only adjudicator to whom a litigant will ever have access, given the limited availability of federal review, either in the form of habeas, removal jurisdiction, or Supreme Court certiorari.[25]

The question of whether a looming election actually influenced a judge's decision in a given case is necessarily less obvious than whether a decision impacted a past campaign supporter.[26] But because this pressure can apply subconsciously, even the judge might not realize she has shifted her thinking. And litigants with cases before judges who must face voters to retain their jobs can never be sure whether that judge is deciding solely on the facts and law or instead with an eye to electoral ramifications. Prospective pressure thus has the potential to influence judicial decisions in "more pernicious and less potentially self-correcting" ways than retrospective gratitude.[27]

Such pressure undermines constitutional values on what can be called both "micro" and "macro" levels. On a micro level, the fear of electoral retaliation endangers procedural due process for individual litigants seeking their constitutionally guaranteed "fair trial in a fair tribunal."[28] On a macro level, it undermines the judiciary's essential countermajoritarian role in our constitutional system, for the obvious reason that judges may be reluctant to side with unpopular litigants or uphold controversial rights out of fear of sparking voter discontent.[29] This leaves a far less than adequate check on majoritarian branch activities that may endanger constitutional rights and effectively undermines the countermajoritarian check essential to the preservation of American constitutional democracy.

The conclusion here is that judicial retention by means of either reelection or reappointment violates the Constitution's guarantee of procedural due process. Though due process may not strictly mandate life tenure for all judges, it does demand at the very least a form of tenure secure enough to prevent judges from having to worry about pleasing voters or the popular branches while on the bench, or from making decisions on the bench with an eye to how they will affect the judge's future employment prospects.

The chapter proceeds in three parts. The first part examines the current judicial elections landscape, explaining the pervasiveness of majoritarian retention methods. The second part explains why the Supreme Court's holding in *Caperton* misses the mark for due process purposes by focusing on backward-looking gratitude to a campaign contributor as a potential due process violation, instead of focusing on forward-looking influence over a judge's decision making. The final part explains why judicial elections violate due process in both the micro and macro senses—as applied to individual litigants, and as a matter of broader constitutional theory.

JUDICIAL SELECTION AND RETENTION: THE CURRENT LANDSCAPE

The Topography of State Judicial Selection and Retention

States select their judges through a patchwork of methods in various combinations: appointment, merit selection, regular elections, retention elections, and some unusual outliers, such as legislative appointment in Virginia.[30] However, elections remain the most common means of determining who sits on state courts and who stays there. Currently, judges in thirty-nine states must face elections to remain in office—either partisan reelection or nonpartisan reelection, or uncontested, up-or-down retention election after initial appointment.[31]

Originally, most states appointed their judges, though a few outliers employed elections for at least some judges starting in the 1810s.[32] That trickle became a flood amidst the rise of Jacksonian democracy in the 1830s and 1840s, as well as concurrent economic and fiscal crises that triggered a wave of state constitutional conventions.[33] Frustrated by what they saw as the patronage politics of appointments and coziness between judges and those in the other branches of state government, people believed judicial elections "promised a *less* partisan and *less* politicized bench that would be emboldened to act as a stronger check and balance against other branches."[34] By the time of the Civil War, twenty-four of the thirty-four states had established an elected judiciary, and new states subsequently admitted to the union also adopted popular election of some or all judges, until the admission of Alaska in 1959.[35]

Judicial elections fulfilled reformers' hopes "in at least one respect," as the first generation of elected judges blocked far more legislation than their appointed predecessors.[36] However, as party politics and their attendant corruption began to play an increasing role in judicial elections, "it became apparent that this new system was no panacea," and in the late 1800s and early 1900s, the pendulum swung towards other types of reform.[37] Nonpartisan judicial elections emerged in some states, although they also eventually suffered from some of the same problems as partisan elections.[38] Around the same time, prominent jurists and legal scholars also began advocating "merit selection" to expand the pool of judicial candidates beyond merely politicians' friends.[39] In 1940, Missouri became the first state to adopt such a plan. Though merit selection systems vary somewhat by state, most include "a permanent, nonpartisan commission composed of lawyers and nonlawyers" appointed by a variety of public and private officials to recruit and screen candidates. The commission then forwards a list of qualified individuals to the executive, who must make an appointment from the list. The appointed judge serves a year or two and then must face a retention election, in which he or she runs unopposed and must win a majority of the vote to win a full term on the bench.[40]

Today, judges in fifteen states must run for partisan reelection, including all judges in Alabama, Louisiana, New Mexico, Ohio, Texas, and West Virginia.[41] Term lengths run from four to fourteen years, with six and eight years the most common.[42] An additional nineteen states hold nonpartisan reelection, with six- and eight-year terms again common. And eighteen states rely on judicial "retention elections" in which voters are asked only whether or not they wish to retain the judge currently holding the seat. If the judge loses, the process to fill the vacancy starts over again. In these states, terms after a retention election range from four years, mainly for lower courts, to twelve years for the supreme and appellate courts in California and Missouri.[43] An additional five states use purely gubernatorial or legislative reappointment for subsequent judicial terms.[44] The rest either reappoint judges through merit commissions[45] or have life or nonrenewable tenure. The latter category includes only three states: Massachusetts, New Hampshire, and Rhode Island.[46] Once appointed, judges there hold their jobs until age seventy or, in Rhode Island, for life.[47]

Before roughly 1980, judicial elections were, according to Professor Jed Shugerman, "sleepy and low key," with "relatively inexpensive campaigns."[48] But they have since transformed into what he calls "judicial plutocracy," with businesses "capitalizing on socially conservative issues and pouring money into key races" and trial lawyers spending more in response (or sometimes vice versa) prompting a flood of advertising and attention, including attack ads and sound bites.[49] In the 2000s, judicial elections cost $200 million in direct campaign contributions, up from about $60 million the decade before.[50]

The Problem of Judicial Retention

Percentage-wise, fewer judges in retention elections are defeated than those in other types of elections, suggesting that merit selection/retention election plans have to some extent achieved their aim of reducing political competition for judgeships.[51] However, this in no way removes the threat to due process posed by the requirement of *any* judicial election to remain on the bench, because an election provides a means for voters to remove judges with whose decisions they disagree.[52] Indeed, it could well be that retention elections are often uneventful because judges who face them, knowing that they will face check by election, intentionally avoid doing anything to upset the electorate.

The reason for the suggested dramatic shift in constitutional focus from initial selection to retention is the simple fact that how judges are chosen in the first place matters far less from a due process standpoint.[53] Every method of initial selection has pluses and minuses. The pitfalls of judicial elections have been well documented, particularly with campaign spending rising to the almost astronomical levels seen in *Caperton*.[54] However, it is worth noting that the concentrated "patronage, cronyism, and capture" of gubernatorial and legislative appointments is what initially spurred citizens to adopt such elections.[55] Though the merit system is more insulated from popular politics—at the very least, it makes it harder for any one group to gain control of the selection process—it also cannot escape them entirely, and for several decades it has produced less diversity on the bench than other systems.[56] The key point to recognize is that ensuring that a judge would not have to worry about how to remain on the bench once she got there would blunt the drawbacks of each selection method.

The Supreme Court has never even noted, much less adopted the selection/retention distinction advocated here. Its most extensive discussion of judicial elections came in the 2002 case, *Republican Party of Minnesota v. White*,[57] which dealt with whether a state could restrict judicial candidates' ability to announce their views on disputed legal and political issues. Justice Scalia's majority opinion held that such a limitation violates the First Amendment and in so holding explicitly downplayed the differences both between judicial and legislative elections and between state court judges and legislators more generally.[58] Unlike judges in "countries where judges neither make law themselves nor set aside the laws enacted by the legislature," Justice Scalia wrote, American state judges are not completely separated "from the enterprise of representative government," inasmuch as they "have the power to 'make' common law" and "immense power to shape the states' constitutions as well."[59] He therefore concluded that it is perfectly appropriate to subject state judges to elections, because their role and lawmaking power differ significantly from that of federal judges, and are more closely related to the functions popular branches perform. Justice Scalia's logic is highly questionable. After all, the very same rationale could just as easily apply to federal judges, who also on occasion "make law" and "set aside the laws enacted by the legislature."[60] Indeed, the very fact that, as Justice Scalia emphasized, state judges "set aside the laws enacted by the legislature" underscores the need for their separation from the legislature. Justice Scalia's opinion also puzzlingly ignores the fact that a judge's job is radically different from that of a legislator, because it requires resolution of individual cases in which the rights of individual litigants are at stake.[61] Regardless of whether that judge is in a common law state court system or an Article III tribunal, constitutionally dictated due process protections of life, liberty and property apply.[62]

In the same opinion, Justice Scalia—perhaps inadvertently—identified the real issue:

> [E]lected judges—regardless of whether they have announced any views beforehand—*always* face the pressure of an electorate who might disagree with their rulings and therefore vote them off the bench. . . . So if, as Justice Ginsburg claims, it violates due process for a judge to sit in a case in which ruling one way rather than another increases his prospects for reelection, then—quite simply—the practice of electing judges is itself a violation of due process.[63]

Justice Scalia presents this comment as one element of a parade of horribles, enabling him to ridicule the idea that electorally based judicial retention violates due process. But in the process, he unknowingly makes the case for the opposite view. While Justice Scalia was correct to challenge Justice Ginsburg for failing fully to commit to the logical implications of her argument, he does so in order to support the conclusion that judicial elections do not violate due process. But his own logic demonstrates exactly how such elections do in fact, contravene the dictates of due process. Similarly, the very fact that state judges can "set aside the laws enacted by the legislature" is the very reason why state judges need to be insulated from electoral pressure. Otherwise, if judges invalidate a popular law, voters could simply oust them in favor of different judges who will uphold it, undercutting one of the main reasons for having a separate judicial branch in the first place. It is difficult to understand how Justice Scalia could so readily ignore obvious threats to state judicial independence that unambiguously contravene long-established constitutionally dictated standards of neutrality.

Unlike Justice Scalia's majority opinion, both the concurrences and dissents in *White* evince varying levels of discomfort with judicial elections. However, they all stop short of suggesting that judicial elections violate due process. As Justice Scalia noted, Justice Ginsburg's dissent comes closest to following this concern to its logical conclusion.[64] Most notably, Justice Ginsburg's dissent observes that a judge's knowledge that his success and tenure in office depend on certain outcomes represents a "direct, personal, substantial, and pecuniary" interest sufficient to threaten a litigant's right to due process.[65] Her statement is of special significance, given that the Court's judicial independence due process cases have never required proof of actual bias, but instead have sought to prevent "even the probability of unfairness."[66] Thus, when one "cannot know for sure whether an elected judge's decisions are based on his interpretation of the law or political expediency,"[67] but a prophylactic measure would eliminate that uncertainty, due process—in Justice Ginsburg's formulation in her opinion in *White*—errs on the side of overprotection. This is in direct contrast to what Justice Stevens suggests in his *White* dissent: "In the absence of reliable evidence one way or the other, a State may reasonably presume that elected judges are motivated by the highest aspirations of their office."[68]

The Court's next consideration of the due process implications of a judicial election-related issue came seven years later, in *Caperton*. There the Court once again bypassed an opportunity to explore the due process ramifications of judicial retention, perhaps because the facts of the case concerned only the initial selection process. However, the facts of *Caperton* illuminate why popularly based judicial retention is inherently incompatible with both procedural due process and broader countermajoritarian constitutional values.

CAPERTON AND GRATITUDE AS A DUE PROCESS VIOLATION: TOO MUCH AND NOT ENOUGH

In *Caperton*, the Court held that although in most situations campaign contributions by a prospective litigant or attorney do not give rise to a probability of bias sufficient to constitutionally require a judge's recusal,

Blankenship's "significant and disproportionate influence on placing [Justice Benjamin] on [his appeal] by raising funds or directing the judge's election campaign" was sufficient to pose "a serious risk of actual bias—based on objective and reasonable perceptions," in violation of the Due Process Clause of the Fourteenth Amendment.[69]

In one way, the Court's rationale for its decision in *Caperton* fits well with its previous cases invoking the due process right to an independent adjudicator. The judge in question in *Caperton* insisted that there was no evidence that he had been biased or that he was "anything but fair and impartial," a conclusion that the Court did not dispute.[70] However, because of the "difficulties of inquiring into actual bias, and the fact that the inquiry is often a private one, the Due Process Clause has been implemented by objective standards that do not require proof of actual bias," the Court reasoned.[71] "Otherwise there may be no adequate protection against a judge who simply misreads or misapprehends the real motives at work in deciding the case."[72] Such standards govern the constitutionality of "[e]very procedure which would offer a possible temptation to the average man as a judge . . . which might lead him not to hold the balance nice, clear and true," to use the oft-quoted phrase from *Tumey v. Ohio*, the Court's foundational judicial independence decision.[73]

Despite this sweeping language, the Court has acknowledged that it is impossible to root out all bias and interest.[74] It therefore confined its earlier judicial independence decisions to two categories of situations that could give rise to a due process violation: those in which the judge had a direct financial interest in the outcome of a case, and those involving nonsummary contempt procedures where the judge had such strong emotional ties from prior proceedings that he would be unlikely to rule fairly.[75]

Nonsummary contempt adjudication is rare, and the most recent case in the contempt line, *Mayberry v. Pennsylvania*, is from 1971.[76] In *Mayberry*, a criminal defendant repeatedly insulted both the judge and the proceedings; after the trial ended, the judge charged the defendant with contempt and found him guilty.[77] While acknowledging that "not every attack on a judge . . . disqualifies him from sitting," the Court noted that the insults at issue in this trial were so vicious that due process required contempt adjudication before a different judge.[78] Today, in an era of even coarser public dialogue, it seems unlikely that the Court would go quite as much out of its way as the *Mayberry* Court did in explaining how appalled it was by the defendant's conduct.[79] Nonetheless, the contempt cases remain good law—a fact illustrated by Justice Kennedy's citation of *Mayberry* in the majority opinion in *Caperton*.[80]

Unlike the pecuniary interest cases, the contempt cases rest upon a backward-looking anger rationale: that direct personal insults are so likely to color a judge's judgment of a particular litigant that it would deny due process for that judge to rule in the future on contempt charges stemming from those insults. These decisions never claimed to be broadly applicable. Rather, they attempted to confine their holdings to very specific factual settings. Though also based on the idea that backward-looking emotions can taint a judge's decision making, this anger arguably presents a more direct due process violation than *Caperton*-style gratitude, because the person acting as judge is also the complaining party. Such conflicts are also easier to detect: a judge will always owe many people for his job, but anger is case-specific.

The direct financial interest cases have had more widespread applicability, yet at the same time sparked greater uncertainty. *Tumey v. Ohio* is the classic illustration of this category. There the Court unanimously found that a "mayor's court," where the mayor-acting-as-judge was paid only if the defendant was convicted, violated the Fourteenth Amendment's due process guarantee.[81] This "direct, personal, pecuniary interest in convicting the defendant" made it impossible for the judge-mayor to serve as the impartial adjudicator that due process requires.[82] This was so even though "[t]here are doubtless mayors who would not allow such a consideration . . . to affect their judgment" in the particular case: "The requirement of due process of law in judicial procedure is not satisfied by the argument that men of the highest honor and the greatest self-sacrifice could carry it on without danger of injustice."[83]

Subsequent cases elaborated and expanded upon what constituted the "direct, personal, pecuniary interest" sufficient to violate due process. In *Ward v. Village of Monroeville*, for example, the Court held that a mayor violated litigants' right to due process by sitting as a judge in a court whose "fines, forfeitures, costs, and fees" made up roughly half of total village revenues.[84] The mayor played a role in managing the town's finances and also had responsibilities for revenue production and law enforcement; applying *Tumey*, the Court held that the mayor's interest in keeping the village coffers filled provided enough "possible temptation" to find against defendants when he might not otherwise have done so.[85]

Ward was perhaps more important and considered more of a step forward than the Court realized at the time. In *Ward*, the mayor did not stand to gain directly or risk losing income as a result of his decisions; only the town did. Yet that interest was still sufficient to violate due process. One could argue that achieving healthy town finances provided indirect financial benefit to the mayor by satisfying voters and helping him remain in his elected position, but it is unclear from the decision how much the mayor-judge was paid for that job, if at all. In any event, it is clear that the judge-mayor's financial incentive to decide cases a certain way found to exist in *Ward* was both less personal and less financially direct than in *Tumey*, and more analogous to the dilemma faced by elected state judges (though, for reasons we will explain, not nearly as problematic).

Similarly, in *Aetna Life Insurance Co. v. Lavoie*, the Court held that an Alabama Supreme Court justice violated due process by participating in a case that would help determine the law that would govern his *own* lawsuit against one of the parties, pending in a lower court.[86] The 5–4 decision he authored "had the clear and immediate effect of enhancing both the legal status and the settlement value of his own case."[87] While the justice's decision in the disputed case did not necessarily lead to *guaranteed* financial gain, unlike the rulings at issue in *Tumey* and *Ward*, it did give rise to a strong probability that the justice would succeed in his pending suit and receive money as a result. This, the Court held, constituted the requisite direct pecuniary interest sufficient to violate due process, because it had the effect of making the justice "a judge in his own case."[88]

Importantly, the "direct, personal, substantial, pecuniary" interest cases[89] all rely on a rationale grounded in a concern over a judge's temptation due to the possibility of *forward*-looking financial gain: A judge who hears a case in which he has a *prospective* financial incentive to decide a certain way deprives litigants of a neutral adjudicator and thus violates their right to due process. In *Tumey*, for example, that incentive came in the form of a direct payment that would result in a decision in favor of a particular litigant; in *Ward*, the Court deemed it sufficient that the money resulting from a particular judicial decision went to the city government, which the mayor-judge played a major role in running. The interest in *Lavoie* was filtered through another layer: state law governing insurance suits that would benefit the judge through resolution of a separate litigation. But to the Court, the case before the Alabama justice was sufficiently dependent on the outcome of the case in which the justice's financial interests were at stake to be constitutionally defective.

In contrast to all of the preexisting case law, the decision in *Caperton* rests on the potential of *past* financial benefit to skew a judge's decision making. The petitioners argued that although Blankenship's campaign support did not amount to a bribe or criminal influence, Justice Benjamin "would nevertheless feel a debt of gratitude to Blankenship for his extraordinary efforts to get him elected," thereby creating a "temptation . . . as strong and inherent in human nature as was the conflict the Court confronted in *Tumey* and [*Ward*], as well as [in the contempt cases]."[90] Justice Kennedy, speaking for the Court, accepted that argument, holding that Blankenship's lavish spending in support of Justice Benjamin's campaign, combined with the timing of that spending, raised a "serious risk of actual bias," such that for Justice Benjamin to hear Blankenship's case would constitute a violation of due process.[91]

Justice Benjamin's failure to recuse himself at the very least gave rise to a strong impression of unfairness that would have caused the party opposing Blankenship to doubt the legitimacy of the result. But it was a far less obvious due process violation than those found in the prior judicial independence cases, and a less glaring threat to due process than judicial retention elections in general. First, in *Tumey* and *Ward*, as with judicial reelections, the risk is that a *future* financial incentive will sway the judge's decision making. That financial benefit might be a certainty, as in *Tumey*, or merely a possibility, as in *Lavoie*, but in either event it hinges on decisions to be made by the judge in cases currently before her. In *Caperton*, the only prospective financial benefit that Justice Benjamin could conceivably receive from deciding in favor of Blankenship would be the cultivation of Blankenship's support in the next election, which was eight years away when Justice Benjamin last ruled on the case.[92] It is conceivable, of course, that the Court could deem this consideration a sufficient threat to independence to constitute a constitutional violation as a future benefit case; after all, the day a judge is elected she may reasonably be thinking about the need to prepare for reelection. However, the Court in *Caperton* chose not to focus on such a future-centric analysis but instead focused solely on the backward-looking factor of gratitude.

None of this is to say that *Caperton* should have come out the other way, or that gratitude can *never* constitute a sufficient influence on a judge's thinking to violate litigants' rights.[93] Rather, the point is that *Caperton*'s gratitude rationale simultaneously proves slightly too much and not nearly enough. Judges will always owe their job to *someone*, and often someone who may at some point appear before them or be directly impacted by their decisions. But that in and of itself should not be considered constitutionally problematic. In addition, it would be difficult to sort out *when* gratitude is sufficient to deprive a litigant of an independent adjudicator. By contrast, the threat that a judge might make decisions on the basis of what might win him another term in office (and thus ensure his continued livelihood) looms constantly and fits with the rationale underlying the Court's hallmark cases concerning the right to an independent adjudicator: the prospect that future financial gain will influence and perhaps skew judges' decisions on the bench. *Caperton* thus avoids consideration of the greater structural concern that retention poses through the pressure of having to face voters, regardless of campaign spending.[94]

Despite the *Tumey* line of cases, the *Caperton* opinion does not expressly raise concerns about the possibility that a future election would improperly influence Justice Benjamin's decisions. Though Justice Kennedy attempted to limit *Caperton*'s holding to the "extraordinary situation" at hand, his majority opinion employs broad language that raises as many questions as it answers. In defining the "objective standards" under which a judge's partiality violates due process, he wrote, "the Court has asked whether, 'under a realistic appraisal of psychological tendencies and human weakness,'" the interest "poses such a risk of actual bias or prejudgment that the practice must be forbidden if the guarantee of due process is to be adequately implemented."[95] This language set off an avalanche of criticism and dissection, exemplified by the "Forty Questions" Chief Justice Roberts posed in his dissent. Furthermore, Justice Kennedy's language closely resembles the emotional tie at issue in the contempt cases, minus the limited applicability to situations involving case-specific anger.[96] For present purposes, it is enough to note that it is extremely unclear what "practice" must be forbidden on the basis of *Caperton*: private financing of judicial elections? Spending over a certain amount on a judicial campaign (and if so, how is that amount is determined)? Judges hearing cases that involve campaign supporters?

To take the narrow view, if hearing a case involving the person to whom a judge owes his position constitutes a due process violation, then Article III judges are arguably violating due process on a fairly regular basis.[97] After all, federal judges more directly owe their position to the president who appointed them and the senator who recommended them than Justice Benjamin did to Blankenship. As generous as Blankenship's support was, it is impossible to know whether it was the determinative factor in Justice Benjamin's electoral victory. The Court in *Caperton* itself says that "proving what ultimately drives the electorate to choose a particular candidate is a difficult endeavor, not likely to lend itself to a certain conclusion."[98] It is much easier for an Article III judge to get a sense of who was instrumental in her appointment, since Article III judges are selected by a far smaller pool of individuals.

Yet implicit in the very structure of Article III—generally considered the gold standard for ensuring an independent judiciary—is the idea that backward-looking gratitude alone, even significant gratitude for the position that provides one's livelihood, cannot be deemed a due process violation. Instead, Article III is set up to remove any *prospective* incentives to decide cases a certain way. Once on the bench, Article III judges never have to seek reappointment, do not have to worry about their salary declining, and are therefore free to render decisions that might upset the president and the political party that appointed them.[99] For example, consider Justice Souter's vote in *Bush v Gore*,[100] or Justice Ginsburg's vote against President Clinton's position in *Clinton v. Jones*.[101] They decided cases differently from what their appointing president and party might have preferred, which suggests that they did not feel bound by any sense of gratitude. Conversely, the chance that federal judges might be grateful to their benefactor also does not constitute a due process violation.[102]

When one combines the structure of Article III with the long history of cases holding that the prospect of future financial consequences poses the most serious danger to the guarantee of a neutral adjudicator, the core due process threat comes into focus. Requiring judges' continuance in office to turn on the will of the voters or majoritarian branch officials whose jobs depend on the approval of the voters is itself the problem, because it provides judges with a prospective financial interest in maintenance of their livelihood in potentially every decision they make on the bench. In this way, a judge's desire to avoid upsetting voters in order to keep his job is driven by financial concerns in much the same way as the judge in *Tumey* might have been. Indeed, in certain ways, the threat to judicial independence may be even greater in the reelection context than in *Tumey*, because the loss of livelihood is a far greater financial concern then the loss of a possible supplement to the judge's salary.

It is true that, unlike *Tumey*, the threat of a particular judicial decision to a judge's livelihood in the reelection context is far more speculative and diffuse. But it is impossible to know *ex ante* exactly which judicial decisions are likely to attract voter attention. One should be willing to concede, if only for purposes of argument, that the large majority of judicial decisions are sufficiently technical or esoteric as to completely escape the attention of the voters. However, as is so vividly demonstrated in subsequent discussion,[103] this is by no means always the case, especially where sensitive constitutional issues are raised. To the contrary, many of the issues that arise in the course of state court litigation concern hot-button issues with various segments of the populace, often triggering the interest of powerful interest groups. The problem, of course, is that it is impossible *ex ante* to separate the cases which might engender public retaliation from those that do not pose such a risk. Because subjecting adjudicators to such coercive influences on their decision making *always* constitutes an unambiguous violation of due process, the conclusion is inescapable that *all* state judges must be provided with protection of their retention in a manner that satisfies due process. If the inescapable choice is between overprotection or underprotection of a constitutional right, it should hardly be controversial that the choice must be in favor of overprotection if at all possible. Granted, judges have to be selected somehow. As I wrote many years ago, "[R]eality forces us to tolerate some bias," or else "there would probably be no one left to adjudicate anything."[104] However, "[t]he degree of bias that we are willing to tolerate should be limited . . . by our ability to avoid it."[105]

Types of bias that most threaten independent adjudication break down primarily into two categories, in addition to the rare situation of physical intimidation: 1) Financial stake in the outcome of a case. This includes a direct stake, as in *Tumey*, and cases where a judge may gain or lose money in the future based on how he decides—such as *Ward*, *Lavoie*, and any case a judge decides differently based how it will look to voters in an upcoming election. 2) Some personal bias towards a party in the case, along the lines of emotional ties such as friendship, animosity, or family connections.[106] These vary mostly in degree, not kind; each "is potentially threatening, and it would be difficult to measure just how much temptation" exists in each instance.[107]

Popularly grounded methods for determining judicial retention are fraught with the potential for just these types of bias. This situation arguably presents the greatest threat to adjudicatory independence.[108] As Alexander Hamilton wisely noted in *Federalist* No. 79, "a power over a man's subsistence amounts to a power over his will."[109] The Supreme Court essentially concurred in this assertion in *Tumey*.[110] It did not matter whether the judge-mayor in *Tumey* was *actually* biased, nor did it matter that the payments he received from each conviction were relatively small: The mere perception of unfairness to which the financial interest gave rise was damaging enough.[111]

This coercive pressure on state judges is different in both degree and kind from mere personal preferences or prejudices, such as whether someone is a baseball fan or a member of the Catholic Church. Unlike purely personal traits, future electoral pressure is inherently undesirable in judges and arguably a concern in all cases, at least potentially. Moreover, it is easily avoidable. Electorally based judicial retention exists out of tradition, not necessity.[112] States could therefore resolve the danger to which the practice gives rise either by providing for life tenure without elections or via other reappointment mechanisms that do not require a judge to submit her candidacy to the diffuse and unpredictable mass of voters.

Following the thread in *Caperton* to its logical conclusion could lead to a wholesale upending of judicial elections on due process grounds, and the Court appears to want to avoid this result, especially given the current ubiquity of judicial elections and institutional inertia in their favor.[113] Granted, the Court is a passive institution that must wait for a case to be brought, and *Caperton* did not squarely present the issue of whether judicial retention violated due process. But the Court has not really bothered to consider the question in any context. As in the campaign finance realm, where cases like *FEC v. Wisconsin Right to Life*[114] begat more sweeping change in *Citizens United*,[115] it is likely that someone would bring a case if the Court hinted that it was troubled by the due process implications of existing state judicial retention practice.

Granting state judges Article III-style life tenure or some variation on it, such as service until a mandatory retirement age, is the most obvious prophylactic measure designed to remove the due process threat that current retention processes pose. However, it is not necessarily the only option. As Professor Henry Monaghan has observed, "what relieves judges of the incentive to please is not the prospect of indefinite service, but the awareness that their continuation in office does not depend on securing the continuing approval of the political branches" or the voting public.[116] Consequently, fixed, nonrenewable terms of service could arguably protect due process as well.[117] After all, if a judge's term is not renewable, one might conclude that the judge cannot reasonably fear that a decision one way or the other in a particular case will result in her losing employment.

Even in the federal system, proposals have been made for such tenure. For example, Professor Steven Calabresi has advocated fixed, eighteen-year nonrenewable terms for Supreme Court justices, in part because such terms would be long enough to allow justices to adjust to their role and perform their most effective work, while also allowing for moderate, regulated turnover that insulates the Court's membership as a whole from short-term political trends.[118] However, although shorter terms might not "substantially influence" justices' behavior on the Court, they introduce "the risk that justices might tailor their judicial behavior, even if only slightly, to maximize post-Court employment opportunities."[119] While the Supreme Court is obviously not a perfect metaphor for lower state courts, a similar calculus would conceivably apply to setting state judges' nonrenewable terms, balancing the desire for occasional turnover with the need to protect independence.

Four-, six- and eight-year terms are common in lower state courts, with states' highest courts often having slightly longer tenures, such as ten- and twelve-year terms.[120] If state judges were no longer allowed to seek reelection or reappointment, terms lengthier than those that currently exist would probably be needed to achieve the proper mix of turnover and independence. Because people tend to become state judges at a younger age, state judicial terms might need to be longer than those Professor Calabresi proposes for U.S. Supreme Court justices to ensure that judges not be concerned about their prospects of future employment and the possibility of displeasing a possible future employer while on the bench.[121]

POPULARLY BASED RETENTION METHODS
AND AMERICAN CONSTITUTIONALISM

Requiring judges to submit to popularly grounded methodologies to remain in office violates core constitutional values both in theory and in practice. In terms of constitutional theory, this pathology operates on both the "micro" and "macro" levels.[122] Microconstitutionalism involves the individual litigant's right to procedural due process. Macroconstitutionalism, on the other hand, concerns the broad, foundational principles inherent in the Constitution—"the basic notion of limited government," with majoritarian branches and majority will" constrained by a binding, written, countermajoritarian Constitution, enforced by an independent "judiciary."[123] Linking the two is the perception of fairness, which is fundamental to both individual dignity and systemic, institutional legitimacy in a constitutional system that "holds itself out as promoting" equality and meaningful participation in its processes, as our justice system does."[124] But no matter how long a judicial term is made, there always will exist the possibility of a judge's concern about postjudicial employment. As a result, the threat to judicial independence will remain. Hence the only means of removing the possibly coercive input caused by judicial concern about continued employment is requiring life tenure.

Appearance of Fairness

The appearance of fairness is one of the most fundamental values underlying constitutional rights on both micro and macro levels. It matters not just to individual litigants, but to broader perceptions of systemic legitimacy. The public is more likely to trust and participate in a justice system that it sees as fair.[125] Conversely, if people believe otherwise, their respect for the rule of law may deteriorate.[126] To put it in more practical terms, even if a judge finds against you, the result is likely to be more satisfying if you can be sure he ruled on principle, not out of personal or political calculation. The decision might be the same one he would have reached otherwise, but the difference in *appearance* is enough to increase your trust in both the result and the system that produced it.

Of all the values informing the due process guarantee, the perception of fairness "most clearly dictates use of a truly independent adjudicator."[127] Accuracy means little on its own if litigants have no confidence in the result. *Tumey* is illustrative. There the Court invalidated the defendant's conviction for an offense, not because the result was inaccurate, but because the procedure used to reach that result was itself unfair and, perhaps even more important, could never satisfy the appearance of fairness.[128] As long as the judge received payments only if he found the defendant guilty, the defendant would never be able to know for certain whether the judge ruled against him because the judge actually believed he was guilty or because of financial enticement.[129] An independent adjudicator was required to satisfy due process, independent of accuracy.[130]

Post-*Tumey* cases up to and including *Caperton* have reiterated the importance of adjudication that *appears* fair. As the Court observed in *In re Murchison*,

> [O]ur system of law has always endeavored to prevent even the probability of unfairness. . . . Such a stringent rule may sometimes bar trial by judges who have no actual bias and who would do their very best to weigh the scales of justice equally between contending parties. But to perform its high function in the best way "justice must satisfy the appearance of justice."[131]

Because the appearance of fairness so depends on the presence of an independent adjudicator, it should come as no surprise that judicial retention elections endanger this due process value more than any other means of judicial appointment. Studies suggest that elected judges modify their decisions because of electoral pressures.[132] Indeed, a judge may adapt her thinking without even realizing she is doing so; thus, reliance on something like recusal requests to address the problem falls woefully short. The point is that as long as processes of judicial retention exist, so too does the possibility that elected state judges will decide cases differently out of fear of losing their jobs. Thus, the appearance of unfairness is inextricably tied to the uncertainty of retention.

Given the difficulty of separating actual from perceived bias in the electoral context, state judicial retention by reelection inherently violates the Constitution's guarantee of due process. Though a step removed from the remuneration at issue in *Tumey*, this financial motivation is direct and powerful enough to pose a structural threat. The prophylactic measure of ending state judicial retention by reelection is necessary to ensure independent adjudication in state courts, especially as state governments cannot justify such elections as a matter of necessity.

Microconstitutionalism: The Value of an Independent Adjudicator

Microconstitutionalism centers on the need to preserve the dignity of the individual inherent in the liberal social contract. It does so through the constitutional protection of procedural due process. Microconstitutionalism applies any time the state is in a position to deprive an individual of life, liberty, or property, including in every judicial proceeding, no matter how insubstantial or subconstitutional the issue involved. It serves as a shield against the immense power of the state and an assurance that the Bill of Rights is not an empty promise. More concretely, microconstitutionalism encompasses the procedural protections commonly included under the rubric of due process.

The Supreme Court has long taken an instrumental view of procedural due process, holding it is intended to protect persons "from the mistaken or unjustified deprivation of life, liberty, or property."[133] But the value and power of microconstitutionalism extend well beyond the mere desire for an accurate result. It also ensures the individual dignitary interests underlying the Constitution's guarantees[134]—the appearance of fairness, equality, and the chance to meaningfully participate in a proceeding in which one's rights are at stake. Popularly based judicial retention threatens protection of all of those values, because a judge deciding a case based on factors other than her view of the law and evidence is far less likely to reach an accurate result or treat the litigants fairly.

The presence of an independent adjudicator is thus the most fundamental element of the microconstitutionalism embodied in the Due Process Clause. Without it, as I wrote many years ago, "the values of due process cannot be realized," "[r]egardless of what other procedural safeguards are employed."[135] Indeed, "the rights to notice, hearing, counsel, transcript, and to calling and cross-examining witnesses . . . are of no real value . . . if the decisionmaker bases his findings on factors other than his assessment of the evidence before him."[136] For instance, "if the individual seeking to enforce his rights is black, and the adjudicator is racially biased" and would never find in favor of a black person, other procedural guarantees mean nothing.[137] History further bolsters the case that the right to an independent adjudicator "constitutes the floor of due process." Such a right was "considered a crucial element of procedural justice by the common law, by those that established the law of the colonies, and, perhaps most important, by the Framers of the United States Constitution."[138]

When one applies the standard of judicial neutrality dictated by the Due Process Clause to popularly based methods of judicial retention, the unconstitutionality of such methods should become obvious. It should not be difficult to see how the pressure of a looming election could taint a judge's ability to reach accurate decisions in the cases before her. This pressure could influence both the judge's positive and normative decision making, and, perhaps more important, create a general atmosphere in which the judge's electoral concerns inevitably take priority over her desire to reach an accurate result in the first place. A judge who is concerned that finding for a particular litigant may upset voters and cause him to lose his job is no longer primarily concerned with accuracy. This also deprives the litigant of the chance to convince the decision maker of the merits of his case, because the judge's mind is already largely closed. As described above, this electoral pressure differs from other personal biases because it is always a potential concern that is impossible to eliminate altogether.

Eliminating the practices of judicial reelection and reappointment would also augment the instrumental value of other due process safeguards. For example, the right to an oral hearing and the right to counsel mean little if the judge presiding over the proceedings is under externally imposed pressure to find against the litigant exercising those rights.

Due process does not rest on a utilitarian desire for accuracy alone. It also encompasses "noninstrumental," dignitary values such as the appearance of fairness, equality, and the chance to participate in a proceeding where one's rights are at stake.[139] These values are part of our constitutional tradition, run through a range of Supreme Court cases, primarily in the criminal realm, and form the basis for decisions such as *Tumey*.[140] Though these values are worth pursuing for their own benefit, they also support instrumental goals, and likewise depend on the participation of an independent adjudicator.[141] For instance, state judicial elections threaten equality and participation, which reflect the individual's dignitary interest in having a chance to play a role in proceedings that affect her and influence the decision maker to rule in her favor. If a judge is predisposed to find for one side for reasons outside the merits of the case—such as, for present purposes, fear of electoral reprisal—then procedural inequality exists. Those whose position in a case would conceivably be more palatable or less upsetting to a majority of voters gain a built-in advantage; those on the opposite side come in behind. Similarly, a party's participation has a dramatically reduced chance of affecting the outcome of a case, and little value overall, if electoral pressure means the judge has a powerful incentive to find against that party.

An adjudicator who injects irrelevant factors into the decision making process—for example, a judge deciding a case based on how his decision will impact a future judicial election—also undermines the procedural values of predictability, transparency, and rationality. Under such circumstances, he abandons the course set by the law and impedes individuals' ability to plan their behavior.[142] By contrast, the absence of other procedural safeguards does not necessarily present the same threat. For instance, a litigant who is unable to give an oral argument in his case may still benefit from procedural rationality if he knows in advance that he is not entitled to such a hearing and can plan accordingly.[143] No such alternative exists for litigants facing trial or other proceedings before a judge unduly influenced by electoral pressure.

Finally, electoral pressure also compromises litigants' ability to know the "why" of court decisions affecting their cases. A judge who (a) *consciously* decides a case differently based on majority sentiment is almost certainly not going to admit it, and (b) one who *subconsciously* decides a case differently because of electoral pressure will also not be able to articulate the true reasons for his decision. Either instance leaves the affected individual without a true or satisfactory explanation of why the court decided the way it did. Officials are generally under no obligation to accurately explain the reasons for their decisions in informal settings.[144] However, judges generally *are* obligated to explain their decisions, and they cannot fulfill that duty without the kind of decisional independence that reelection and retention elections endanger.

Macroconstitutionalism: Understanding the Dangers of Popular Constitutionalism

Beyond the threat they pose to individual due process, popularly based methods of judicial retention also endanger what might be called macroconstitutionalism—the countermajoritarian governing structure that ensures the rule of law and protection of constitutional rights on a societal level. This structure simultaneously allows democratic input while protecting minority rights. Without it, there is little point in having a written constitution, because the legislature or executive can simply override it at any time.[145]

By clear design, the Constitution casts the prophylactically insulated federal judiciary in a distinctive role. Vested with the judicial power to decide individual cases and controversies, federal judges are protected by the prohibition of reducing their salaries and life tenure to provide independence and allow them to restrain the popular branches if and when those branches contravene the Constitution.[146] "Without this, all the reservations of particular rights or privileges would amount to nothing," Alexander Hamilton wrote in *Federalist* No. 78.[147] Unlike the legislative and executive branches, the federal judiciary is structured so that it is insulated from popular fervor, while maintaining a tie to the representative branches through the appointment process. It is not the government's policy-making engine, though it may nonetheless end up making law. It is an integral part of a constitutional scheme of self-government that combines majoritarian and nonmajoritarian aspects in the service of something greater than "statistical democracy" or "brute forms of preference aggregation."[148]

State courts were never conceived of in quite the same way. The Constitution says nothing explicit about state courts or how they should be structured, which helps explain the wide variety of state court structures and judicial selection and retention mechanisms that have existed over the years. Despite differences between the federal and state court systems, however, since ratification of the Fourteenth Amendment, the Due Process Clause applies equally to state as well as federal courts. State judges perform a function fundamentally different from that of elected state representatives, who act on behalf of the voters who placed them in office.[149] State courts have the same constitutionally imposed duty to uphold constitutional rights that Article III tribunals do.[150] They also matter in the greater constitutional scheme, because they routinely adjudicate federal constitutional claims and defenses, including §1983 civil rights suits, equal protection claims, and myriad criminal procedure issues, with federal review a remote possibility at best. Though state courts may have more diverse responsibilities than Article III courts, they are similarly entrusted with the obligation to safeguard rights that protect unpopular views or groups against the power of the majority. And unless they are free to render rights-protective decisions that may be unpopular with a majority of citizens,[151] they cannot ensure minority rights. But the problem with popularly based methods of judicial retention for purposes of macroconstitutionalism extend far beyond the concern over minority rights—as important as the preservation of those rights is to our constitutional system. The primary concern, rather, is that the entire structure of countermajoritarian constitutionalism is severely undermined when those who interpret the Constitution's provisions are subject to majoritarian pressure. Indeed, as Article V all too clearly shows,[152] the Constitution is by its nature a countermajoritarian document. It demands supermajorities to alter its provisions, *precisely because it is designed to limit simple majorities*. It is, then, highly illogical—indeed, nonsensical—to vest in those who are vulnerable to majoritarian pressures the final say as to the meaning of what is at its core a countermajoritarian document.

As currently constituted, state court systems that require judges to stand for reelection or retention to remain on the bench have effectively reduced their judicial branch to a majoritarian instrument. Steven Croley describes this as the "majoritarian difficulty," the flipside of Bickel's "countermajoritarian difficulty": Rather than asking how unelected and unaccountable judges can be justified in a regime committed to democracy, we should instead consider whether "elected/accountable judges can be justified in a regime committed to constitutionalism."[153] After all,

> [C]onstitutionalism entails, among other important things, protection of the individual and of minorities from democratic governance over certain spheres. When those charged with checking the majority are themselves answerable to, and thus influenced by, the majority, the question arises how individual and minority protection is secured.[154]

And, as I have argued, as long as state judges must face voters to remain on the bench, our system risks denying due process to large swaths of citizens over crucially important rights.

Despite their inherently illogical foundation in the theory of American constitutionalism, popularly based methods of state judicial retention seem to draw strong scholarly support from the intellectually fashionable theory of "popular constitutionalism." Despite the scholarly prestige of the academics who have shaped this theory in recent years, the serious flaws in this system are readily apparent in the oxymoronic nature of the phrase. "Constitutionalism," by its very nature, contemplates a system committed to the rule of law and imposition of principled restraints on majorities.[155] Hence the very notion of a popularly grounded form of constitutionalism is incoherent: To the extent that the system is popularly based, it is a system devoid of constitutionalism as generally understood in American political thought.

As explained in chapter 1, popular constitutionalism posits that the final authority to interpret the Constitution lies not with courts but with "the people themselves," whatever that means, in a way that somehow amorphously extends beyond the ability to alter the Constitution via the amendment process.[156] Judicial review exists, according to advocates of popular constitutionalism, as "only one of many mechanisms by which the people's will could be enforced"—with, notably, the people's will paramount.[157] As should be immediately apparent, popular constitutionalism is difficult to define with any real level of precision,[158] and it is unclear how it would or could ever work in practice: Who, exactly, are "the people themselves"? How do we know what they want? Are they not already expressing their views on the Constitution—and who is best suited to interpret it—by generally assenting to judicial decisions?

To the extent that judicial elections "suggest what a vigorous practice of popular constitutionalism might entail," we have years of results from which to gauge their success—or lack thereof.[159] Simply put, they are all quite "popular", but with little or no "constitutionalism."[160] As David Pozen notes, "[e]lected judges will generally seek to avoid a backlash at all costs," so "the safest strategy for incumbent judges facing reelection is to simply preserve the status quo and avoid making any segment of the population angry enough about a decision to protest (and thus threaten the judge's reelection bid)."[161]

Not surprisingly, this forced judicial restraint can end up at odds with a judge's duty to enforce the constitutional rights of unpopular minorities. Indeed, how could we possibly expect any other result? As Professor Pozen has correctly noted, "when pusillanimous judicial interpretations of the Constitution merely reproduce and reinforce prevailing beliefs. . . . the courts contribute nothing distinctive to the 'discursive formation of popular will upon which democracy is based.'"[162] For a countermajoritarian constitutional system to remain viable, the courts must function as more than a majoritarian echo chamber.[163]

The leading scholarly advocate of popular constitutionalism is Larry Kramer. Kramer pays essentially no heed to the Constitution's inherently countermajoritarian tradition, structure or text, or to courts' special ability to protect rights and enforce values embodied within that structure.[164] He excoriates those who believe in judicial supremacy, or at the very least view courts as specially positioned to settle constitutional rights, describing them as anti-democratic, modern-day high federalists who disdain "ordinary people."[165] Of such people, he writes:

> They would not deny or repudiate the underlying core [belief]: that constitutional law is motivated by a conviction that popular politics is by nature dangerous and arbitrary; that "tyranny of the majority" is a pervasive threat; that a

democratic constitutional order is therefore precarious and highly vulnerable; and that substantial checks on politics are necessary lest things fall apart.[166]

As this chapter's exploration of popularly based methods of judicial retention clearly shows, what Kramer is really challenging is not advocacy of judicial supremacy but rather the very essence of American constitutionalism. In any event, his analysis demonstrates that concerns about the possibility of a tyranny of the majority are entirely justified.

The sad irony of the entire popular constitutionalist attack on judicial review is that far from being anti-democratic, constitutionalism paradoxically helps to *ensure* democracy—to allow it to flourish.[167] On this point, Tocqueville was characteristically prescient: "Under some constitutions the *judges* are *elected* subject to frequent reelection. I venture to predict that sooner or later these innovations will have dire results and that one day it will be seen that by diminishing the magistrates' independence, not judicial power only but the democratic republic itself has been attacked."[168] As Dean Post and Professor Siegel note, "[s]upport for judicial finality in the protection of constitutional rights may reflect the simple idea that in certain contexts we want citizens to hold rights against their governments that are as secure and as reliable as the private rights that they hold against their fellow citizens."[169] Truly independent courts are capable of enforcing those rights; those where judges are subject to retention and reelection turn the quest for enforcement into a roll of the dice that endangers the rule of law. "[B]oth common sense and practical experience dictate that the provisions of the Constitution will effectively be deprived of all legal force and meaning if the very majoritarian branches regulated and controlled by that document are allowed to act as the final arbiters of the countermajoritarian limitations which the document imposes upon them."[170] Both judicial retention elections and gubernatorial and legislative reappointment methodologies effectively provide (albeit indirectly) the majoritarian branches with that type of final say. A system grounded in principles of constitutionalism—as ours is—is seriously undermined as a result.

CONCLUSION

State judicial elections are employed across most of the nation, a practice voters support in the abstract even if they cringe on encountering a long ballot of judicial candidates. Yet tradition has never been enough to justify continuing a practice that violates the Constitution. And tying judges' continued tenure on the bench to the voters' will violates the constitutional guarantee of procedural due process by providing a future financial incentive for judges to decide cases far differently from the way they would otherwise. The very argument used to justify judicial elections—as an opportunity to hold judges accountable—renders such elections unconstitutional, especially because it is clear that voters have in fact used judicial elections to hold judges responsible for unpopular, yet arguably legally sound decisions.

One might reasonably ask, why eliminate the whole institution when we cannot know for sure that any particular judge is actually deciding cases differently in response to future electoral pressure? That, though, is precisely the point: we can rarely, if ever, know with certainty that a judge decided a matter differently because of electoral pressure. Yet that such pressure exists as a general matter is simple common sense. It is exactly for this reason that due process demands a prophylactic safeguard of judicial independence. Any of the perceived benefits of judicial reelection or retention elections cannot constitutionally outweigh the psychological toll such elections take on judges and the danger they pose to both individual litigants' due process rights and the broader enforcement of constitutional rights. Judicial reelection and retention elections threaten accuracy, fairness, the chance for individuals to meaningfully participate, and courts' ability to protect minority rights. Purely as a constitutional matter, they are not worth the cost.

In *Caperton*, the Supreme Court for the first time found a due process violation linked to judicial elections, but in doing so the Court adopted a constitutional rationale that proved too much by identifying backward-looking gratitude as the source of that violation. The real problem in *Caperton* was not the possibility of judicial gratitude to whoever helped put the judge on the bench, any more than when a federal judge adjudicates a case involving the president who appointed her. The problem, rather, was that state court judges at some point after their initial selection will have to rely on politically based retention methods in order to hold onto their jobs. This knowledge and constant pressure threatens sitting judges' decisions in a way that is directly comparable to the situations in the Court's other key cases on constitutional threats to judicial independence. With the number of high-stakes judicial elections only likely to increase, the Court will almost certainly have a chance to revisit the issue in the future. It should do so in a more comprehensive and principled fashion than it did in *Caperton*.

CHAPTER FIVE

Constitutionalism, Democracy, and the Pathology of Legislative Deception

INTRODUCTION

Some Supreme Court decisions withstand the test of time.[1] They are universally recognized as the fulcrums of modern constitutional law, even if they were decided before the turn of the prior century. If students learn nothing else in their constitutional law courses it is the names (if not the actual holdings) of these decisions. A few of these decisions are known primarily because we love to hate them.[2] In contrast, there are numerous Supreme Court decisions that are effectively buried, even before the justices who authored them are buried themselves.

There also exists a third, less easily described category of Supreme Court decisions that are not readily classifiable under either of the other headings. They are not nearly as well known as the doctrinal giants of constitutional law. Nevertheless, they generally receive respectful, if not extensive treatment in the casebooks, largely because there is a widely shared sense that they are somehow of substantial significance in the flow of American constitutional or political theory. The problem, however, is that no one is exactly sure how or why.

One such a decision is *United States v. Klein*,[3] a case whose importance to the shaping of American political theory has never been fully grasped or articulated by scholars,[4] and whose meaning has been comprehended by the federal judiciary—including the Supreme Court itself—virtually not at all.[5] The position taken here is that once the Court's decision in *Klein* is appropriately dissected and extrapolated, both judges and scholars will be in a position to grasp the essence of an extremely important—yet often ignored or misunderstood—precept of American democratic and constitutional theory that lies at the hidden core of the *Klein* opinion.

In *Klein*, the post–Civil War Supreme Court held unconstitutional a federal statute that sought to employ Congress's constitutional power to make exceptions to Supreme Court appellate jurisdiction[6] as a vehicle for requiring the Court to deem the issuance of a presidential pardon to be conclusive proof of disloyalty on the part of former Confederates.[7] A finding of disloyalty mattered greatly because those found to have been disloyal were statutorily disabled from recovering property seized by the federal government. In this chapter, I undertake to glean a vitally important, yet largely unrecognized, element of democratic theory from the reasoning contained in the *Klein* opinion that declared this legislatively directed rule of evidence unconstitutional, and to explore its essential role in the healthy operation of the American political process. Derived from *Klein* is the need for a dynamic, intersecting relationship among three important actors in the American political system: the elected branches of government, the electorate that chose them, and the unrepresentative judiciary. In this relationship, it is, paradoxically, the most undemocratic branch of government that is to stand as the policeman of the democratic process, seeking to assure the continuing viability of representative democracy and the integrity of the fiduciary relationship between the elected and the electorate.

It would surely not be a startling revelation to suggest that, in the American constitutional system, it is the insulated judiciary that is intended to police the elected branches of government. Indeed, much of this book has been devoted to explicating and defending this precept. What is derived here from *Klein*, however, is a far more subtle precept of American political theory: that the judiciary has the constitutional power and obligation to assure that Congress not deceive the electorate as to the manner in which its legislation actually alters the preexisting legal, political, social, or economic topography. The legislative deception that is of concern, it should be emphasized, does not relate to the legislators' private motivation in enacting the legislation, or what incidental or collateral effects the legislation may have, beyond its direct and immediate impact. Instead, the focus here is exclusively on the much more fundamental concern about deception as to what the legislation actually accomplishes.

One might wonder how Congress could possibly attempt to deceive the electorate as to the direct impact of its legislation. After all, the words of the statute presumably tell us what the law does. On occasion, ambiguity may exist as to what a statute means or exactly how it will impact the legal and political worlds, either due to inartful drafting or a conscious legislative choice, embodied either explicitly or implicitly in the body of the statute, to delegate common-law-making power to the courts or, on occasion, to agencies empowered to administer the statute.[8] But ambiguity is surely not the same as deception. The deception focused upon here does not arise from the operative substantive provisions of the statute. It is accomplished by other means.

Legislative deception may take one of two forms, which are appropriately described as "micro" and "macro" deception.[9] When a legislature engages in micro deception, it leaves the generalized substantive law intact, but legislatively directs that a particular litigation (or group of litigations) arising under that law be resolved in a manner inconsistent with the dictates of that preexisting generalized law. In the case of macro deception, in contrast, the legislature leaves substantive law unchanged on its face, but alters it in a generally applicable manner by enacting procedural or evidentiary modifications that have the effect of transforming the essence—or what can appropriately be described as the law's "DNA."[10] In the former situation, the legislature has altered the reach of the substantive law in specific applications. In the latter, it has sought to alter preexisting controlling law generally, but has done so through the use of indirect procedural or evidentiary manipulation. In both situations, the legislature has purported to leave the controlling law unchanged, but in reality has manipulated the application of that law, either in specified instances or more generally. As a result, the essential elements of the democratic process will have been undermined, because the electorate may have been deceived as to the nature and extent of its chosen representatives' political commitment in voting for or against that legislation. A legislator's vote for or against a proposed substantive law means little if the legislature has furtively altered the reach or impact of that law by resorting to a form of legislative shell game.

In both micro and macro deception, the legislature accomplishes this sleight-of-hand without explicitly informing the electorate of how its procedural legislation has transformed the political, social, and economic landscape. As a result, the deception effectively denies the electorate the opportunity to hold its representatives accountable. When members of Congress vote for or against proposed legislation, they are making a political commitment that enables the electorate to judge them. This process of political commitment facilitates protection of the essential elements of the American democratic process: representation, accountability, and checking.[11] A voter cannot judge her elected representative on the basis of that legislator's vote on legislation when the legislation in question amounts to something approaching a sham, due to the manipulative effect of accompanying procedural or evidentiary devices.

The key theoretical insight that may be gleaned from *Klein* is that the judiciary—the one governmental branch insulated from the electorate—provides the only effective means of assuring that the democratic process operates in the manner necessary to the attainment of the normative goals that underlie the nation's chosen form of representative government. It does so by policing the legislative process to eliminate both micro and macro legislative deception.

There are a number of reasons why this significant aspect of American democratic theory—namely, the need to have the unrepresentative judiciary police possible legislative deception—may have been lost in the doctrinal and theoretical shuffle in the years since *Klein*. First, there existed an alternative rationale for the Court's finding of unconstitutionality that more clearly and directly implicated the judiciary's traditional role in the constitutional process, and much of the post-*Klein* analysis has centered on this question.[12] Second, the *Klein* Court itself may not have fully grasped the theoretical implications of the point that it was making.[13] Third, the post-*Klein* Supreme Court has been less than forthright in either its explication or application of the legislative deception aspect of *Klein*. On occasion, the Court has described the *Klein* holding in what are largely obscure and misleading terms.[14] On other occasions, it ignored blatant violations by Congress of the democratically imposed limits on its authority to manipulate the judicial process, without either acknowledging, or perhaps even comprehending, the serious stakes involved for purposes of the success of American democracy.[15]

The first section of this chapter focuses on the facts and holdings of *United States v. Klein*. In doing so, it describes the alternative conceivable constructions of the Court's opinion.[16] The second section seeks to place *Klein* within the broad framework of American political theory. It explicates the connection between democratic theory, legislative accountability, and the potential harms of legislative deception.[17] The chapter then posits, and seeks to respond to, potential criticisms of the legislative-deception model fashioned here.[18] It proceeds to examine the manner in which the Constitution authorizes the judiciary to perform the policing function necessary to eliminate instances of legislative deception. In so doing, it explains how congressional use of the judiciary to implement the devices of legislative deception threatens fundamental dictates of constitutionally protected separation of powers.[19]

All of the dictates of democratic theory expounded upon here derive from the theoretical seed planted by the Court in its opinion in *Klein*. Perhaps due to recognition of the important political theory that lies implicitly at the heart of the *Klein* decision, that case will be promoted from the type of constitutional purgatory in which it presently resides to the place where it belongs: among truly significant Supreme Court decisions, recognized for their contributions to the foundations of American political theory.

THE MYSTERY OF *UNITED STATES V. KLEIN*

The Facts and Holding of Klein

United States v. Klein was one of the last Supreme Court cases during Reconstruction to invalidate congressional legislation. Throughout Reconstruction, a primary concern of the Republican-controlled Congress was the loyalty of Southerners pardoned after the Civil War. The legislation challenged in *Klein* was designed to ensure that those who were pardoned would not receive preferential treatment. Klein, an administrator of an estate, sued on behalf of that estate to recover property seized from the decedent and sold by the federal government pursuant to the Abandoned Property Collection Act of 1863. That legislation authorized the Treasury Department to collect abandoned or captured property in any territory involved in the insurrection. However, it also enabled the owner of the seized property to recover the proceeds from its sale upon proof of loyalty. Under an earlier judicial ruling, a claimant would be deemed loyal for purposes of the 1863 Act if he had received a presidential pardon. In *Klein*, the decedent had received a pardon, the Court of Claims entered judgment in favor of the estate, and the government appealed.

While the government's appeal was pending, Congress passed the Act of July 12, 1870,[20] declaring pardons inadmissible as evidence to establish loyalty in cases under the 1863 Act. The Act directed the Supreme Court to dismiss, for want of jurisdiction, appeals from judgments that denied recovery to pardoned individuals. The law further provided that receipt of a pardon containing recitation of the pardoned acts without a disclaimer of participation in those acts would constitute conclusive evidence of disloyalty, which effectively meant that the Supreme Court must reverse judgments awarding recovery to pardoned individuals.[21] In other words, the legislation made evidence of a pardon inadmissible *in support* of a claimant and admissible *against* a claimant.[22] Klein challenged the 1870 Act on the grounds that it violated separation of powers. The government argued that the 1870 Act was constitutional because Congress had employed its power to make exceptions to the Supreme Court's appellate jurisdiction pursuant to Article III's "Exceptions Clause"[23] as a means of precluding Supreme Court review.

The *Klein* Court rejected this argument and held the 1870 Act unconstitutional.[24] The Court found the congressional action to be constitutionally defective because it required the Court to "ascertain the existence of certain facts and thereupon to declare that its jurisdiction on appeal has ceased, by dismissing the bill. What is this but to prescribe a rule for the decision of a cause in a particular way?"[25] After describing the law's jurisdictional directive, the Court asked rhetorically, "Can we do so without allowing one party to the controversy to decide in its own favor? Can we do so without allowing that the legislature may prescribe rules of decision to the Judicial Department of the government in cases pending before it?"[26] The constitutional problem, said the Court, was that under the law the judiciary was "forbidden to give the effect to evidence which, in its own judgment, such evidence should have, and is directed to give it an effect precisely to the contrary."[27]

The Court then provided several conceivable grounds to explain its decision. It is at this point that the analysis becomes murky. All of the rationales suggested in the Court's opinion are framed in brief, cryptic terms. Some of them, when taken literally, make little sense in terms of the basic principles of American democracy. More important, the Court did not appear to grasp the magnitude of the issues with which it was dealing from the perspectives of American constitutional and political theory. It is likely for these reasons that *Klein* has played so limited a role in the shaping of modern American constitutional law. The discussion that follows explores the various interpretive permutations and combinations to which the Court's opinion in *Klein* may give rise. After that discussion, the chapter describes the important insight of democratic theory that should be deemed to lie at the heart of the *Klein* decision, even if (as seems likely) the *Klein* Court itself may have failed to recognize the full theoretical implications of its own conclusions.

The Alternative Constructions of Klein

Construction 1: Congress May Not Dictate to the Courts How to Interpret the Constitution. Although Congress purported to employ its presumably broad power under Article III, section 2, to make exceptions to the Supreme Court's appellate jurisdiction, the Court correctly rejected this effort as little more than a sham: "[T]he language of the proviso shows plainly that it does not intend to withhold appellate jurisdiction except as a means to an end. Its great and controlling purpose is to deny pardons granted by the President the effect which this court has adjudged them to have."[28] While the statute dictated that pardons were not to be considered by the Supreme Court on appeal, the Court "had already decided that it was our duty to consider them and give them effect, in cases like the present, as equivalent to proof of loyalty."[29] The Court's point appears to be sound. In a society governed by a countermajoritarian Constitution, the very majoritarian branches limited by that document may not usurp the function of interpreting the document's terms. This is nothing more than a summary restatement of the reasoning of both Hamilton in *Federalist* No. 78[30] and Chief Justice John Marshall in *Marbury v. Madison*. While several scholars have challenged this assertion of judicial supremacy, it surely is not inconsistent with prevailing doctrinal and theoretical notions of judicial power for the Court to assert this authority.[31] Even if one were to postulate a very different model of the judicial role, whereby each branch of government could determine for itself the extent of the constitutional limits on its authority,[32] the congressional action invalidated in *Klein* would still have been unconstitutional. Rather than simply state that the pardon means what Congress believes it means, Congress sought to have the judiciary invoke the congressional determination as part of the adjudicatory process. If Congress wishes to make use of the legitimacy of the politically insulated federal judiciary, it must simultaneously allow the judiciary to make its own determinations.[33]

If this were all the Court had held, the case would still be important as one of a number of Supreme Court assertions of its ultimate authority to interpret the terms of the Constitution. But the Court immediately proceeded to embark down some very cryptic—and, on occasion, misguided—lines of analysis.

Construction 2: Congress May Not Prescribe "a Rule of Decision in Causes Pending" in Its Favor. After noting that the primary purpose of the law was "to deny to pardons granted by the President the effect which this court had adjudged them to have," thereby seemingly invoking the principle of judicial supremacy in constitutional interpretation, the *Klein* Court immediately proceeded to shift its reasoning to a much less compelling logic. The opinion noted that in the law, "the denial of jurisdiction to this court, as well as to the Court of Claims, is founded solely on the application of a rule of decision, in causes pending, prescribed by Congress."[34]

By means of a rhetorical question, the Court then provided the second conceivable rationale for its holding:

> What is this but to prescribe a rule for the decision of a cause in a particular way? In the case before us, the Court of Claims has rendered judgment for the claimant and an appeal has been taken to this court. We are directed to dismiss the appeal . . . . Can we do so without allowing one party to the controversy to decide in its own favor? Can we do so without allowing that the legislature may prescribe rules of decision to the Judicial Department of the government in cases pending before it?[35]

Here the Court appears to be saying one or both of two things: First, Congress may not constitutionally allow one party to decide the case in its own favor, and second, Congress may not "prescribe rules of decision" to the courts in pending cases. In terms of the strength of the Court's rationale, however, a great deal depends upon which of the two points the Court intended to make.

Recall the fundamental premise of constitutional democracy that the Court may not invalidate a federal statute unless that law violates the Constitution. What, one may ask, is unconstitutional about Congress directing either result, assuming such direction does not usurp the judicial power to interpret the Constitution? While the Court never really answers this question, in one sense it is not difficult to find the constitutional basis for a holding that prohibits Congress from directing the result in a particular case. The resolution of individual cases—including the process of the application of general law in fact-specific contexts—clearly falls within the concept of "judicial" power, as a definitional matter. Thus, Congress may not constitutionally adjudicate individual disputes, because to do so would constitute the performance of a nonlegislative function, in violation of Article I's vesture in Congress of nothing more than the "legislative power."[36] If Congress may not itself resolve individual litigations, its direction to the courts—the one branch vested with the "judicial power"—as to how to resolve specific disputes is constitutionally problematic, on two grounds. First, it effectively constitutes an improper performance by Congress of a judicial function. Second, it disrupts the judiciary's performance of its constitutionally intended function. This is, then, simply a matter of separation of powers.

It is by no means clear, however, that the Court intended to confine its constitutional rationale to the legislative resolution of an individual case. This is so for two reasons. First, the legislation challenged in *Klein* appeared to do far more than simply resolve the individual litigation pending before the Court. Rather, it was framed in the traditionally general terms that characterize legislation, applying to all cases in which pardons had been issued to former Confederates. Second, the Court's opinion expressed constitutional concern with more than a congressional effort to legislatively resolve an individual litigation. Indeed, the Court's suggestions that Congress lacks constitutional authority either to "decide [a litigation] in its own favor" or "prescribe rules of decision" in cases pending before the courts make little constitutional sense. Of course, if by the former suggestion the Court meant simply that Congress may not prescribe the result in an individual case, for reasons already discussed, the point would be sound. The Court's statement, though, does not appear to be so confined, because its logic is not limited to the decision of an individual case in which the government is a party in the government's favor. Rather, the Court's statement would apply to congressional resolution of *all* litigation in which the government is a party.

On the other hand, if Congress seeks to influence the resolution of an individual case, even one in which the federal government is a party, simply by altering the subconstitutional landscape through enactment of generally applicable legislation affecting the outcome of the particular case, it is difficult to understand why the legislation is unconstitutional. Congress possesses the power to alter the general law in constitutionally valid ways, and that change in general law must control the outcome of relevant litigation, even in pending cases.[37] Put bluntly, the Court is simply wrong in its statement that Congress lacks constitutional authority to "prescribe rules of decision to the Judicial Department of the government in cases pending before it," even in those to which the government is a party, at least to the extent the statement was intended to extend beyond legislative resolution of a particular litigation or the resolution of issues of constitutional interpretation.[38]

Construction 3: Congress May Not Prohibit the Court from "Giv[ing] the Effect to Evidence Which, in Its Own Judgment, Such Evidence Should Have." Thus far, we have seen that the Court in *Klein* provided two probably sound rationales for its decision: that Congress may neither control the judiciary's interpretation of the Constitution nor direct the resolution of an individual suit. In addition, we have seen that the Court may have seriously undermined the force of these holdings by suggesting the insupportable rationale that Congress may not, through the enactment of generally applicable legislation, alter the governing rule of decision in a pending litigation. Lost in all this, however, is the most subtle and insightful—yet also most controversial—of the possible rationales for the Court's conclusion that the statute purporting to restrict its jurisdiction was unconstitutional

The Court put forth this rationale in its attempt to defend its broad (and largely misguided) assertion that Congress may not prescribe rules of decision in pending cases. In defending this assertion, the Court sought to distinguish its earlier decision in *Pennsylvania v. Wheeling and Belmont Bridge Co.*,[39] where after an earlier decree in the Supreme Court that the bridge, in the then-state of the law, was a nuisance and must be abated, Congress passed an act legalizing the structure and making it a post road; and the Court, on a motion to enforce the decree, held that the bridge had ceased to be a nuisance by the exercise of congressional power and denied the motion.[40] The *Klein* Court distinguished *Wheeling Bridge* because in that case "the court was left to apply its ordinary rules to the new circumstances created by the act," while "[i]n the case before us no new circumstances have been created by legislation."[41] In *Klein*, in contrast, "the court is forbidden to give the effect to evidence which, in its own judgment, such evidence should have, and is directed to give it an effect precisely contrary."[42] This sentence establishes that the *Klein* Court did not mean what its earlier words literally suggest because, if it did, it would have been impossible to distinguish *Wheeling Bridge*: Congress's statute legalizing the bridge clearly prescribed a rule of decision in a pending case, and the Court there had absolutely no problem with such congressional action. In distinguishing the *Wheeling Bridge* decision, though, the *Klein* Court made clear what so troubled it about the challenged statute in *Klein*: The law forbade the judiciary from giving the effect to the evidence that it deemed it should have. The key problem, then, was not that Congress had changed the governing rule of decision, as it had in the statute upheld in *Wheeling Bridge*. Rather, the constitutional problem with the statute challenged in *Klein* was that Congress had *not* changed the governing rule of decision. Instead, it had sought to control the outcome of the case, not by altering the governing substantive law, but instead by manipulating the evidentiary inferences the judiciary could make in applying that preexisting substantive law.

There are two conceivable constitutional difficulties with this congressional control of evidentiary inferences, though the Court did not really make clear which of the two gave rise to its concern. First, the Court could have been troubled by congressional control of evidentiary inferences because it deemed the manner of resolution of individual suits to be exclusively a judicial function. So characterized, the judicial authority would not only extend to determining the outcome of particular litigation; it would also include the power to determine the significance of particular evidence within a category of litigation. Second, the *Klein* Court's distinction of *Wheeling Bridge* underscores the Court's concern with congressional attempts to alter substantive law indirectly through manipulation of applicable procedure. Congress may seek to change existing law by altering or amending the preexisting legal landscape through substantive legislation (as the *Klein* Court found Congress had done in the *Wheeling Bridge* situation), or it may instead seek to do what amounts to the same thing by purporting to leave existing law in place but altering that law indirectly through procedural or evidentiary manipulation (as the Court apparently concluded Congress had sought to do in the legislation overturned in *Klein*). The former method is constitutional, the Court concluded, while the latter is unconstitutional.

THE IMPORT OF *KLEIN* FOR AMERICAN CONSTITUTIONAL AND POLITICAL THEORY: FASHIONING THE "LEGISLATIVE DECEPTION" MODEL

After parsing the Court's opinion in *Klein*, one is left with five conceivable constitutional dictates growing out of the case: (1) Congress may not control or direct the Court's interpretation of the Constitution; (2) Congress may not dictate the outcome of an individual litigation; (3) Congress may not dictate the rule of decision in pending cases; (4) Congress may not dictate the rule of decision in cases in which the federal government is a party; and (5) Congress may not alter the substantive law by dictating how a court should weigh competing evidence. The first possibility finds support in the Court's opinion, and, for reasons previously mentioned,[43] constitutes a legitimate means of maintaining separation of powers and constitutional supremacy. In contrast, while the third and fourth possibilities find an arguable basis in both the text of the opinion and subsequent Supreme Court interpretations of *Klein*,[44] neither makes sense as an abstract principle, in light of accepted principles of separation of powers and constitutional structure. As long as the controlling rule of decision does not reverse a judicial decision already made[45] or attempt to provide a controlling interpretation of the Constitution, there exists no reason, in either constitutional theory or doctrine, why Congress may not enact subconstitutional, generally applicable rules of decision, even for pending cases in which the federal government is a party, which have the effect of deciding a particular case in the government's favor.

The *Klein* Court's language, when taken literally, may be thought to support these broader—and largely indefensible—pronouncements of constitutional structure. When put in context, however, it appears likely that the opinion intended to make a far less expansive—but nevertheless insightful and foundational—point about the nature of the relationship between the legislative and judicial branches. The Court was saying that while Congress has authority to enact governing generally applicable substantive law, it may not dictate to the court how to resolve cases brought pursuant to that law, unless it formally alters the substance of that law accordingly.

As previously noted, constitutional prohibition of the legislative resolution of cases may apply on two levels, micro and macro. On the micro level, the restriction prohibits legislative resolution of individual litigations in a manner inconsistent with controlling law, absent a corresponding alteration in that law. This concern is clearly reflected in the *Klein* opinion,[46] even though one might debate exactly how the principle applies to the facts of that case itself.[47] On the macro level, the prohibition extends to even more generalized directives as to the use of evidence or procedures in the resolution of categories of cases.[48] In both situations, the Court is saying that while Congress may prescribe the generalized subconstitutional law that the judiciary is to interpret, apply, and enforce in the course of adjudications, it may not direct how the adjudication is to be resolved, either on the specific or general levels.

When stated in such a "bottom line" fashion, neither the micro nor macro level of judicial protectionism is free from doubt. On the micro level, a formalist rationale for branch separation is by no means universally accepted.[49] Thus, in the minds of some, congressional performance of what is technically a judicial function may not be inherently unconstitutional, if a sufficient justification is deemed to exist. On the macro level, if taken literally, the rationale would prevent Congress from providing any evidentiary presumptions or substance-specific procedural directives—hardly a feasible conclusion in the modern world of judicial-legislative interaction. Moreover, an argument could be fashioned that the greater power to legislate substantive law subsumes the lesser power to establish the generalized method for adjudicating that law. Indeed, one might arguably characterize the "substantive law" as a single package that includes both the substantive directives enacted by Congress *and* whatever evidentiary or procedural restrictions Congress has chosen to impose on the adjudication of those directives.[50] It may be, then, that by attempting to distinguish the *Wheeling Bridge* decision from the case before it, the *Klein* Court was groping towards a very different theoretical rationale. Indeed, this is quite probably the case, though the Court itself may not have fully grasped the subtle ramifications of the distinction it was drawing.

In *Wheeling Bridge*, Congress had chosen to alter the generally applicable governing substantive law legislatively, in a constitutionally permissible manner. Where Congress has done this, it is the duty of the court, even in the course of a preexisting pending suit,[51] to enforce the substantive law as it has been altered, unless, of course, it finds the alteration to violate the Constitution. But in *Klein*, Congress did not directly alter governing substantive law; both before and after the challenged statute had been enacted, the controlling law remained the same: an individual found to be "disloyal" during the rebellion could not reacquire previously seized properties.[52] However, before enactment of that law, in light of relevant judicial precedent, evidence of a pardon would be deemed by the courts to constitute proof that the individual had, in fact, been *loyal*. In contrast, following enactment of the challenged statute, courts would have to deem evidence of a pardon to constitute conclusive proof that the individual had been *disloyal*.[53]

In addition to the serious constitutional difficulty that such a law would effectively preempt judicial authority to interpret the ramifications and implications of a specific constitutional provision (the executive's power to issue pardons),[54] the legislation also altered the meaning of the prior law, but did so only indirectly—arguably furtively—through the device of an evidentiary presumption imposed by Congress on the courts. Both before and after enactment of the statute, controlling substantive law was that "disloyal" Confederates were legally disabled from reacquiring their seized property. Even had no interpretation of a constitutional term been involved, the challenged statute achieved a fundamental alteration in substantive law through means other than a direct alteration in that law. The end result was that while the controlling substantive law purportedly remained the same, in reality the essence of that law had been effectively transformed into something very different.

When the dust settled, then, it was possible that the public had become the victim of a type of political shell game: Congress had effectively deceived the electorate as to what the governing substantive law actually was.[55] If rationalized on the basis of judicial concern over this legislative deception, the macro version of the restriction on legislative power to dictate the resolution of cases appears not nearly as unreasonable as it might at first have seemed. Instead of constitutionally prohibiting any form of procedural or evidentiary directive to the judiciary, this "legislative deception" model limits the reach of the constitutional restriction on congressional power to impose evidentiary presumptions to situations in which the procedural or evidentiary modification imposed by Congress has the effect of altering the essence of the underlying substantive law. Of course, it will not always be a simple matter to distinguish between the two situations. For present purposes, however, suffice it to say that a procedural or evidentiary modification should be deemed to alter the essence of applicable substantive law when, as a result of the procedural or evidentiary modification, the law's impact on citizens' primary behavior is so significant as to alter a reasonable voter's perception of her elected representative on the basis of that representative's vote on the relevant substantive legislation.[56]

This legislative-deception rationale also explains the micro version of that restriction. Viewed from the perspective of the legislative-deception model implicit in *Klein*, the prohibition on the legislative resolution of individual suits is explained as an effort to prevent Congress from altering the legal and political impact of the controlling generalized substantive law in specific contexts without also simultaneously altering that substantive law itself. Were Congress permitted to leave controlling generalized law intact but simultaneously direct the resolution of particular disputes in a manner inconsistent with the judiciary's assessment of the controlling substantive law, Congress would be able to deceive the electorate into believing the law had remained the same, while in reality it had not.

When viewed together, the constitutional concerns about both micro and macro legislative manipulation of the judicial decision-making process can be rationalized by one overriding constitutional concern: the fear that Congress might undermine the sound operation of the representative democratic process by enlisting the judiciary as a co-conspirator in a plan to deceive the electorate. It is this synthesis of the macro and micro concerns about congressional disruption of the democratic process by means of the legislative deception of the electorate achieved through congressional manipulation of the judicial process that lies at the theoretical core of *Klein*. It is this focus on the concern with the vital need to prevent legislative deception that should be gleaned from the *Klein* opinion as its greatest contribution to American political and constitutional theory.

The following section considers the validity of the *Klein* Court's implicit concern over the danger of legislative deception from the perspective of both democratic and constitutional theory. While a number of potential difficulties plague the theory of legislative deception,[57] the concern that underlay much of the analysis contained in the Court's opinion in *Klein* is central to the preservation of democratic values. When a legislative body employs evidentiary or procedural mechanisms or legislative resolution of individual litigations to indirectly alter the "DNA" of its substantive law, a significant danger exists that the legislative body is misleading the electorate into believing that the law remains unchanged. In such a situation, the electorate is unable to judge its legislators on the basis of their support for or opposition to proposed legislative change, because it has been confused as to whether any such change has actually been implemented.

LEGISLATIVE DECEPTION, POLITICAL COMMITMENT, AND DEMOCRATIC THEORY

The Centrality of the Electoral Process in Democratic Theory

The concept of constitutional democracy necessarily implies that the bulk of subconstitutional policy choices will be made by those who are representative of and accountable to the electorate. In the words of a leading theorist, "everything necessary to [democratic] theory may be put in terms of (a) legislators (or decision-makers) who are (b) legitimated or authorized to enact public policies, and who are (c) subject or responsible to popular control at free elections."[58]

Through the process of elections, a democratic system assures that, on some basic level, those who make the bulk of normative policy choices will represent the positions held by those who elected them. In this sense, the democratic process ensures that individuals will be able to control their lives, if only indirectly. The process is by no means perfect. A legislator faces many decisions, and that she agrees with voters on one issue does not ensure that they will agree on another issue.[59] But the value of the electoral process is highlighted by considering the various undemocratic alternatives—for example, monarchy or dictatorship. An imperfect representative process fosters the values that underlie democracy far more than even a benevolent dictatorship would.[60]

It is true that once elected, the chosen representative is not bound to adopt the normative positions held by the electorate's majority on every—or, indeed, any—piece of proposed legislation.[61] But that presumption underlies the second function of the electoral process: accountability.

Even under the version of democratic theory that posits an extremely limited role for the electorate in making policy choices,[62] the voters are assumed to play an important role on Election Day by determining whether their elected representatives have represented them acceptably. Absent this principle, the essential element of democracy is lost. Without the ability to oust elected officials deemed unrepresentative of its wishes through the electoral process, the electorate has no means of either ensuring that government represents it or checking those vested with governing power. This, in short, describes what can be appropriately called the "political commitment" principle.[63]

Skeptics might respond that while the political commitment principle may make sense purely as a theoretical matter, on a practical level it breaks down. The attack on the political commitment principle proceeds in the following manner: The stark reality is that rarely is the populace aware of, much less have a serious interest in, the content or impact of federal legislation. But the realities are far more complex than this simplistic argument suggests. The populace's awareness of and concern with proposed legislation is similar to the impact of advertising on consumers. It is often said that half of a company's advertising efforts are likely wasted; the problem is that no one knows which half that is. Similarly, there can be little doubt that *some* legislation is of enormous interest to different segments of the electorate. This is true of proposed laws dealing with such subjects as the environment, welfare, health care, foreign policy, trade, gun control, tax relief, defense spending, drug regulation, and criminalization or decriminalization of behavior. Other laws may be of much narrower interest, but nevertheless remain of great significance to well-defined, albeit more limited, interest groups. It is impossible for anyone—especially a court—to determine in an individual case exactly which laws are matters of public interest. Thus, the safest course is for a reviewing court to proceed on the assumption that the electorate is aware of all legislation enacted by its chosen representatives.

Political Commitment and Legislative Deception

Macro Deception. When legislative deception occurs, the legislators purport to make a political commitment by voting for or against proposed substantive legislation. However, through contemporaneous or subsequent procedural or evidentiary modification or the legislatively dictated resolution of individual litigations,[64] the legislative body will have altered the essence—or what can be called the "DNA"—of that underlying substantive law. It would be as if Congress had enacted "law A," but, through indirect means, had surreptitiously transformed it into "law B," or even "law not A."

An illustration of such legislative deception is *Michael H. v. Gerald D.*,[65] where California purported to give substantive rights to a biological father, but indirectly altered this law through use of an irrefutable evidentiary presumption that the husband of the mother is the biological father. When the dust has settled, through indirect resort to an evidentiary presumption, the law effectively denies the biological father any rights.

Another arguable example of legislative deception through procedural manipulation is a process in which the legislature enacts a substantive cause of action designed to compensate individuals who have been personally injured by a defendant's wrongdoing, yet—either simultaneously or subsequently—dictates to the court use of a broad-based statistical model in the adjudication of those causes of action. In such a situation, the court would be required to award damages for what are, as a substantive matter, supposed to be nothing more than individualized determinations of liability, even absent any actual proof that the individual plaintiff had, in fact, been injured by the legally proscribed behavior of the defendant. As a practical matter, such legislation creates a type of "compensa-tax," whereby companies that have engaged in behavior deemed to give rise to a socially unacceptable risk of harm will be made to transfer wealth in order to benefit classes of victims injured by such behavior, whether by the defendant or others similarly situated. Thus, through use of legislatively directed evidentiary presumptions, Congress will have implemented what is known as the "public" model of modern tort theory, even though on its face the governing substantive law purports to implement the generally very different "private rights" model of tort theory, which is premised on individualized determinations of liability.[66] Such legislation may or may not be socially or morally justifiable, but that is not the question posed by the legislative-deception model. The issue, rather, is whether the face of the substantive directive comports with what the law actually does in practice.

There can be little doubt that legislative deception is far more invidious to the operation of the political commitment principle than such conceivable legislative practices as broad legislative delegation or secret legislative voting. In the case of legislative delegation, at least the electorate is put on notice that its legislators have declined to make a political commitment through their votes for or against proposed legislation, and may judge them accordingly at the polls.[67] Even when secret legislative ballot is employed, at least members of the electorate are placed on notice not to rely on how their legislators voted on proposed legislation and instead to judge them on alternative bases. In contrast, when legislation is deceptive in the manner just described, members of the electorate have been defrauded into believing that their legislators' vote for or against a proposed law actually achieves goals discernible on the statute's face when the reality is far different. When Congress simultaneously alters the essence of a substantive law indirectly through procedural or evidentiary means, the legislators' vote on the substantive portion of the law is effectively rendered a sham. When Congress subsequently alters the DNA of the substantive reach of the statute, the electorate is likely unaware that its current legislators have in reality made a political commitment very different from the one made by the earlier Congress. In short, while the legislative delegation and secret ballot models contemplate no political commitment on the part of elected representatives, the legislative-deception model is concerned with preventing false political commitments and the consequent disruption of the populace's performance of its intended checking role through the electoral process. Although in the former situations the voters are put on guard, in the latter situation the voters are lulled into a false sense of security about the political commitments made by their elected representatives.

Micro Deception. Congress may deceive the electorate about the state of controlling law through manipulation of the resolution of specific litigations, as well as through adoption of generalized and manipulative procedural or evidentiary rules. When Congress attempts to resolve individual litigations, it purports to leave the generalized controlling law unchanged, but indirectly effects alterations in the application of that law in specific situations by the legislative direction to the court.[68]

Despite the compelling nature of the micro legislative-deception rationale to explain the decision in *Klein*,[69] it has had a surprisingly rocky time of it in post-*Klein* doctrine. The Supreme Court has played fast and loose with both its recognition and application of the micro deception explanation. In *Robertson v. Seattle Audubon Society*,[70] for example, the Court reversed a decision of the Ninth Circuit holding an act of Congress to be a violation of separation of powers under the principles of *Klein*. The plaintiffs in two consolidated cases had challenged the statute on grounds that it directed a particular outcome in pending cases without changing the actual substance of the underlying applicable law. The appellants argued that the National Forest Service and the Bureau of Land Management's guidelines for implementing a particular forestry management plan conflicted with the directives of prior environmental statutes.[71]

Meanwhile, Congress enacted legislation that established the "Northwest Timber Compromise."[72] The provision (embedded in an appropriations bill) established a plan to increase timber harvesting in some areas and decrease it in other areas. In it, Congress referred to the two pending cases within the Ninth Circuit by name and case number and insulated sections (b)(3) and (b)(5) from judicial review.[73] Essentially, the new law provided that for purposes of judicial review, if the agencies acted pursuant to the requirements identified in the preexisting environmental legislation, then they would satisfy the statutory requirements of the preexisting environmental statutes. Congress presumably could have specifically identified those preexisting laws. Instead, it referenced the specific cases in which the statutes had been considered. In response to this provision, the district courts dismissed the actions for want of jurisdiction and the plaintiffs appealed to the Ninth Circuit.

The Ninth Circuit held the new law unconstitutional under *Klein*,[74] finding that Congress had exceeded its constitutional authority by directing a particular result in a pending case without repealing, amending, or changing the underlying substantive law. The Ninth Circuit found that Congress had not modified the underlying law but instead had enacted a provision within an appropriations bill that directed the court to reach a specific result and to make certain factual findings within the two pending cases.[75] This was deemed to be a threat to judicial independence, and therefore a violation of separation of powers.

In reversing the Ninth Circuit, the Supreme Court held that the provision actually did modify the substantive law embodied in the preexisting provisions and therefore did not direct particular findings in particular cases without changing controlling law.[76] In response to the argument that the legislation specifically mentioned the pending cases by number and therefore constituted an attempt to interfere with the judicial power, the Court explained that Congress did so merely because those cases contained references to the underlying statutes Congress was modifying.[77] The Court concluded that whether or not Congress lacked constitutional authority to decide individual cases, the legislative enactment in question "compelled changes in law, not findings or results under old law."[78]

There are two troubling features of the Supreme Court's decision in *Robertson*. First, it is difficult to understand how a statute that expressly directed a result in two specifically mentioned pending litigations could be deemed not to resolve specific litigation. Second, whether or not the Court was correct in its assessment of the specific situation involved in *Robertson* itself, it is surprising that the Court would suggest that the constitutionality of a congressional attempt to alter the outcome of litigation without simultaneously altering preexisting general substantive law is an open question.

As to the former point, it is at least arguable that the *Robertson* Court was correct in concluding that the congressional action had, in fact, altered preexisting law; the statute did, after all, provide that specified behavior would now be deemed to satisfy certain statutory requirements that it had not previously satisfied. However, it would probably be wise for the Court to hold that any legislation that directs findings in specifically referenced litigation should categorically be deemed to violate *Klein*, if only as a prophylactic effort to avoid legislatively created confusion and deception. If Congress is truly changing substantive law, it can do so without express reference to specific pending cases, and therefore any case-specific reference in legislation should automatically be deemed suspect.

Moreover, whether or not the Court was correct in its assessment of the specific situation involved in *Robertson* itself, it is surprising that the Court would even raise the possibility that the constitutionality of a congressional attempt to affect the outcome of litigation without simultaneously altering preexisting general substantive law is an open question. There is absolutely no conceivable context in which Congress could constitutionally alter the result in a specific litigation without simultaneously altering preexisting general substantive law. It should be a matter of concern that the Supreme Court could even countenance such a possibility. Whether or not the Court agreed with the Ninth Circuit's application of the *Klein* standard under those particular facts, there should have been no doubt about the validity of the general principle that the lower court had invoked.

Potential Difficulties with the Legislative-Deception Model

While this description of how legislative deception negatively impacts the political commitment principle provides the rationale for the legislative-deception model, a number of gaps remain to be filled and potential criticisms to be considered. Five difficult questions need to be answered: (a) If Congress has openly adopted the procedural or evidentiary modification of the substantive law, or has openly legislated the resolution of a particular case, how can it be thought that the public has been deceived? (b) Even in situations in which procedural or evidentiary modifications have transformed underlying substantive law, would not individuals directly affected by the alteration be properly incentivized to communicate its existence to the electorate? If so, why would there be any need to have the judiciary police legislative deception? (c) Is it reasonable to presume that the electorate is even aware of, much less actually cares about, how its chosen representatives vote on legislation? (d) Since all procedural and evidentiary rules will inevitably impact the enforcement of substantive rights in some way, why are all such rules not deemed to be impermissible alterations of a preexisting substantive political commitment? Yet, if it is conceded that all procedural and evidentiary rules may in some sense impact the substantive rights being enforced, why disapprove of such a connection only in certain contexts? (e) Is it really feasible to determine whether a particular procedural or evidentiary modification has, in fact, altered the essence, or "DNA," of a particular substantive statute? Each of these questions can be answered satisfactorily, and as a result, both the content and rationale of the legislative-deception model will become more understandable.

Openness of procedural or evidentiary modification. It is true that a legislative body does not implement the deception through the adoption of secret codicils. Either contemporaneously or subsequently, the legislature modifies the substantive statute through open processes.[79] Thus, one might reasonably question the characterization of this alteration as "deceptive"; it is there, on the statute books for all to see. What may not be so readily recognizable to the public eye, however, is the true connection between procedural or evidentiary modifications and the transformation of the substantive law being enforced. The modifications that are of concern, though technically open and available for all to see, are analogous to small-print boilerplate that deceptively alters the terms provided for in larger print in the body of a contract. There is little question that such small-print contractual modifications are appropriately characterized as "deceptive," even though as a technical matter the alteration is there for the consumer to read.[80] Society does not demand that all consumers possess the perspicacity of an experienced attorney. Like a deceptive small-print alteration in a consumer contract, a procedural or evidentiary rule that alters the essence of underlying substantive law implements its change in a manner not likely to be recognized by most political consumers. The important functions of electoral checking and accountability are thereby significantly undermined.

It is true that we shall not be able to ascertain empirically, in the individual case, whether a procedural or evidentiary modification actually has misled the electorate. Indeed, in certain politically celebrated contexts, it may be quite clear to all concerned what Congress is actually attempting to do substantively, even when it seeks to do so indirectly through procedural or evidentiary manipulation. In some situations, then, it may seem overly formalistic to draw a rigid, categorical distinction between direct substantive change and indirect alteration through resort to procedure or evidentiary presumptions. But the fact that we cannot be sure in an individual case whether use of indirect forms of modification will actually deceive the electorate should not dictate rejection of the legislative-deception model. It is, rather, far wiser to risk overprotection than underprotection.

Communication by interested groups. For much the same reasons, a court cannot reasonably be expected to determine in an individual instance whether advocacy groups have adequately communicated and explained to the electorate as a whole the nature of the profound alteration of controlling substantive law brought about as a result of simultaneous or subsequent procedural or evidentiary modification. It is simply too unpredictable a safety valve and too difficult a task for a reviewing court to ascertain the adequacy and clarity of political debate in the individual instance. Thus, a court may be required to ignore existence of extensive political debate over a specific proposed procedural modification in order to avoid underprotection in other instances in which it would, as a practical matter, be impossible for a court to make such a determination.

The public's unawareness of legislative votes. It might be suggested that even if the fear of legislative deception were grounded in reality, little turns on this fact as a practical matter, because the public is generally unaware of how its legislators vote on proposed legislation in any event. The first point to note in response is the seeming inconsistency between this challenge to the legislative-deception model on the one hand, and the argument that the public will be readily able to see through the technical distinctions between direct substantive modification and indirect modification through the use of procedural or evidentiary devices, on the other. Presumably, both cannot be true.

This inconsistency underscores the empirical uncertainty that pervades our ability to judge the extent of the public's knowledge and understanding of its representatives' role in the legislative process. Clearly there are many cases in which voters care very much about how their legislators vote on a proposed statute—from Obamacare to trade regulation to environmental controls to proposals to raise or cut taxes. Where it is impossible to know what the public's actual understanding and awareness is in a particular case, it is advisable to adopt a prophylactic approach. Such an approach would presume, in all cases, that the public is both aware of and cares about how its legislators vote in deciding on their electoral retention. Any less formalistic test risks underprotecting the foundations of our democratic system. It is, as already noted, wiser to risk overprotection of the essential elements of American democracy than to risk their underprotection.

The substantive-procedural overlay. As part of its line of cases stemming from *Erie R.R. v. Tompkins*,[81] the Supreme Court has recognized the inevitable intersection between substance and procedure.[82] Moreover, in the Rules Enabling Act, Congress expressly prohibited the Federal Rules of Civil Procedure from abridging, enlarging, or modifying a substantive right.[83]

Far from undermining the legislative-deception model, recognition of this inevitable intersection underscores the importance of protecting against legislative deception through procedural manipulation. While the substantive-procedural intersection in some instances is inevitable, the nature and extent of that intersection may vary. The Rules Enabling Act, it should be recalled, dictates that a Federal Rule of Civil Procedure may not modify a substantive right; yet it simultaneously contemplates the existence of procedural rules that will inevitably impact enforcement of substantive rights in one way or another. If the inevitable impact of a procedural rule on the enforcement of substantive rights automatically modifies those rights in an impermissible way, then no procedural rules could be promulgated. Clearly, the Rules Enabling Act contemplates some inevitable intersection; the question is, how much? For present purposes, however, there is no need to attempt to resolve the mysteries of the Rules Enabling Act. All that we need do is place within a special category those procedural (or evidentiary) rules that do a great deal more than incidentally "affect" or "impact" underlying substantive rights. I refer here to those rules that effectively transform the essence of the underlying substantive rights. One might question whether it is feasible to separate such situations from other substantive-procedural interactions. It is to this question that the analysis now turns.

Ascertaining the "DNA" of substantive law. So far, this chapter has shown that the legislative-deception model is triggered only by evidentiary or procedural rules that alter the "DNA" of underlying substantive law. It has, however, spoken only briefly as to how to determine whether a law's "DNA" has been transformed.[84] It is possible to fashion a reasonably satisfactory rule of thumb that, though not always free from controversy or uncertainty, will provide a reviewing court with the necessary guidance in applying the restrictions of the legislative-deception model.

In deciding whether a procedural rule or evidentiary presumption has transformed substantive law's essence, a reviewing court should draw on the "political commitment" principle by asking itself whether the voters' perceptions of their elected representatives' political commitment, revealed by their votes on the legislation in question, might reasonably be expected to change had they been made aware of the true substantive impact of the law when combined with its related procedural or evidentiary modification. Even if this inquiry turns out not to resolve all problems of application, the fact that a general legal standard may encounter difficulty in its application in specific contexts surely does not disqualify it from use.

Applying this standard to the facts of *Klein*, it is clear that the case was correctly decided. To transform the law from saying that issuance of a pardon allows the individual to recover property ("disloyalty" before the statute challenged in *Klein*) to one saying that issuance of a pardon conclusively prevents such property recovery ("disloyalty" after the challenged statute) dramatically alters the political impact of that law. The chapter has previously provided several additional examples of such impermissible transformations.[85] To be sure, relatively speaking, there will likely be few instances of such deception. This is, of course, as it should be, since it would be extremely problematic were a democratically elected legislative body to seek to deceive the populace with regularity. In those instances in which such deception exists, however, it should not be an impossible task to unearth it.

LEGISLATIVE DECEPTION AND SEPARATION OF POWERS

To this point, the analysis has established that Congress may employ procedural or evidentiary devices to disguise its modifications of governing substantive law and in so doing undermine the democratic goals of checking, accountability, and representation. The fact that legislation undermines even the fundamental elements of the democratic process does not, however, necessarily imply that it is unconstitutional. It is only when those precepts of democratic theory are in some way embodied in or protected by the Constitution that the judiciary may invalidate an enactment that contravenes them. Thus, absent grounding in the Constitution, the legislative-deception model would at most be an elaboration of normative political theory.

When viewed through the lens of *Klein*, the legislative-deception model finds grounding in the Constitution. To be successful, legislative deception must conscript the federal judiciary in the imposition of what amounts to a political fraud on the public. Such a practice violates fundamental notions of judicial integrity embodied in Article III, which expressly insulates the federal judiciary from improper influence by the political branches by guaranteeing judicial tenure and salary.[86]

Prior to the Constitution's adoption, it was not uncommon for colonial assemblies to function "as courts of equity of last resort, hearing original actions or providing appellate review of judicial judgments."[87] The Framers recognized these legislative violations of judicial integrity. In *Federalist* No. 48, Madison warned that "[the legislature's] constitutional powers being at once more extensive, and less susceptible of precise limits, it can, with the greater facility, mask, under complicated and indirect measures, the encroachments which it makes on the co-ordinate departments."[88] The Framers vested the judicial power in an independent and insulated judiciary principally to rectify this.[89]

Article III's guarantee of life tenure and protection against salary reduction prophylactically insulates the judiciary from the majoritarian branches.[90] But to have confined the scope of judicial independence protections exclusively to these institutional guarantees would have rendered the framework fatally vulnerable to legislative erosion. If Congress were able to control either the method or conclusion of the judicial decision-making process, the formal protections of independence would prove to be of little value. Instead, the legislative branch would be in a position to undermine the integrity of the judicial branch and usurp its constitutionally vested authority. Thus, it is appropriate to ground the prohibition on legislative deception in the constitutional guarantee of separation of powers.

None of this analysis is inconsistent with the established understanding that Congress possesses broad power to regulate the jurisdiction of the federal courts.[91] It is one thing to exclude completely the federal courts from adjudication; it is quite another to vest the federal courts with jurisdiction to adjudicate but simultaneously restrict the power of those courts to perform the adjudicatory function in the manner they deem appropriate. In the former instance, by wholly excluding the federal courts, Congress loses its ability to draw upon the integrity possessed by the Article III judiciary in the public's eyes. In contrast, where Congress employs the federal courts to implement its deception, the harmful consequences to that judicial integrity are far more significant. Thus, Henry Hart was correct when he asserted that

> the difficulty involved in asserting any judicial control in the face of a total denial of jurisdiction doesn't exist if Congress gives jurisdiction but puts strings on it . . . .

. . . .

. . . [I]f Congress directs an Article III court to decide a case, I can easily read into Article III a limitation on the power of Congress to tell the court how to decide it.[92]

CONCLUSION

It might be suggested that this chapter illustrates all too vividly what can happen to a Supreme Court decision when scholars get a hold of it. It might be thought that, by attempting to read a model of political theory into a relatively brief and cryptic post–Civil War decision, this analysis seek to twist that decision beyond all recognition. In reality, the argument proceeds, the Court was probably doing nothing more than seeking to assert strong judicial authority at a time of great political stress for, and attempted congressional manipulation of, the federal judicial power.

To a certain extent, the point is well taken. One cannot assert with any level of historical confidence that Chief Justice Chase had thought through a detailed political theory designed to avoid the harms of legislative deception through legislative manipulation of the judicial process. Yet it does seem to be clear that, whatever the chief justice had in mind, the opinion's brief but important distinction of the situation before it from the *Wheeling Bridge* situation must have had something to do with the fear that Congress could employ legislatively imposed evidentiary directives to unconstitutionally disrupt the sound operation of the judicial process. The Court was necessarily concerned about an issue above and beyond the constitutional problem, expressed earlier in its opinion, that Congress was seeking to interfere with the judicial interpretation of constitutional provisions. If that had been the Court's sole concern, it could easily have distinguished its earlier *Wheeling Bridge* decision by simply pointing out that the earlier case had not involved construction of a constitutional provision. It did not seek to distinguish its earlier decision on this ground, however. The Court's focus, instead, was on a separation of powers concern that extended also to the adjudication of subconstitutional questions. The Court's difficulty with the congressional action, then, necessarily included the fear that Congress was improperly invading the judicial province. As noted earlier, there are two conceivable ways in which Congress could invade the judicial province: either by telling the courts how to resolve individual litigations, or by enlisting the federal judiciary in a fraudulent manipulation of the substantive law through use of modifying procedural rules or evidentiary presumptions. Both practices undermine the essence of the nation's commitment to the democratic process. Moreover, both violate fundamental constitutional dictates of separation of powers.

Habeas Corpus, Due Process, and American Constitutionalism

INTRODUCTION

Article I, section 9 of the United States Constitution guarantees the availability of the writ of habeas corpus.[1] The "Great Writ," as it has come to be called,[2] is the primary procedural vehicle through which those detained by the government may challenge the legality of their detentions. Put simply, habeas corpus restricts government's ability to imprison its citizens for any reason it wants—or for no reason at all.

Famously described as the Constitution's only "express provision for exercise of extraordinary authority" in times of crisis,[3] the writ of habeas is subject to one significant qualification. Article I, section 9, clause 2 gives the federal government the power to suspend the writ of habeas corpus "when in Cases of Rebellion or Invasion the public Safety may require it."[4] Suspension of the writ effectively insulates the government's power to imprison its citizens from any and all meaningful judicial oversight. The potentially dramatic consequences of such a suspension on the protection of civil liberties during times of emergencies are almost unfathomable. For example, during a suspension, there would seem to be absolutely no way, either legally or practically, to stop the president from throwing all Jews, all Irish-Americans, or all Democrats in jail. Because the legal mechanism by which they could challenge the lawfulness of their detentions would have been revoked, there would be no way for these individuals to obtain their release or even challenge the lawfulness of their confinement until the suspension of habeas was lifted.

One might be tempted to dismiss these frightening hypotheticals as highly improbable. After all, the suspension power has been invoked only four times in our nation's history, and only once on a national scale.[5] But as the attacks of September 11, 2001, so forcefully demonstrated, given the mercurial nature of world conditions, the unexpected can quickly become stark reality. The subsequent "war on terror" stirred considerable political interest in the suspension power.[6] This renewed interest in turn ignited an intense scholarly debate as to whether a suspension of habeas corpus should be construed to authorize executive detentions that would otherwise be deemed unlawful or unconstitutional.[7] As scholars involved in this debate have all correctly recognized, it is unwise to view the Suspension Clause as a constitutional dinosaur whose predicate conditions of a finding of a "[r]ebellion or [i]nvasion" render it irrelevant in the context of modern warfare. Rather, a panicked or politically ambitious president, in the aftermath of a national crisis, might well be able to convince Congress that an attack on the United States satisfied the constitutional prerequisites of the Suspension Clause, and that the interests of "public safety" required that he be provided with virtually unlimited authority to combat the crisis at hand.[8] It is for this reason that it is important to establish the boundaries of the suspension power now, before another unexpected crisis strikes, so that political leaders will be prevented from using it as a blunt weapon against unpopular minority groups, political opponents, or our constitutional system itself.

On the level of constitutional theory, neither court nor scholar has ever seriously explored the potential tension between the Suspension Clause and the Fifth Amendment's guarantee that life, liberty, or property may not be deprived by the federal government without due process of law. Not surprisingly, then, the relationship between the Suspension and Due Process Clauses remains completely unsettled. Two highly respected scholars have argued that the suspension of habeas corpus "shuts off . . . those rights that find protection and meaning in the Great Writ."[9] Another highly respected scholar has argued that a suspension of the writ does not displace individuals' underlying substantive constitutional rights, but rather shifts the sole responsibility for their enforcement to the executive.[10] All three scholars, however, have missed the mark on this vital constitutional question. This is because they either ignore or misunderstand the textually unambiguous and inescapable impact of the Fifth Amendment's Due Process Clause on the federal government's ability to invoke the Suspension Clause. The thesis of this chapter, simply put, is that because the Due Process and Suspension Clauses are irreconcilable, and because the due process dictate is embodied in an amendment that supersedes anything in the body of the text with which it is inherently inconsistent, it is the due process right that must prevail.[11] The Suspension Clause should therefore be deemed unconstitutional.

It is true, of course, that the terms of the Due Process Clause do not expressly and specifically invalidate the Suspension Clause. In this sense, it might be thought, its preempting impact is by no means as clear as, say, the Twenty-First Amendment's preempting impact on the Eighteenth.[12] But it is surely true that two provisions may be wholly irreconcilable without one expressly repealing the other—a precept long understood by the Supreme Court in judging the impact of a constitutional amendment on preexisting constitutional provisions.[13]

In the case of the Due Process and Suspension Clauses, the first point to note is the unambiguously unrestricted reach of the constitutional right guaranteed by the former provision. By its terms, the Due Process Clause is unlimited in its applicability: It applies in all contexts, without exception. While the provision most assuredly fails to elaborate on how exactly a court is to determine what process is "due" when the federal government threatens life, liberty, or property, it is unambiguous that, whatever that protection is, it is triggered in every such instance. Courts and scholars have long debated the frontiers of the concepts of "liberty"[14] and "property,"[15] as well as the nature of the procedures required when those interests are threatened.[16] But what cannot be disputed is that the summary imprisonment of an individual by the executive authority without any hearing before a fair and neutral adjudicator fails to satisfy the constitutional dictate of due process.[17] Any other conclusion would render the due process guarantee a cynical, Orwellian sham. Yet it is equally clear that once the authority of the Suspension Clause has been invoked, this very conduct by the executive necessarily becomes insulated from any constitutional scrutiny or remedy. Thus, solely because of the exercise of federal authority under the Suspension Clause, the detained individual has inescapably been denied the due process that the Fifth Amendment expressly provides to him.

While this argument, grounded in indisputable precepts of textual interpretation, should be deemed dispositive, there is also strong support for this position in core notions of American political theory. Foundational notions of American constitutionalism provide a strong normative basis for the chapter's thesis. Absent the availability of the writ of habeas corpus (or at least its procedural equivalent), there would be no means of preventing the majoritarian branches of the federal government from assuming the equivalent of dictatorial power. Were the independent judiciary to be unavailable as a check, there is nothing to prevent the executive—authorized by a sympathetic or intimidated legislative branch—from arresting whomever it wants, for whatever reason it wants, for however long it wants. To permit the executive branch to exercise such unrestrained coercive power is consistent with neither due process nor the foundational precepts of American constitutional democracy.

This chapter proceeds in four parts. Initially, it briefly surveys the historical origins of the writ of habeas corpus and the Suspension Clause. In the next part it establishes the inescapable conflict between the Suspension and Due Process Clauses and explains why the latter provision must be found to supersede the earlier one, insofar as the two conflict. Once it is established that the Due Process Clause trumps the Suspension Clause, it is of course necessary to determine exactly what sort of limits the dictates of due process impose in such a context. The third section therefore considers how the Due Process Clause might be interpreted in various permutations of attempted suspension. In the final section, the chapter addresses current scholarly counterarguments, demonstrating their inadequacy, given their failure to come to terms with both the textual and political difficulties necessarily brought on by rejection of the approach advocated here.

THE WRIT OF HABEAS CORPUS AND THE SUSPENSION CLAUSE: A BRIEF HISTORICAL REVIEW

Within the American legal system, the writ of habeas corpus now functions as the primary mechanism for the enforcement of the Fifth Amendment due process guarantee against extrajudicial coercive action by the executive. In this section the chapter surveys the historical origins of the writ of habeas corpus, beginning with its foundational role in the development of England's constitutional monarchy. It then describes the events and debates that shaped the Framers' decision to protect the writ in the Constitution and their debate over whether to recognize a power to suspend the writ.

British Origins of the Writ of Habeas Corpus

Habeas corpus emerged as the English writ of liberty during the constitutional struggles of the seventeenth century, when it was used as a remedy against political arrest by King Charles and his Privy Council.[18] The writ authorized a court to require the king's ministers to produce a person in their custody and explain the basis for the detention so that the court could determine whether the imprisonment was lawful.[19] Sir Edward Coke famously described habeas corpus as inextricably linked with the *legem terrae* provision of Magna Carta, which he translated as "no man [shall] be taken . . . without [due] proces[s] of the Law."[20] Parliament codified the common law procedures in the Habeas Corpus Act of 1679, which ensured that the writ itself would be continually available, that relief sought under it would not be obstructed or delayed, and that the king could not recommit a person released on habeas corpus for the same cause or any pretended variations thereof.[21]

Despite the "spiritual" importance of both Magna Carta and the writ of habeas corpus to the foundations of the unwritten British constitution, their mandates (and the rest of that constitution) were never deemed legally binding on Parliament.[22] Rather, in accordance with the English system of legislative supremacy, Parliament had the power to suspend the protections of the writ at will.[23] Any constraints on its power to do so were based on custom and tradition, rather than on law.[24] Parliament suspended the writ on numerous occasions during the late seventeenth and early eighteenth centuries,[25] usually with respect to a limited class of persons who were suspected of treason.[26] During a suspension, courts were still able to issue the writ of habeas corpus to determine whether the imprisoned individual fell within the bounds of the legislation.[27] If the court determined that the petitioner had been detained pursuant to the terms of the suspension, however, it possessed no further authority to remedy the detention while the suspension legislation remained in force.[28]

Incorporation of the Great Writ into the American Legal System

Like the British, the Framers of the American Constitution recognized that the writ of habeas corpus represented an essential check on executive power. The historical role of habeas corpus within the English system, as well as the important scholarly works emphasizing its role in the preservation of the rule of law, undoubtedly influenced the Framers' decision to guarantee the writ in the body of the new federal Constitution.[29] The common-law writ of habeas corpus had also been employed by courts in all thirteen colonies prior to the American Revolution.[30] Moreover, five fledgling states had incorporated habeas corpus guarantees into their state constitutions around the time the nation won its independence.[31] For example, the Massachusetts provision, which served as a model for the clause included in the first draft of the federal Constitution,[32] provided:

> The privilege and benefit of the writ of habeas corpus shall be enjoyed in this commonwealth in the most free, easy, cheap, expeditious and ample manner;

and shall not be suspended by the legislature, except upon the most urgent and pressing occasions, and for a limited time not exceeding twelve months.[33]

This clause, enacted in 1780, essentially codified English practice by providing for the availability of the writ, subject to a narrow exception for emergencies, which delegated the decision to suspend the writ to the legislature and limited the duration of the suspension.[34]

The Framers' decision to protect the writ of habeas corpus in the new Constitution was relatively uncontroversial. Participants in the Convention debates seemed unanimous in their belief that the maintenance of a strong writ of habeas corpus was essential to the preservation of individual liberty.[35] Indeed, the fact that the writ was one of the very few individual rights that the Framers chose to mention explicitly in the original Constitution underscores its foundational role within the new constitutional democracy.[36]

The delegates at the Philadelphia Convention disagreed, however, over whether and under what circumstances the Constitution should recognize a federal power to suspend the writ.[37] Parliament[38] and at least five colonies[39] had suspended the writ during the American Revolution, so it seems likely that a number of the Framers had experienced the benefits and drawbacks of a suspension. On one hand, it was thought that a suspension of habeas corpus allowed an executive to react quickly and decisively in responding to a crisis. Massachusetts, for example, suspended the writ in response to Shays's Rebellion, authorizing the governor to "command, and cause to be apprehended, and committed . . . any person or persons whatsoever, whom the Governour . . . shall deem the safety of the Commonwealth requires should be restrained of their personal liberty."[40] The act allowed the governor immediately to order the arrest of several individuals whom he suspected of inciting the riots.[41] On the other hand, removal of the traditional judicial remedy of release from unlawful executive detention necessarily imperils individual liberty. In fact, the response to Shays's Rebellion also reveals the darker element of the suspension power, because the suspension enabled the governor to detain suspects incommunicado for over seven months after their initial arrests without affording them any opportunity to rebut the charges.[42] It is thus unsurprising that a proposal to recognize a suspension power in the federal Constitution engendered an intense, albeit brief, debate among the delegates to the Constitutional Convention.

The initial draft of the Suspension Clause, proposed by Charles Pinckney, granted to the legislative branch the exclusive power to suspend the writ but limited the duration of any suspension to no more than twelve months.[43] According to James Madison's notes from the Philadelphia Convention, John Rutledge argued that habeas corpus should be declared inviolable, because he could not conceive of any circumstance that would justify a nationwide suspension.[44] Additionally, James Wilson contended that a suspension power was not necessary to provide executive authority in times of crisis, because the judiciary possessed the power to respond flexibly to an emergency while still providing individual due process. He noted that judges could simply retain their customary discretion as to whether to retain or grant bail in "important cases."[45] In his protest against inclusion of a suspension power, Wilson seems to have recognized the need to provide an individual with at least some opportunity to contest the underlying basis for his detention, even if an emergency rendered a full trial temporarily impracticable. A judge, he argued, could assess the grounds for the detention within the context of a preliminary, but still adversarial, bail hearing.[46] Despite these protests, however, a vote was called to cut off further debate, and the delegates passed the clause.[47]

Other opponents of the Suspension Clause feared that the federal government was likely to use this power to oppress states and state officials who disagreed with its policies. During the ratification debates, for example, Luther Martin argued that:

> [I]f we gave this power to the general government, it would be an engine of oppression in its hands, since whenever a State should oppose its views, however arbitrary and unconstitutional, and refuse submission to them, the general government may declare it to be an act of rebellion, and suspending the habeas corpus act, may seize upon the persons of those advocates of freedom . . . and may imprison them during its pleasure in the remotest part of the union.[48]

Thomas Jefferson agreed and privately urged Madison to remove the Suspension Clause from the Constitution and replace it with a clause rendering the writ of habeas corpus inviolable.[49] Martin's criticism reflected the pervasive fear of tyranny that underscored the Framers' decision to build the Constitution around an elaborate system of prophylactic checks and balances.[50] A federal power to suspend habeas corpus would concentrate power in the hands of the federal government by enabling Congress and the president to suspend the writ under the pretext of an "emergency" in order to imprison their political opponents. Martin also wisely, if unintentionally, highlighted a potentially fatal flaw in the proposed constitution's ability to protect individual liberty: its lack of a structural safeguard to ensure that any suspension satisfied the constitutional prerequisites.[51]

Despite these protestations at both the Convention and state ratification levels, the Framers ultimately decided to append the Suspension Clause to the habeas guarantee in the body of the Constitution.[52] The Convention eventually adopted Gouverneur Morris's proposal, which narrowed the criteria for suspension to the two-prong test of the existence of a "Rebellion or invasion" and a finding that "the public safety may require it."[53] During the evolution of the proposal, Pinckney's express guarantee of the privilege of the writ, as well as the proposed restriction on the duration of the suspension, were removed.[54] The Suspension Clause was originally placed in the judiciary article, after a provision guaranteeing a jury trial in criminal cases.[55] The Committee on Style later moved it to Article I, section 9, which contains the limitations on the powers of Congress.[56] The proposed constitution of the new federal government recognized the foundational nature of the right to be free from arbitrary imprisonment by ensuring the availability of the writ of habeas corpus. The clause also imposed restrictions on the legislative power to suspend the writ, which represented a marked departure from the English practice. Subsequent discussion, however, will demonstrate that the core due process requirements of the Fifth Amendment irreconcilably conflict with the outer bounds of the suspension power. As a result, the Due Process Clause supersedes the Suspension Clause.

THE IMPACT OF THE DUE PROCESS CLAUSE
ON THE SUSPENSION CLAUSE

The Implications of Textual Interpretation

While the Suspension Clause's history is instructive, it plays no direct role in support of the argument that the Suspension Clause is no longer valid. The argument turns not on an interpretation of the Suspension Clause itself, but rather on construction of the text and values of the Fifth Amendment's Due Process Clause. This discussion fashions an argument grounded in textual interpretation, while the discussion that follows explores the normative implications of the Due Process Clause for the foundations of American political and constitutional theory.

The textual argument proceeds in three steps. First, the Supreme Court's due process jurisprudence, however confusing its contours might be at the margins, has always embraced two core principles that have served as a baseline for the constitutional guarantee: that freedom from coercive government custody is a protected "liberty" interest, and that "due process of law" requires, at minimum, provision of notice and hearing before a neutral adjudicator to determine the lawfulness of the detention. Second, exercise of the suspension power necessarily enables the executive to behave in a manner inherently—indeed, blatantly—inconsistent with these fundamental dictates of due process. Finally, in light of this inherent inconsistency, the Due Process Clause must be deemed to supersede any conflicting exercise of the suspension power by virtue of its location in an amendment to the body of the Constitution.

Constitutional Baseline for Procedural Due Process

Scholars have often lamented that procedural due process doctrine is confusing,[57] unpredictable,[58] and even incoherent.[59] This frustration, however, applies solely to controversial issues on the outer frontiers of due process—for example, when the Court must determine whether a statutorily created entitlement constitutes a "property" interest protected by the Clause,[60] or whether "due process of law" mandates that an individual receive a specific type of procedure before being deprived of a constitutionally protected interest.[61] Despite this uncertainty at the margins, however, the Supreme Court has clearly and consistently articulated two fundamental baseline tenets of procedural due process: (1) that an individual's interest in avoiding imprisonment by the government is a fundamental "liberty" interest that triggers the protections of the clause,[62] and (2) that "due process of law" requires, at a minimum, that an individual receive notice and a hearing before a neutral adjudicator to determine the lawfulness of that individual's detention.[63] Put bluntly, it is indisputable that when it locks someone up and throws away the key, without providing her with a fair and orderly process by which to challenge her detention before a neutral adjudicator, the executive violates the Fifth Amendment guarantee that "[n]o person shall be . . . deprived of life, liberty, or property, without due process of law."[64]

Prior to delving into the particulars of due process doctrine, it is first necessary to articulate the provision's core operational principle: that a deprivation of "liberty" entitles a person to "due process of law." This statement is so simple and indisputable that the Court's due process analyses often seem to take it for granted.[65] Nevertheless, it requires elaboration in two respects. First, this constitutional directive necessarily bars anyone charged with the power of constitutional interpretation from concluding that what is acknowledged to be a constitutionally protected liberty interest is not entitled to "due process of law."[66] Second, it makes clear that temporary, as well as permanent, deprivations of recognized interests trigger the protections of the Clause.[67] The Fourteenth Amendment, the Court has held, "draws no bright lines around three-day, 10-day or 50-day deprivations."[68] Thus, it is no answer to an individual imprisoned unlawfully for one week without a hearing that he regained his freedom at the end of that week. The Fifth Amendment prohibits the deprivation of liberty without due process and nowhere refers to satisfaction of a minimum period of restraint. To be sure, neither "life, liberty, or property" nor "due process of law" are self-defining terms. But it is important to make clear at the outset that however the terms are defined, establishing a deprivation of the former necessarily triggers the procedural protections of the latter.

While it is true that establishing this fact does not automatically tell us what "due process" necessarily entails, it is not all that difficult to discern a consensus as to the procedural core of the concept. The Supreme Court and scholars have always agreed that an individual's interest in avoiding wrongful confinement is a "liberty" interest protected by the clause.[69] The Court has described freedom from executive detention as the "most elemental of liberty interests," emphasizing that it has "always been careful not to 'minimize the importance and fundamental nature' of the individual's right to liberty."[70] Scholars have described this interest as so ingrained in our legal tradition that it creates a "rebuttable presumption" that executive detention is impermissible.[71] Even proponents of a rigidly historical conception of "liberty" agree that an individual's interest in freedom from physical constraint is protected by the clause.[72] The Supreme Court has previously granted constitutional protection to wages,[73] bank accounts,[74] welfare benefits,[75] and even gas stoves purchased through conditional sales contracts.[76] A fortiori, even relatively limited physical detentions must trigger the clause's protections. Thus, requiring some level of "due process" before an individual can be imprisoned by the government should be—and indeed is—an absolutely uncontroversial assertion.

Once it is established that the protections of the Due Process Clause are triggered by governmental detention, it is necessary to determine what procedures are dictated by that concept. Currently, the Court determines the type and amount of process due in a given case by applying the three-part balancing test established in *Mathews v. Eldridge*.[77] This test does not, a priori, mandate any specific procedures. Nonetheless, the Court has established three "essential principle[s]" of due process: "notice and opportunity for hearing appropriate to the nature of the case,"[78] which must be conducted by a neutral adjudicator.[79] In the Court's words, "For more than a century the central meaning of procedural due process has been clear: 'Parties whose rights are to be affected are entitled to be heard; and in order that they may enjoy that right they must first be notified.'"[80] In order to give these rights meaning, "[o]ne is [also] entitled as a matter of due process of law to an adjudicator who is not in a situation which would offer a possible temptation to the average man as a judge . . . which might lead him not to hold the balance nice, clear and true."[81] While exigent circumstances might require the court to forego some other procedures, these three core elements may not be displaced.[82] To be sure, the form and timing of the required notice and hearing will vary on a case-by-case basis.[83] For present purposes, the point is simply that the Court has consistently held that aggrieved individuals must receive some meaningful opportunity to challenge the deprivation of a constitutionally protected life, liberty, or property interest.[84]

Implications of the Exercise of the Suspension Power for Due Process

As in the discussion of the baseline of procedural due process, it is necessary to begin the analysis of the operation of the Suspension Clause with a few basic statements about how exercise of the suspension power would function in practice. First, a suspension of habeas corpus necessarily revokes the authority of the judiciary to order the release of any individual detained by the executive pursuant to the suspension.[85] In other words, suspension of habeas corpus effectively operates as a bar to detainees' ability to obtain their release from government custody. Second, the removal of the remedy of habeas corpus precludes the judiciary from conducting a hearing to analyze the lawfulness of the detention.[86] Several prominent scholars readily acknowledge that a suspension of habeas corpus "shut[s] off" an individual's due process rights.[87] Yet absent an individual right to such a hearing, one cannot be assured that an imprisoned individual will be afforded due process during a suspension.[88]

It is true that, within our modern legal system, the writ of habeas corpus is not the only procedural vehicle through which a person imprisoned by the government is able to challenge the merits of her detention before a court.[89] As Trevor Morrison has pointed out, a prisoner detained pursuant to a valid suspension could theoretically file suit in an Article III court under one of any number of writs, including a writ of injunction or mandamus.[90] If a court were to provide a detainee with a hearing under one of these writs, and were deemed to possess the power to order the detainee's release if convinced that the detention was unlawful, then the argument would end there, because the requirements of due process of law would then be satisfied. But under such an approach, the impact of the congressional exercise of the suspension power would, as a practical matter, be rendered meaningless. Thus, it seems more likely that a judge would view such a suit as an attempted end-run around the suspension of habeas and would likely dismiss it out of hand.[91]

If one were to consider the potential impact of a suspension, its irreconcilability with even the most basic notion of due process becomes readily apparent. Imagine, for example, that a large terrorist cell with the avowed goal of overthrowing the U.S. government launches a coordinated attack on multiple American cities. To resist this "invasion," Congress authorizes a nationwide suspension of the writ of habeas corpus for any individual who, in the view of the executive, has participated in the attacks, is suspected of participating in the attacks, or has obstructed the government's investigation of the attacks. The minority political party, skeptical of this drastic measure, holds protest rallies on Capitol Hill and urges local officials to refrain from enforcing the law. In response, the president arrests these lawmakers and protesters, and orders his subordinates to identify and arrest any other citizens who could conceivably threaten to undermine her policy.[92]

If a suspension has the effect of removing all judicial avenues by which a detainee could obtain release, as it must to be effective, then it necessarily removes all judicial power to correct any executive abuse of the suspension power. As a result, the president would be free to imprison whomever she wants for the duration of the suspension—and there is no constitutional requirement that a suspension be time-limited. Thus, the president would be free to use that power to ensure that the suspension persists indefinitely. More important for present purposes, the president need not (and in this scenario, does not) provide the detainees with any procedural protections whatsoever. There exists absolutely no basis on which to suggest that, once the suspension power has been exercised, a court would possess any legal authority to terminate such a frightening constitutional travesty. There is similarly no reasonable basis on which to argue that such a scenario satisfies even the most minimalist version of due process. Thus, in this situation the exercise of the suspension power would directly conflict with the Fifth Amendment's guarantee that any individual imprisoned by the government is entitled at minimum, to notice and a hearing before a neutral adjudicator.

The Impact of a Constitutional Amendment on Inconsistent Text in the Body of the Constitution

The textual argument fashioned here rests on a fundamental—and, for the most part, uncontroversial—rule of textual interpretation that predates the framing of the Constitution and has been repeatedly affirmed by the Supreme Court. Where the reconciliation of two conflicting laws (when those laws possess the same legal status)[93] is legally or physically impossible or even merely "impracticable," "[t]he rule which has obtained in the courts for determining their relative validity is that the last in order of time shall be preferred to the first."[94] Justice Story, for example, reasoned that when there is a "positive repugnancy" between two laws, "the old law is repealed by implication only pro tanto, to the extent of the repugnancy."[95] The Court more recently noted this general rule in *Watt v. Alaska*, where it recognized that the "more recent of two irreconcilably conflicting statutes governs."[96]

This interpretive principle applies with even more force in the context of a constitutional amendment, which, by definition, is designed to make a "formal revision" to the original document.[97] To determine whether two constitutional provisions irreconcilably conflict, the Supreme Court first ascertains each provision's constitutional function.[98] While of course explicit repeal or indisputable evidence of the drafters' intent to repeal would be probative, it is important to emphasize that neither constitutes a necessary condition. Rather, the Court requires only that the principles embodied by the provisions be fundamentally irreconcilable.[99] If the two constitutional provisions directly conflict, then the directives of the earlier provision are necessarily limited or revoked by the amendment.[100]

A classic illustration of this interpretive trumping process is the Supreme Court's conclusion in *Seminole Tribe of Florida v. Florida*[101] that the Eleventh Amendment, which limits the jurisdiction of the federal judiciary to adjudicate claims against states,[102] supersedes Congress's power under a synthesis of the Commerce[103] and Necessary and Proper Clauses[104] (both contained in the body of the Constitution's text) to authorize suits against states.[105] The Court reached this conclusion despite the fact that the Eleventh Amendment includes no express repeal of the otherwise plenary power embodied in the original text.

This example demonstrates that the logic underlying the argument that the Due Process Clause repeals the Suspension Clause, to the extent they are in conflict, does not depend on the acceptance of some obscure canon of statutory interpretation. Rather, it mirrors the way in which scholars and judges have always resolved cases of irreconcilable conflict between constitutional provisions. If the Eleventh Amendment trumps Article I and the Thirteenth Amendment trumps the Fugitive Slave Clause, then it is also reasonable to conclude that the Due Process Clause of the Fifth Amendment trumps the Suspension Clause of Article I, section 9, to the extent the two are in inescapable conflict.

This is precisely the situation that exists with regard to the Suspension and Due Process Clauses. The Suspension Clause establishes a power that authorizes the executive to imprison individuals without allowing them any procedural rights, for indefinite periods. The Due Process Clause, however, subsequently imposed an unequivocal limit on the federal government's power to detain individuals summarily by guaranteeing, without exception or limitation, that "no person shall . . . be deprived of life, liberty, or property, without due process of law."[106] "Due process of law," at its textual, historical, and doctrinal cores, at minimum requires the provision of notice, hearing, and a neutral adjudicator. Employing the interpretive process that has indisputably been endorsed by the Supreme Court, the limitations imposed by the Fifth Amendment necessarily supersede the power conferred on the political branches of the federal government by the Suspension Clause to summarily imprison individuals absent any procedure, hearing, or judicial review of the legality of the governmental action. As a result, to the extent it is inconsistent with the dictates of due process, the suspension power has been rendered unconstitutional.

Foundational Precepts of American Constitutionalism

The dictates of textual interpretation described in the prior discussion, standing alone, provide sufficient support for the contention that the Due Process Clause supersedes the Suspension Clause, to the extent the two are inconsistent (which they most assuredly are). However, there exists an equally powerful alternative foundation for the argument: the fundamental precepts of American constitutionalism. As made clear throughout this book, this phrase refers to a core precept of American political theory: the preeminence of the rule of law through a process of checking both the majority's unlimited power over the minority and government's unlimited power over the individual and unlimited authority over the populace. While the inherently adversary nature of the nation's form of political interaction is well established in American history,[107] the essential premise of our system is that whoever gains political power may not suppress the minority for no reason other than ideological disagreement or the desire to gain a competitive advantage. It is no secret that the Framers were centrally concerned with the dangers of tyranny.[108] The mere fact that those exercising political power acquired that power lawfully will not necessarily validate the unlawful or tyrannical exercise of that power.

If we were to recognize the power of the majoritarian branches of the federal government to suspend the writ of habeas corpus, we would necessarily be accepting the possibility that at some time in the future, a president of the United States may imprison all of her political opponents for no reason other than that they oppose her rule. Similarly, once the Suspension Clause has been invoked, a president could employ this unrestrained power to suppress or arrest unpopular racial or religious minorities. With habeas corpus suspended, the judiciary would be powerless to prevent such blatant violation of fundamental constitutional rights.[109] We must accept that, in the aftermath of a "[r]ebellion or [i]nvasion," however those terms are ultimately defined, a president would be empowered to employ the suspension power to effectively transform the nation into a dictatorship. And under the inherent logic of the Suspension Clause, we must accept that the judiciary would be absolutely powerless to stop such invidious—and otherwise blatantly unconstitutional—action.

The Supreme Court's eloquent warning in *Ex parte Milligan* should be recalled:

> This nation, as experience has proved, cannot always remain at peace, and has no right to expect that it will always have wise and humane rulers, sincerely attached to the principles of the Constitution. Wicked men, ambitious of power, with hatred of liberty and contempt of law, may fill the place once occupied by Washington and Lincoln; and if this right is conceded, and the calamities of war again befall us, the dangers to human liberty are frightful to contemplate. If our fathers had failed to provide for just such a contingency, they would have been false to the trust reposed in them. They knew—the history of the world told them—the nation they were founding, be its existence short or long, would be involved in war; how often or how long continued, human foresight could not tell; and that unlimited power, wherever lodged at such a time, was especially hazardous to freemen.[110]

As the *Milligan* Court recognized, the nation cannot stake its constitutional system on a mere hope that future presidents will decline to view national crises as an opportunity to aggrandize their own power. Nor can we ever really know how a president or her advisors will respond to an emergency.

It is important to recognize that once the power of the judiciary to issue the writ of habeas corpus is revoked, all other constitutionally protected liberties are, as a practical matter, revoked as well. For example, were the executive to summarily arrest individuals for exercising their right of free expression, there would be no opportunity for the judiciary to provide meaningful protection of that right. Were the executive to arrest individuals without satisfying the requirements of the Fourth Amendment, the courts would be unable to enforce that constitutional right. Suspension of habeas corpus would thus effectively revoke not only the due process right to a hearing but all other constitutional rights, substantive or procedural, that a court might enforce through resort to the vehicle of habeas corpus.

It should also be emphasized that there exists no constitutional requirement that a suspension be time-limited. Rather, it lasts for the period of the rebellion or invasion. Indeed, once the Suspension Clause has been invoked, it is by no means clear that either the judiciary or Congress would have constitutional authority to overrule the executive's continuing decision that the circumstances originally justifying that invocation no longer exist. In any event, such a situation could conceivably continue for extended periods. Thus, had Congress suspended the writ after the attacks of September 11, 2001, the continued presence of terrorist cells within the borders of the United States would likely have justified extension of the suspension indefinitely.

One could reasonably ask why, if the availability of the writ of habeas corpus is so foundational an element of American constitutionalism, the very Framers who drafted a document so sensitive to the dangers of tyranny failed to recognize that fact. To the contrary, it could be argued, they are the ones who inserted the Suspension Clause into the body of the Constitution in the first place. The flaw in such an argument, however, should be obvious: it proves far too much. The Framers also omitted virtually any reference to individual right protection, so much the same argument could be made with regard to the First Amendment right of free expression, the Fifth Amendment right against self-incrimination, and all of the other provisions of the Bill of Rights. Yet it would be difficult to deny that most or all of these provisions are today widely thought of as core elements of American political theory and as part of the modern tradition of American constitutionalism. These facts give rise to an important insight: the core concepts of our political theory were a work in progress at the time of the framing. That the Framers were merely groping towards an understanding of the central premises of American constitutionalism is a concept that has evolved, been refined, and gained force over the years.

The other insight to be drawn from the Framers' failure to include a Bill of Rights in the original document is that core precepts of American constitutionalism derive not only from those who framed the original document, but include those who ratified it and demanded enactment of a Bill of Rights as a condition for their doing so.[111] Indeed, it is by no means clear that those who drafted the document recognized the full implications for the principle of judicial review of the guarantees of independence for federal judges included in Article III.[112] Core precepts of the modern version of American constitutionalism, then, derive in significant part from adoption of the Bill of Rights in general and the Due Process Clause in particular, as well as from certain provisions of the original document. As Professor Zechariah Chafee has written, "[w]hen imprisonment is possible without explanation or redress, every form of liberty is impaired."[113]

ANTICIPATING COUNTERARGUMENTS

The case is compelling that the Due Process Clause supersedes the Suspension Clause. Puzzlingly, however, the argument appears never even to have been suggested by scholars, much less judicially accepted. It is therefore likely to seem counterintuitive to many and to engender considerable scholarly opposition (perhaps reflexively). It is appropriate, then, to anticipate and respond to the plausible arguments that could be raised against the theory advanced here.

Three such arguments can reasonably be anticipated: (1) the fact that the argument fashioned here has never been suggested before demonstrates its inconsistency with the historical understandings of the relationship between the two constitutional provisions; (2) the widely accepted construction of the Suspension Clause as requiring congressional authorization, rather than merely unilateral executive action, provides a sufficient check on the exercise of arbitrary executive power, rendering a further judicial check unnecessary; and (3) in times of national crisis, such as invasion or rebellion, the executive needs unfettered discretion to act in the national interest, and the exercise of judicial review under such circumstances would therefore present a serious threat to national security. None of these arguments, however, justifies rejection of the theory advanced here.

The Argument From Originality

Normally, the originality of a scholarly argument is thought to reflect positively on the scholar who fashioned it. In the present context, however, the argument's originality may in many ways be more of a detriment than a benefit. If the Suspension Clause is as fundamentally inconsistent with the dictates of due process and core notions of American constitutionalism as argued here, then why has no one ever posited this before?

There are two responses. First, the fact that the power under the Suspension Clause has so rarely been exercised—only four times in the nation's history[114]—has rendered the issue seemingly more academic than real. In fact, even in academic circles, until very recently the Suspension Clause received virtually no attention. Moreover, by definition, the clause's invocation occurs solely at times of great national stress, during which the population's instinct is to draw together. Anyone who raises constitutional questions about the validity of the suspension power at such a time would risk being labeled unpatriotic. In short, when there exists no basis for invoking the clause, there has been little or no scholarly interest in the issue, because it is purely hypothetical, but when the issue is all too real, there is, as a practical or political matter, no opportunity to consider it in a thoughtful manner.

The primary flaw in the counterargument grounded in the theory's lack of historical acceptance is that it risks proving too much. The same could be said of the unconstitutionality of the so-called separate-but-equal concept,[115] the constitutional protection of commercial speech,[116] the unconstitutionality of quasi-in-rem jurisdiction,[117] and the constitutional right of privacy.[118] In each of these situations, the Court chose to develop a constitutional right despite its historical lack of acceptance. The argument for the Due Process Clause's supersession of the Suspension Clause is far more obvious and indisputable, textually and theoretically, than the arguments in support of any of those rights.

The Implications of the Requirement of Congressional Authorization

On its face, the Suspension Clause is silent as to which organ of government possesses the authority to invoke it. Although President Lincoln asserted the constitutional authority to do so unilaterally,[119] it is generally thought today that the authorization of the legislative branch is required.[120] It might be suggested that as long as the president lacks the authority to exercise the power of suspension unilaterally, the requirements of American constitutionalism are satisfied.[121]

The initial response to this assertion is that even if the textually based contention advanced here is accurate,[122] this counterargument is beside the point: The Constitution, through the addition of the Fifth Amendment, has made the choice for us. Even from the perspective of political or constitutional theory, however, this counterargument is seriously flawed. If one were to accept the notion that a requirement of congressional authorization for executive action exhausted the Constitution's separation-of-powers demands, there logically would be no need for judicial review of *any* legislatively authorized action. Yet that, of course, would be inconsistent with established American practice. We demand judicial review of the constitutionality of even legislatively authorized executive action because we recognize the centrality of countermajoritarian enforcement of the Constitution's countermajoritarian directives. Neither the legislative nor the executive branch qualifies to provide this check.

This concern is of special importance in the context of the Suspension Clause because, by its very nature, that power will be invoked only in times of great national crisis. It is at these very times that dissenting minorities are most vulnerable to majoritarian infringement.[123] Reliance on an elected Congress as the sole check on an elected president would make little sense under these circumstances.

Finally, there is an even more dispositive response. At most, congressional authorization of executive suspension could provide a sufficient constitutional check on executive power over a general situation. It is not responsive to the individual's constitutionally protected interest in due process to remedy unlawful detention. One could easily imagine a situation in which the general need for suspension exists, but there nevertheless exists no legal or factual basis for the arrest *of a particular individual*. He might have been arrested mistakenly, for ulterior political motives, or out of racial or religious prejudice. In such a situation, it is of little benefit to this particular individual that Congress determined a need for a general suspension of the writ.

Due Process, Suspension, and the Needs of National Security

The final counterargument asserts that the interests of due process must give way to the interests of national security in times of invasion or rebellion. Thus, suspension must supersede the Fifth Amendment's due process guarantee.[124] At the outset, in response to this argument, it is important to recall the dispositive force of reliance on textual construction. Because the due process guarantee is unlimited and unqualified in its reach, and appears in the form of a subsequently enacted amendment, it indisputably supersedes the inconsistent directive in the Suspension Clause purely as a matter of textual interpretation. If anything, the argument grounded in national security effectively underscores the point, because it highlights the inconsistency between the two provisions.

More important, this counterargument ignores the truly frightening scenarios—ones that are, unfortunately, far from inconceivable—that might result from the total preclusion of judicial enforcement of the Due Process Clause necessarily flowing from invocation of the Suspension Clause.[125] Absent such enforcement, what is there to legally stop an executive—already politically empowered by the wave of patriotism that inevitably accompanies a crisis of national security—from immediately imprisoning all of her political opponents? Unless and until advocates of suspension are able to provide an adequate response to this question, it is impossible—or, at the very least, extremely dangerous—to accept their argument.

In any event, the inherent flexibility of the due process guarantee should provide a sufficient means by which to ensure appropriate room for executive discretion in the face of a national emergency. In the presence of an invasion or rebellion, the judiciary will no doubt recognize the need to provide the executive with more deference than might otherwise be appropriate. This flexibility, however, does not necessarily preclude judicial ability to remedy invidious or obviously mistaken detentions through provision of the core due process notions of notice and some form of meaningful hearing before a neutral adjudicator.

PROCEDURAL DUE PROCESS DURING AN ATTEMPTED SUSPENSION: WHAT IS THE PROPER JUDICIAL ROLE?

The analysis to this point has established that individuals retain their right to "due process of law," regardless of the availability of the writ of habeas corpus. This section explores exactly how the Due Process Clause would apply in various permutations of attempted suspension.

The analysis begins by considering detainees' procedural due process rights during a blanket suspension of habeas corpus similar to the one described previously: a situation in which habeas has been suspended and the executive chooses to detain individuals summarily.[126] The second permutation considers a situation in which habeas has been suspended, but the executive has chosen to provide to those detained some form of intra-branch hearing. In this context, assuming that the Due Process Clause constrains the suspension (as argued here), the analysis examines the court's role in ensuring that "executive due process"—that is to say, hearings provided by a civilian executive tribunal—complies with the constitutional requirements of the Fifth Amendment. Third, the analysis asks whether suspension legislation limiting the duration of detention is unconstitutional. In the fourth and final permutation, the chapter briefly discusses a reviewing court's role in evaluating the sufficiency of process afforded by military tribunals or commissions.

This discussion fashions two different "levels" of a court's procedural due process analysis.[127] "First-level" due process analysis involves the constitutional question of what procedures are necessary to satisfy the dictates of "due process of law" in a given case, as well as how that standard is to be applied to determine whether the executive has satisfied it. "Second-level" analysis, in contrast, refers to the adjudicator's performance of the individualized fact-finding function to determine whether the arrest was in fact lawful. The court will proceed to perform this second-level function if and only if it has determined that the procedures provided by the executive, if any, fail to satisfy the court's first-level analysis of what procedures are constitutionally required.

As a final point of emphasis, it should be noted that this discussion involves an interpretation of the Due Process Clause, not the Suspension Clause. As established in the prior discussion, a suspension of habeas corpus must be unconstitutional unless it satisfies the demands of the Due Process Clause. One might disagree with the elements of the due process analysis proposed here, but whatever one decides that "due process" requires in a given case, it still overrides the suspension power to the extent the two are deemed inconsistent.

Suspension of Habeas Corpus Absent Provision of Executive Due Process

Suppose that the constitutional prerequisite of a "[r]ebellion or [i]nvasion" has been satisfied. Imagine further that Congress has decided to take the bold step of suspending the writ of habeas corpus nationwide and has enacted legislation granting the executive unfettered discretion to arrest and detain any individual whom he deems to be a threat to national security. Pursuant to this limitless authority, the president orders the arrest and imprisonment of all individuals of Irish descent for the duration of the suspension. Once her officers identify a person as "Irish" (a rather haphazard inquiry in and of itself), they immediately arrest that person without providing her with any process whatsoever—no opportunity to see any evidence against her (at least in part because no evidence need exist), no access to counsel, and no hearing to challenge the basis of her detention.

Of course, this hypothetical scenario represents the most extreme permutation of the suspension power, but we must always keep in mind that any argument that the Suspension Clause is constitutional necessarily deems such a situation to be acceptable.[128] Because the Suspension Clause itself imposes no requirement on the executive branch to provide its detainees with individual hearings, we must at the outset proceed on the assumption that the executive will choose not to do so.

As demonstrated earlier, the government violates the core dictates of the Due Process Clause when it summarily and indefinitely detains its citizens. As also established previously, to satisfy due process, government must provide an adequate hearing before a neutral adjudicator. A detainee thus must have access to a court in order to satisfy this constitutional guarantee. But it will not always be immediately clear what the court's role would be in this situation. In deciding this question, the reviewing court must determine what procedures are required by due process in this specific context. Then, still as part of this first-level analysis, it must determine whether whatever procedures actually have been provided by the executive satisfy those constitutional requirements. Of course, if, as hypothesized here, absolutely no procedures are provided, the answer to that question would be obvious: The detainee has been denied due process. At that point the court will necessarily turn to the second-level due process inquiry: determining whether, on the basis of facts proven at a constitutionally appropriate hearing, the individual's detention was lawful.

Type and Scope of Procedures Required to Satisfy Due Process

The "essential principle" of due process of law is that an individual deprived of her liberty must be provided with "notice and opportunity for hearing appropriate to the nature of the case."[129] In invoking a "first-level" due process analysis, an Article III court would have the opportunity to determine whether the procedures actually provided to the detainee by the executive, both before and immediately following arrest, satisfy these foundational constitutional requirements.[130] Indeed, the political insulation of the Article III courts likely makes them the most neutral forum available to adjudicate detainees' due process claims.[131]

This is not to imply that the court's "first-level" analysis of the constitutional requirements of due process will always be easy or straightforward. Even if it is clear that the executive has failed to provide any process at all, the court will still have to determine the type, terms, and timing of the notice and hearing mandated by the Due Process Clause. One may assume, arguendo, that a detainee will seek a full evidentiary hearing reminiscent of a criminal trial, because that type of hearing will give her the fullest opportunity to contest the sufficiency (or even the validity) of the government's evidence against her.[132] The executive, by contrast, will presumably argue that providing the detainees with any process at all will unduly undermine national security interests because such a hearing could force the government to divulge sensitive state secrets that might compromise its ongoing efforts to thwart the "[r]ebellion or [i]nvasion" that precipitated the suspension.

At that point it will fall to the judge to define the requirements of due process of law in the context of a blanket suspension. The Supreme Court's due process jurisprudence provides little concrete guidance on this question. To the contrary, the Court has repeatedly emphasized that due process is "not a technical conception with a fixed content unrelated to time, place and circumstances."[133] Under well-established Supreme Court doctrine, to determine what procedures are constitutionally required in a particular case, a reviewing court will invoke the test of *Mathews v. Eldridge*, under which it balances three factors to determine which procedures are necessary to satisfy the dictates of "due process of law" in a given case:

> First, the private interest that will be affected by the official action; second, the risk of an erroneous deprivation of such interest through the procedures used, and the probable value, if any, of additional or substitute procedural safeguards; and finally, the Government's interest, including the function involved and the fiscal and administrative burdens that the additional or substitute procedural requirement would entail.[134]

The problems with this balancing approach are arguably many,[135] and the outcomes of courts' application of it have on occasion proven difficult to predict.[136] Nonetheless, the case-by-case flexibility it prescribes is valuable in the context of a social or political crisis, because it allows the courts to strike "the proper constitutional balance" during a period of ongoing domestic upheaval.[137]

The major "first-level" issue for the court will likely involve the detainee's claim that he is constitutionally entitled to a live hearing. Applying the *Mathews* test, the court should first note the gravity of the private interest at stake in this case. Freedom from wrongful detention is generally considered the most fundamental of liberty interests, particularly when that imprisonment is of indeterminate and possibly indefinite length. To be sure, *any* forced custody is sufficient to trigger the protections of the Due Process Clause.[138] But a detainee's interest is potentially magnified in the context of modern warfare, because conflicts such as the "war on terror" are unlikely to have a finite and conclusive resolution.[139] Moreover, it is not inconceivable that the government could continue the suspension of habeas corpus indefinitely, by arguing either conclusorily that it needs additional time to identify and apprehend all of the parties involved in the "[r]ebellion or [i]nvasion" or that the "public [s]afety" requires continued suspension in order to prevent similar attacks in the future. Not only have the individuals who have been imprisoned under a blanket suspension already suffered a deprivation of their most fundamental liberty interest, but they also face the strong possibility of indefinite wrongful imprisonment.[140]

In assessing the private interest at stake, the Supreme Court has often considered whether the individual's protected interest can be fully remedied by post-deprivation damages. Essentially, if the individual can obtain full retrospective relief if she later establishes that the government deprivation was wrongful, her private interest in obtaining immediate process is diminished.[141] The availability of compensatory damages for individuals wrongfully detained during a suspension has been a hot-button issue in recent scholarship interpreting the Suspension Clause.[142] For purposes of Due Process Clause interpretation, however, the crucial point is that the damage done by a wrongful executive detention must, simply as a matter of common sense, be deemed irreparable. It would be absurd to posit that a post hoc damage award could reasonably compensate a wrongfully imprisoned individual, arrested and imprisoned without any meaningful opportunity to challenge the accuracy or lawfulness of her detention, for the tangible and intangible harm done by the arbitrary conduct of the executive.[143] As a general matter, the Court has refused to "embrace[] the general proposition that a wrong may be done if it can be undone,"[144] which logically leads to the conclusion that the Due Process Clause cannot be interpreted to allow the government to "buy" the right to imprison individuals when the writ of habeas corpus is unavailable. As a general matter, the idea that a subsequent award of damages can adequately remedy continuing unlawful confinement is clearly preposterous. To be sure, if no remedy were sought or available during the unlawful confinement, the award of damages is far better than nothing. However, it is no answer to one continuing to be unlawfully confined who seeks direct judicial intervention to end that confinement that her requested relief is being denied because of the availability of a damage award following her release.

In deciding what specific procedures must be provided, the court will have to balance the gravity of the individual's fundamental interest in physical liberty against the public interest at stake if the government were forced

to provide every detainee with a full evidentiary hearing. The "public interest" component of the *Mathews* balancing test usually includes an assessment
of the administrative and financial burden that would flow from the holding
of the required hearings,[145] but this will likely not be the primary argument
made by the government. More probable is that the government will argue
that national security interests could be seriously compromised by providing individual detainees with the opportunity to review and challenge the
evidence against them, which in turn would compromise the public interest in preventing future attacks.[146] Although the Court minimized similar
concerns in *Hamdi v. Rumsfeld*[147] (when, it should be emphasized, the Suspension Clause had not been invoked), it is conceivable that the argument
could carry more weight if the country were embroiled in a serious, ongoing domestic conflict.[148] It is crucial to note, however, that the existence of
an ongoing "[r]ebellion or [i]nvasion" should influence only the timing or
scope of the hearing, not the availability of some meaningful proceeding
in the first instance.[149] Although the *Mathews* test provides the reviewing
court with the power to tinker with the timing or terms of the proceeding, as a constitutional floor, the Due Process Clause demands that anyone
imprisoned by the government receive some form of meaningful hearing.[150]
To accommodate the government's interest in not divulging sensitive information, the court might adapt or even limit particular elements of the hearing. Similarly, the judge might order a change of venue to a different federal
court if particular regions of the country have been ravaged by the rebellion
or invasion. She might even decide to postpone the hearing until after the
immediate crisis has passed. But whatever the court interprets due process to
require in the context of a blanket suspension, it must include some form of
a meaningful individualized hearing.[151]

The specific terms of the hearing will likely be determined by the
court's analysis of the second *Mathews* factor: "the risk of an erroneous
deprivation of such interest through the procedures used, and the probable value, if any, of additional or substitute procedural safeguards."[152]
Recall that in this version of the "blanket suspension" scenario, the
executive has thrown the detainees in jail without providing them with
any process whatsoever. Any "additional procedural safeguards" will
therefore necessarily be designed, under *Mathews*, to reduce the risk of
an erroneous imprisonment. The *Mathews* framework requires the court
to attempt to weigh the benefit of each of these individual procedures in
light of both the grave interest at stake for the detainees and the government's legitimate interest in both protecting sensitive information and
devoting as much of its attention as possible to abating the national crisis.

Determination of the Adequacy of Procedures Already Provided by the Executive

Once the reviewing court determines what procedures are required by due process under the specific circumstances of the individual case, it must determine whether the procedures provided by the executive, if any, satisfy those requirements. This represents the second step in the first-level due process inquiry. In this context, the "first-level" analysis by an Article III court functions as a necessary and appropriate safeguard to ensure that tribunals provided by the executive afford the detainees a constitutionally sufficient level of process.

As a preliminary matter, one may reasonably wonder whether so-called executive due process is an oxymoronic concept. As noted earlier, a neutral adjudicator is one of the three essential requirements of due process of law.[153] This requirement logically applies to both levels of the due process analysis: the adjudicator must not only be "neutral" with respect to the "second-level" factual determination (that is, the individualized determination as to the lawfulness of the detention) but also with respect to the "first-level" question of what due process requires in the context of a suspension. It would hardly make sense—or be consistent with due process—to allow the executive branch itself to have the final say as to whether the procedures it has provided to determine the lawfulness of detention actually satisfy due process. Such "protection" of constitutional rights effectively amounts to no process at all. That determination must be made by the independent Article III court, since it is difficult to imagine that any adjudicator chosen by the executive branch who is herself part of the executive branch (and whose position within that branch therefore ultimately turns on exercise of the unreviewable discretion of the president himself) could satisfy the due process requirement of a neutral adjudicator in making it. One should therefore be skeptical as to whether an executive adjudicator can ever meet the standard for adjudicatory neutrality that the Supreme Court has fashioned, regardless of what specific procedures have been provided. Although the Supreme Court has held that an executive agency is capable of functioning as a neutral adjudicator,[154] it has never confronted the question in the context of a deprivation of liberty or, equally important, in the context of a suspension of habeas corpus, which enables the president to arrest and detain without the availability of any judicial review. A reasonable adjudicator who is part of the executive branch or subject to direct executive control would certainly fear that if she invalidated a presidential determination that a given detention was justified, she might quickly lose her position.

The Supreme Court first articulated a standard for adjudicatory neutrality in *Tumey v. Ohio*, in which it required a judge to recuse himself if he had a "direct, personal, substantial, pecuniary interest in reaching a conclusion against [the defendant]."[155] In that decision, the Court adopted an objective test in which "[e]very procedure which would offer a possible temptation to the average man as a judge . . . or which might lead him not to hold the balance nice, clear and true between the State and the accused" violated due process.[156] At the very least, it would be reasonable to assume that the intra-branch executive adjudicator would have a subconscious desire to avoid invalidating the decisions made by her superiors, leading her to defer to her fellow executive officials' assertions that certain procedures were not "really required" to fail the constitutional requirements of neutrality and independence.[157] To be sure, some executive adjudicators might be able to "hold the balance true" on even the "first-level" question, but the Due Process Clause has never required proof of actual bias in order to invalidate an adjudicatory framework for lack of neutrality.[158] Rather, the realistic risk of bias—the appearance that the adjudicator might favor the claims of one side over the other—is sufficient to undermine her neutrality for purposes of the Due Process Clause.[159]

This argument is wholly consistent with the Court's current doctrine governing judicial review of administrative action; the availability of review of constitutional questions by an Article III court is a long-standing and undisputed tenet of administrative law.[160] It should also be noted that the judicial review of the procedural scheme established by the executive tribunals would not intrude upon their core function of making "second-level" factual determinations regarding the grounds of the detention, because any cases in which the procedures were held to be constitutionally inadequate would be remanded to the tribunals. Moreover, a small number of judicial rulings would likely be necessary to inductively clarify the procedures that the tribunals would be required to apply.[161]

Legislative Limitation on the Duration of Suspension

Assume a situation in which Congress suspects that the president might abuse the suspension power and therefore attempts to limit this danger by specifying a maximum length of time that an individual may be detained without the filing of formal charges. More specifically, assume that this hypothetical suspension legislation requires the secretary of defense to provide each U.S. Court of Appeals with an updated list of detainees on a weekly basis. If the government could not secure a criminal indictment of the detainee within twenty-one days of the initial arrest, the detainee could petition the circuit court for release.[162] In this permutation, the reviewing court is required to make a "first-level" determination of whether postponing any hearing for twenty-one days (or whatever the specified period) is constitutionally acceptable.

As has been emphasized throughout, *any* deprivation of liberty, no matter how temporary, necessarily triggers due process protections. This means that as soon as an individual is imprisoned by the government, she becomes constitutionally entitled to notice and a hearing before a neutral adjudicator. Yet this type of statute would allow the executive to arrest people without providing them with any process at all, so long as the detention did not exceed the statutory time limit. Moreover, nothing in the statute precludes the executive from repeatedly arresting the same individuals and detaining them for periods that stop just short of the statutory maximum.[163] This permutation, then, irreconcilably conflicts with due process and is therefore unconstitutional. The legislative attempt to prevent abuse of the suspension power is immaterial, as it does not remedy the fundamental constitutional defect of this type of legislation—namely, that it allows the executive to imprison individuals without providing them with the core requirements of due process. In any event, even if one were to assume the acceptability of such a legislative scheme for due process purposes, judicial review would have to be available to assure executive compliance with it.

Military Commissions

The final permutation involves a suspension of habeas corpus combined with a provision for individual hearings in front of military commissions, rather than before an Article III court—even when the detainee is a civilian. In *Ex parte Milligan*, the Supreme Court held that, at least in the absence of a formal suspension of the writ of habeas corpus, a civilian detainee could not be tried before a military commission while the federal courts were open and able to hear the case.[164] This holding conclusively limited military trials to individuals who physically participated as enemy combatants, as well as those rare cases in which the federal courts are "actually closed, and it is impossible to administer criminal justice according to law."[165] Thus, were one to accept the conclusion advocated here (although, it should be noted, not accepted by the Court in *Milligan*) that the constitutional dictate of due process survives a suspension of habeas, the alternative provision of a hearing before a military commission, rather than a court, would categorically fail to satisfy constitutional requirements—at least when the defendant is a civilian citizen.[166]

It is conceivable that the suspension legislation would order the military commission to make only the "second-level" due process determination as to whether the ongoing detention in the particular case before it was justified on its facts. In this context, the military commission would perform the same function as the civilian executive tribunal considered earlier. Because it would have to apply civilian, rather than military law, it would also be subject to "first-level" review by an Article III court to assure that it satisfied constitutional requirements of neutrality. The concerns over adjudicatory neutrality of military commissions would thus largely mirror doubts previously expressed in this chapter about executive tribunals.[167]

Second-Level Due Process

Where the reviewing court has concluded that the executive's detention procedure has failed to satisfy due process, it will then need to proceed to the second level of the due process inquiry. This means that the court will itself have to determine the accuracy and lawfulness of the detentions, employing the procedures it has already determined are required as part of its first-level due process analysis.

Of course, if the first-level decision that the executive's method of detaining an individual has failed to satisfy due process has finally been made at the appellate level, this second-level inquiry will not be conducted in the first instance by the appellate court itself. The initial inquiry will instead be conducted by the trial court on remand. However, it is important to keep in mind that whatever court makes the second-level inquiry into the specific facts of the individual case, its processes will have to satisfy the constitutionally established requirements of adjudicatory neutrality.[168]

REJECTION OF SCHOLARLY ARGUMENTS FOR THE SUPERIORITY OF THE SUSPENSION CLAUSE

The Argument from Original Understanding

Professor Amanda Tyler has argued that the Suspension Clause supersedes the Due Process Clause, rather than the other way around. In her view, suspension of habeas corpus "does not simply remove a judicial remedy but 'suspends' the rights that find meaning and protection in the Great Writ."[169] Indeed, she argues that the "very purpose of suspension" is to allow Congress to override core due process safeguards to enable the executive to combat a national crisis effectively.[170] Suspension thus operates as an "on/off" switch for individual due process rights "and possibly other portions of the Constitution as well."[171] Remedies other than habeas corpus remain available to address collateral claims, but the courts cannot use any of these remedies to order the discharge of the detainee.[172]

Tyler and David Shapiro (who has fashioned a similar argument) base their case on the historically "coextensive" relationship between the writ of habeas corpus and Magna Carta.[173] After the writ of habeas corpus became the primary vehicle for the enforcement of the due process rights embodied by Magna Carta, contemporary English legal scholars began to equate the right to be free from unlawful detention with the central role of habeas corpus in guaranteeing that right.[174] Tyler and Shapiro note that the Framers drew their understanding of the writ, and its relationship to due process, from their knowledge of the work of English scholars such as Blackstone and Coke, as well as their first-hand experience with suspensions prior to the Philadelphia Convention.[175] Thus, Tyler and Shapiro assume, the Framers presumably intended to insert the English understanding of the inextricable link between habeas corpus and due process of law into the American Constitution.[176] The fact that the Due Process Clause was added in an amendment does not, Tyler and Shapiro assert, undermine their argument in the slightest. In Tyler's words, "[t]o be sure, the Bill of Rights, with its Due Process Clause, was not part of the original constitutional text; there was, all the same, widespread understanding that it would be added shortly following ratification."[177]

This reasoning is flawed to say the least. Mystifyingly, it chooses, turning constitutional interpretation on its head, to ignore an unambiguous textual directive—namely, that the guarantee of due process applies in all contexts and situations—in favor of some vague and wholly unsupported assertion of original intent. Instead of accepting the natural implication of orderly modes of interpretation that an unambiguous amendment necessarily trumps inconsistent provisions in the body of the Constitution[178]—Tyler and Shapiro actually reverse the relationship. Under their analysis, the body of the text is somehow thought to supersede that inconsistent amendment.

Even if Tyler or Shapiro were to point to some supporting documentation of this counterintuitive inversion (which they do not), the argument would still be ineffective in altering the inescapable implications of the traditionally accepted mode of interpretation. External expressions of intent may not operate as contradicting codicils to otherwise unambiguous constitutional text. It was, after all, the text, not the unstated codicil, that was ratified. Thus, no credence should be given to an originalist argument that seeks to divine what the Framers "intended" to accomplish by including a limited suspension power in the original Constitution and later amending the document to include an unequivocal guarantee that no person can be imprisoned without "due process of law." Privileging unstated "original intent" over the unambiguous text makes no sense.

Finally, purely as a doctrinal matter, Tyler and Shapiro ignore the well-established judicial holding that the Due Process Clause serves as a check on otherwise authorized congressional power to limit federal court jurisdiction.[179] This is so, even though—as in the case of the Suspension Clause—enactment of Article III and the Fifth Amendment's Due Process Clause occurred relatively closely in time. Indeed, no court has even considered, much less accepted, such a line of argument. It is simply too late in the day to argue that the Due Process Clause is incapable of modifying the Constitution's original text on the grounds that it was widely understood at the time of ratification that a due process clause would soon be adopted. As an amendment, the Due Process Clause trumps inconsistent text.

Did the Framers foresee the irrevocable conflict between the Suspension and Due Process Clauses? It does not appear that they devoted sufficient attention to the text or the meaning of the Due Process Clause to anticipate the issue.[180] But it is clear that the initial decision to recognize a suspension power was a controversial one,[181] so much so that three state delegations dissented from ever permitting Congress to suspend the writ.[182] It is also clear that the Framers defined "tyranny" as the accumulation of power by a single person or branch of government,[183] and that they consciously chose to institutionalize prophylactic methods for controlling government and preventing the accretion of power by any single branch.[184] Finally, we also know that James Madison declared that the "great object" of the Bill of Rights was to "limit and qualify the powers of Government."[185] Thus, even though they probably never expressly contemplated the argument that the Due Process Clause supersedes the suspension power, it seems clear that the Framers were moving towards that very conclusion.

Challenge to the Suspension of Habeas as a Substitute for Individual Due Process

Professor Tyler offers an additional argument to support her position by suggesting that the requirements of due process can be satisfied during a suspension by allowing detainees to challenge the validity of the suspension legislation itself.[186] Much like her other arguments, however, this contention fails to justify an abandonment of the individual due process guarantee, because it fails to satisfy the specific interests sought to be protected by that guarantee. At the outset, it should be emphasized that her contention is wholly inconsistent with the very concept of suspension: if the writ of habeas corpus has been suspended, by what procedural avenue might a detainee obtain judicial relief in order to challenge the validity of the suspension itself? The whole point of the suspension was, presumably, to preclude such review. More important, Tyler's argument ignores the explicit text of the Fifth Amendment, which confers a right to due process of law upon each individual "person" who has been deprived of his or her "life, liberty, or property."[187] The Court has never suggested that a detainee's individual due process rights can be satisfied by judgment in a case to which she was not a party, in which she did not have the opportunity to defend her own interests and, indeed, which was not even about her.[188] It is certainly conceivable that although the suspension might be found as a general matter to satisfy the constitutional standard imposed by Article I, section 9, the individual detainee in question might nevertheless have been improperly, maliciously, or incorrectly taken into custody. This could be due to either a simple mistake by the arresting authority or the executive's ulterior political motivation in seeking to imprison an opponent. Review of the generic validity of the suspension itself, in such situations, would hardly satisfy the Fifth Amendment's requirement of due process *for the individual detainee.*

CONCLUSION

The questions addressed in this chapter cut to the very core of the principles of democratic government. The Framers chose to adopt a written Constitution in order to restrain democratic government within a set of carefully delineated boundaries as a means of ensuring that it would not be able to arbitrarily employ its power to repress the very individuals to whom it is accountable.[189] The writ of habeas corpus has historically served as the primary check on executive power by ensuring that all individuals imprisoned by the government receive due process of law. Yet to this point, scholars and the Court seem to have agreed unanimously that suspension effectively removes all judicial oversight over exercises of the executive detention power, at least while they are taking place. It is mystifying that all involved to this point have been so willing to risk the foundations of democratic government by trusting the executive, historically considered to be the branch of government most susceptible to tyranny, given that the president, as commander in chief, has full control of the nation's military.

Exercise of the suspension power inevitably confers upon the president an unchecked power to suppress minority groups and political opponents, or whomever else, in the exercise of her whim, she chooses to suppress. It is impossible to reconcile the exercise of such unrestrained and unchecked authoritarian power with the nation's constitutional commitment to the rule of law and steadfast aversion to tyranny. Therefore, in order to preserve the foundations of American constitutionalism—the system that guarantees continuation of democratic government—the Suspension Clause must be viewed as limited by the Due Process Clause and superseded insofar as the two provisions are found to be inconsistent. This is a conclusion, moreover, that follows from application of long-accepted and -applied precepts of textual construction. To conclude otherwise would not only imperil individual and minority rights; it would also pose a grave danger to the foundational elements of our constitutional structure.

Conclusion

The American constitutional system is a paradox on multiple levels. It is paradoxical in both its theoretical foundation and its mode of implementing its values. Its theoretical foundation proceeds on an assumption of what I have called throughout this book "skeptical optimism"—the simultaneous belief in both the possibilities of human flourishing and the dangers of the dark side of the human psyche. In a manner characteristic of the Framers' pragmatic approach to the art of politics, they chose to foster the benefits of the former and deter the harms of the latter by means of a delicately structured form of constitutional democracy.

That those who framed our Constitution intended to establish just such a structure is conclusively evidenced by the very nature of the document they promulgated. Unlike its British predecessor, it is in written form; it is framed in unambiguously mandatory, rather than merely hortatory, language; and it can be altered only by a complex process of supermajoritarian approval. It does not follow that there should be only one conceivable interpretation of the often ambiguous language included in the document's various provisions—one grounded in a so-called originalist understanding of the words at the time of ratification. It merely means, rather, that any appeal to or binding directive premised on the countermajoritarian force of the Constitution must be grounded ultimately in a linguistically plausible construction of the words contained in the document itself, disciplined by considerations of principled interpretive analysis.

Equally essential to the constitutional plan is the vesting of ultimate interpretive and enforcement power in a judiciary that is prophylactically insulated from majoritarian political pressure. Indeed, the primary lesson of American constitutionalism is that absent the vesting of ultimate inter-pretive and enforcement power in a judiciary prophylactically insulated from the bulk of political pressures, the very idea of an effective counter-majoritarian constitution is a nullity or, even worse, a cynical deception.

Although a number of respected scholars strongly differ with this model of American constitutionalism (for seriously flawed reasons, as explained in chapter 1), it is probably safe to say that the overwhelming majority of constitutional scholars simply assume the correctness of this traditionalist model of the nation's constitutional system. But when one considers the implications of this formalist traditional model for specific issues of judicial independence, the issues become far more controversial.

The first task one must undertake in grasping the proper implications of the formalist traditional model of American constitutionalism for specific issues of judicial independence is to create a taxonomy of judicial indepen-dence, much as chapter 2 has done. In understanding the delicate balance between democracy and countermajoritarianism, it is appropriate to recog-nize five conceivable versions of judicial independence: (1) institutional, (2) countermajoritarian, (3) decisional, (4) lawmaking, and (5) judgmental.

Institutional independence refers to the prophylactic protections of sal-ary and tenure included in Article III. While for the most part it should be relatively simple to understand the operation of these protections, situa-tions may arise in which their outer limits are tested. For example, what if Congress were to reduce, not judicial salaries, but judicial support services? What if, in open retaliation for an unpopular judicial decision, Congress were to deny federal judges an increase in salary? While this book places great weight on the value of judicial independence, in certain instances the rigid terms of Article III might well be regarded as authorizing threats to it. Countermajoritarian independence refers to the ultimate authority of the judiciary to interpret and enforce the provisions of the counterma-joritarian Constitution. If the formal traditionalist model of American constitutionalism is not to be rendered a sham, countermajoritarian inde-pendence must be preserved in all instances. Such independence may be rationalized on two levels, which are not mutually exclusive: the macro level, pursuant to which the systemic need for countermajoritarian lim-its on the political branches logically dictates such independence, and the micro level, where purely as a matter of core notions of procedural due process, the need exists for an independent judiciary to check the majori-tarian branches and preserve individual constitutional rights.

Decisional independence refers to the sanctity of the judiciary's ability to decide individual suits, free from control or usurpation by the political branches. It is important to emphasize that decisional independence is not confined to the resolution of substantive constitutional issues. Decisional independence should not be confused with countermajoritarian independence. Rather, decisional independence flows from the constitutional commitment to separation of powers, which vests "the judicial power" exclusively in the judicial branch. Normatively, this form of independence is rationalized as a means of averting an abuse of the judiciary's legitimacy in the eyes of the populace and political manipulation of the judicial function.

Lawmaking independence stands in stark contrast to decisional independence, and the two should never be confused. While decisional independence refers to the ability of the judiciary to resolve individual cases, lawmaking independence refers to the ability to fashion generally applicable law. Because of their formal insulation from the democratic process, the courts have no preemptive power to fashion generally applicable subconstitutional law. In theory, the courts may develop common law interstitially in order to resolve cases where no other applicable law exists, though for the most part the federal courts have been legislatively denied this authority by congressional enactment of the Rules of Decision Act. But even where the courts possess such interstitial lawmaking power, it may be trumped by enactment of controlling legislation, as with any such power. Properly understood, judicial independence should not be understood to vest in the federal courts an ability to trump the legislative process for no reason other than disagreement with the policies embodied in the statute in question.

Judgmental independence in some ways involves a balance between the decisional and lawmaking varieties of judicial independence. It involves the insulation of final judgments from post-judgment legislative alteration. The Supreme Court has chosen to treat judgmental independence the exact same way it treats decisional independence, but there are arguably important differences between the two. While the courts clearly have the exclusive province to decide individual cases before them, the fact remains that it is the task of the political branches to make generally applicable policy choices. In the case of a breach of judgmental independence, the political branches alter (or reject) the understanding of controlling generally applicable law adopted by the courts in individual suits, and seek to open the final judgments of those courts in order to implement the revised or proper understanding of controlling law. Absent any due process issues related to the retroactivity of the legislative policy choice, it is not immediately clear why the political branches' control over generally applicable policy choices does not trump the courts' decisional independence. Of course, in the case of constitutionally grounded decisions, principles of countermajoritarian independence would logically render moot any such questions.

Troubling questions exist surrounding the tension between the institutional independence granted the federal courts by Article III's guarantees of salary and tenure, on the one hand, and the need to discipline federal judges in appropriate circumstances, on the other. In particular, how one blends the institutional guarantee of life tenure with the safety valves provided in the Constitution for removal of federal judges gives rise to troubling issues of judicial independence. Potentially, two alternative standards for removing federal judges from office exist: the "good behavior" language of Article III and the impeachment power provided for in Article IV for the removal of "civil officers" for committing high crimes and misdemeanors. While respected scholars have argued that these two provisions should be construed to provide alternative means of removal, it would be extremely dangerous to view the vague terms of the "good behavior" clause as anything more than a cross-reference to the impeachment power. Any other view would seriously threaten the very institutional independence so essential to the formal traditionalist model of American constitutionalism. Indeed, it is my belief that because of the centrality of institutional independence, the impeachment power should be given an especially narrow construction in the case of the impeachment of federal judges. Under no circumstances should impeachment be permitted solely because of legislative disagreement with the merits of individual judicial decisions.

The institutional protections of judicial independence apply explicitly only to the federal courts. While state courts are both empowered and obligated to enforce federal law (both constitutional and statutory), their judges have never been thought to be protected by Article III's guarantee of lifetime tenure. Indeed, judicial retention elections are commonplace. But while Article III of the Constitution does not apply to state courts, the Due Process Clause of the Fourteenth Amendment most certainly does. And by guaranteeing a neutral adjudicator, that provision mandates not only the appearance but the reality of fairness. Indeed, absent a truly neutral adjudicator, no other element of procedural due process really matters. The question that should arise (but for the most part has not) is whether a judiciary necessarily concerned about the need for majoritarian approval for its retention through the electoral process could ever be considered truly neutral. It is true, of course, that the electorate will not be concerned with the outcome of most individual litigations. But it is impossible *ex ante* to determine which cases will interest the electorate and which will not. On a more systemic level, requiring the judiciary to be accountable to the electorate effectively turns American constitutionalism on its head. While certain modern scholarly theories—for example, "popular constitutional-ism" and "departmentalism"—advocate majoritarian interpretation and enforcement of the countermajoritarian Constitution, that most clearly was not the plan of those who framed it, nor does it make any sense when one recognizes the vital role of the Constitution as a check on majoritar-ian excesses and abuses. Therefore as shocking as it may sound to many, the inexorable logical conclusion, given the structure of American con-stitutionalism, is that methods of majoritarian retention of state judges (whether by electoral or political means) must be held unconstitutional. State courts are both empowered and bound by the Supremacy Clause to enforce and interpret the nation's Constitution. They therefore must be subject to the dictates of judicial independence dictated by that document.

Paradoxically, it is the prophylactically independent judiciary that is best positioned to ensure that the majoritarian branches remain account-able to the majority that elected them. It accomplishes this by policing legislative action to prevent governmental deception. Such deception can be achieved by having the applicable substantive law provide for x while simultaneously or subsequently transforming the underlying DNA of that law through procedural or evidentiary modification. When the dust settles in such a situation, the electorate has effectively been deceived as to what the lawmaking process has actually implemented, thereby undermining its ability to hold its chosen representatives accountable. Of course, there will be many legislative choices that will not be of concern to the overwhelm-ing majority of the electorate. But there will be a number of important situations where this will not be the case, and it will be impossible *ex ante* to separate the one category of legislation from the other. Therefore it is necessary, as a matter of separation of powers, to prevent the legislative branch from conscripting the judicial branch as a co-conspirator in the deception of the electorate. And it is because of the judiciary's insulation from the majoritarian branches of government that we can trust the judi-ciary to police practices of legislative deception.

One seemingly glaring exception to the Constitution's use of a pro-phylactically insulated judiciary to police the majoritarian branches' adher-ence to the document's countermajoritarian dictates is the rarely invoked Suspension Clause, contained within the constitutional guarantee of habeas corpus in Article I, section 9. In the abstract, habeas corpus is one of the cornerstones of the judiciary's authority to check the majoritarian branches, thereby preventing tyrannical rule. Absent habeas corpus, nothing would legally prevent those in power from arresting individuals for reasons of whim, prejudice, or malevolence and throwing away the key. Yet under the Suspension Clause, the majoritarian branches of government have the power to suspend the writ in the presence of extreme circumstances such as revolution or invasion—and it is by no means clear that the judiciary possesses the power to overrule either the governmental conclusion that such circumstances ever existed or, if they did, the conclusion that they continue to exist.

The text of the Constitution is unambiguous about the existence of such governmental power. But at the time of the document's original enactment, those who framed it appear not to have fully grasped the foundational need for an insulated judiciary to serve as a check on the majoritarian branches. This failure appears to have been corrected, however, by subsequent enactment of the Bill of Rights, which in Amendment V guaranteed that individuals may be deprived of neither life, liberty, nor property without due process of law. When habeas corpus has been suspended as a means of judicially checking governmental arrest, there is *no* process, and that cannot rationally be defined as "due process." Therefore the Fifth Amendment must be construed as a revocation of the Article I, section 9's Suspension Clause, because the two simply cannot be reconciled. To underscore the point, imagine a case in which the president has been legislatively authorized to summarily arrest all citizens of Irish descent. Moreover, the authorizing legislation has suspended habeas corpus on the grounds of a serious internal threat to national safety. When those arrested seek judicial relief to enforce their constitutional rights of due process and equal protection, the judiciary declines to provide it on the grounds that its authority has been legislatively revoked. It is difficult to imagine a starker example of tyrannical government—hardly consistent with the constitutional dictates of the Due Process Clause or the foundational precepts of American constitutionalism.

The form of constitutionalism embodied in the American Constitution was truly unique at the time of the nation's founding. It represented a dramatic breakthrough in political thought—a form of streetwise pragmatism as political theory. It represented a carefully structured balance of the Framers' recognition of both the best and worst in human nature. And, despite its ups and downs over the past two hundred plus years, it has managed to continue to perform its intended function with general effectiveness. The republic does, after all, still stand. But modern doctrine has too often failed to recognize the full implications of American constitutionalism for the nature and extent of judicial independence. To be sure, at first glance judicial independence appears inconsistent with the nation's commitment to democracy, where basic policy choices are made by those representative of and accountable to the electorate. But more careful understanding of the complexities of our system demonstrates that, paradoxically, vigorous protection of judicial insulation from the electorate is essential to the continued effective functioning of the democratic process. Only by recognition of this inherent paradox and understanding of its important implications for the need to expand current protections of modern judicial independence can we be assured that the genius of American constitutionalism will survive for the next two hundred years and beyond.

Notes

INTRODUCTION

1. Henry Steele Commager, Introduction to Andrew C. McLaughlin, Foundations of American Constitutionalism vii (1961).

2. *Id.*

3. U.S. Const. Art. V.

4. *See, e.g.*, Paul Brest, The Misconceived Quest for the Original Understanding, 60 B.U.L. Rev. 204 (1980).

5. *See, e.g.*, Bruce A. Ackerman, We the People, vol. 1: Foundations (1991).

6. *See generally* Martin H. Redish, The Adversary First Amendment (2013).

7. *See* Vincent Blasi, The Pathological Perspective and the First Amendment, 85 Colum. L. Rev. 449 (1985).

8. *See Federalist* No. 79 (Hamilton).

9. Tumey v. Ohio, 273 U.S. 510 (1927).

10. 556 U.S. 868 (2009).

11. *See* chapter 2 *infra*.

12. 80 U.S. (13 Wall.) 128 (1871).

CHAPTER ONE

1. Chapter 1 derives from Premodern Constitutionalism, an article I coauthored with Matthew Heins, published in 2016 in the William & Mary Law Review. © 2016 by the *William & Mary Law Review*. Reproduced with permission of the publisher.

2. *See, e.g.*, Bruce Ackerman, We the People, vol. 3: The Civil Rights Revolution (2014) [hereafter Ackerman, The Civil Rights Revolution], asserting that the American people have "amended" the Constitution by popular movement (outside of Article V) numerous times, and that the American Constitution is more than merely the document itself, and Ernest A. Young, The Constitution Outside the Constitution, 117 Yale L.J. 408, 454 (2007), arguing that there exists an "extraca-

nonical Constitution" in the United States. *See also, e.g.*, Michael Stokes Paulsen, The Most Dangerous Branch: Executive Power to Say What the Law Is, 83 Geo. L.J. 217 (1994), claiming that the "coordinacy" of the three branches of government envisioned by the Framers and enshrined in the Constitution forbids judicial supremacy and allows the executive to exercise final interpretive power; Larry D. Kramer, The People Themselves (2004), arguing that the Constitution does not necessarily vest the judiciary with interpretive authority, and that because it is an undemocratic institution, interpretive power should be transferred to "the people."

3. *See* Steven C. Bourassa, Postmodernism in Architecture and Planning: What Kind of Style? 6 J. Architectural & Planning Research 289, 294 (1989).

4. *Id.* at 293; *see* Jürgen Habermas, Modernity versus Postmodernity, 22 New German Critique 3, 4 (1981).

5. *See* Robert Maxwell, Modern Architecture after Modernism, 2 Architecture N.Y. 36, 36–37 (1993).

6. U.S. Const. Amend. III: "No Soldier shall, in time of peace be quartered in any house, without the consent of the Owner, nor in time of war, but in a manner to be prescribed by law."

7. U.S. Const. Art. I § 9 cl. 8: "No Title of Nobility shall be granted by the United States: And no Person holding any Office of Profit or Trust under them, shall, without the Consent of the Congress, accept of any present, Emolument, Office, or Title, of any kind whatever, from any King, Prince, or foreign State."

8. *See* Paulsen, *supra* note 2.

9. *See* Sanford Levinson, Our Undemocratic Constitution (2008); Mark Tushnet, Taking the Constitution away from the Courts 26 (1999).

10. Martin H. Redish & Matthew B. Arnould, Judicial Review, Constitutional Interpretation, and the Democratic Dilemma: Proposing a "Controlled Activism" Alternative, 64 Fla. L. Rev. 1485, 1491, 1495 (2012) (expounding upon the variety of archaeological difficulties that confront each different type of originalist method of interpretation).

11. John McGinnis and Michael Rappaport have persuasively argued that the basic character of the American constitution is "supermajoritarian." *See* John O. McGinnis & Michael B. Rappaport, Our Supermajoritarian Constitution, 80 Tex. L. Rev. 703, 710 (2002).

12. *See* Bourassa, *supra* note 3, at 295, quoting Brent Brolin, The Failure of Modern Architecture 7 (1980): "Modernists' 'indifference—indeed hostility—to harmonious continuity comes from the modernists' violent denunciation of derivative architectural forms.' Today, an eclectic permissiveness prevails with respect to historic form and ornament. [Postmodern architects] appreciate the symbolic function of architecture and the symbolism of historic forms and ornamentation."

13. Here it should be noted that the British "unwritten constitution" is not, in fact, unwritten. Rather, it is a collection of laws and pronouncements like Magna Carta and the Human Rights Act of 1998 that the country views as elements of its constitution. *See* David S. Law & Mila Versteeg, The Evolution and Ideology of Global Constitutionalism, 99 Calif. L. Rev. 1163, 1188 (2011). By "unwritten," then, is meant the absence of a formal single document.

14. Herman Belz, The Constitution in the Gilded Age: The Beginnings of Constitutional Realism in American Scholarship, 13 Am. J. Legal Hist. 110, 114 (1969): "J. Franklin Jameson, in the preface to a book of essays dealing with constitutional developments in the confederation period, stated that many educated persons 'think of our Constitution as having sprung full-armed from the heads of Olympian conventioneers.'"

15. Herman Eduard von Holst, The Constitutional and Political History of the United States 1: 62–63 (1876).

16. Belz, *supra* note 14, at 114: "Explaining that the charters of English trading companies were the embryo of American constitutions, [Brooks] Adams concluded, 'Americans are subject to the same general laws that regulate the rest of mankind; and accordingly . . . they have worked out their destiny slowly and painfully, . . . and . . . far from cutting the knot of their difficulties by a stroke of inventive genius, they earned their success by clinging tenaciously to what they had.'"

17. Alexander Johnston, The First Century of the Constitution, 4 New Princeton Rev. 175, 176–78, 186–87 (1887).

18. *See, e.g., Federalist* Nos. 48 and 49 (Madison). *See also* McGinnis & Rappaport, *supra* note 11, at 722 (advancing an originalist argument that supermajoritarian governance was a uniquely American creation devised to avoid tyranny).

19. Traditionalism, it should be emphasized, should not be deemed synonymous with originalism, nor does espousal of a traditionalist view of the Constitution's animating principles necessitates originalist interpretation. *But see* Steven E. Sachs, Originalism as a Theory of Legal Change, 38 Harv. J. L. Pub. Pol'y (2015). One need not rely on the original meaning of the Constitution's text or the original intent of the Framers to demonstrate that countermajoritarianism is the core element of our constitutional regime; instead, the structural Constitution is itself proof positive of the countermajoritarian principle at its heart.

20. *See* discussion *infra* at 27–36.

21. *See* discussion *infra* at 36–47.

22. *See, e.g.,* Bowers v. Hardwick, 478 U.S. 186 (1986) (upholding the constitutionality of same-sex sodomy laws); Korematsu v. United States, 323 U.S. 214 (1944) (upholding the constitutionality of imprisoning persons of Japanese descent in internment camps during the Second World War); Plessy v. Ferguson, 163 U.S. 537 (1896) (upholding the constitutionality of state laws mandating racial segregation).

23. *See, e.g.,* Levinson, *supra* note 9; H. Jefferson Powell, A Community Built on Words (2002); Martin H. Redish, The Constitution as Political Structure (1995).

24. *Compare* Redish, *supra* note 23 *and* Martin H. Redish & Elizabeth J. Cisar, "If Angels Were to Govern": The Need for Pragmatic Formalism in Separation of Powers Theory, 41 Duke L.J. 449 (1991); Gary Lawson, In Praise of Woodenness, 11 Geo. Mason U. L. Rev. 21 (1988) (all advocating various degrees of formalism) *with* Jesse H. Choper, Judicial Review and the National Political Process: A Functional Reconsideration of the Role of the Supreme Court (1980) *and* Michael J. Perry, The Constitution, the Courts and Human Rights: An Inquiry into the Legitimacy of Constitutional Policymaking by the Judiciary (1982) (both championing functionalism).

25. *See* Richard R. Johnson, "Parliamentary Egotisms": The Clash of Legislatures in the Making of the American Revolution, 74 J. Am. Hist. 338, 339 (1987). Johnson explains that the taught version of American history is not per se wrong to blame King George, but it also fundamentally misses the point, insofar as the only reason the monarch moved the needle was that Parliament acquiesced in his exercise of power and was constitutionally incapable of checking either itself or the monarch. *Id.* at 342.

26. *See* Johnson, *supra* note 25, at 343: "There remained a tradition of belief in a fundamental law that placed limits on the exercise of arbitrary power by any branch of government, a tradition that was to find a receptive audience—and, eventually, a permanent home—in the American colonies. In England, however, political theory and reality moved in tandem toward a magnification of parliamentary power. The Glorious Revolution of 1688 confirmed Parliament's power as guardian and interpreter of the ancient constitution."

27. *See Federalist* No. 78 (Hamilton) (describing a Constitution of limited government); *Federalist* No. 48 (Madison) (arguing for structural checks to ensure limits on executive and legislative power).

28. *See* Daniel A. Farber, Judicial Review and Its Alternatives: An American Tale, 38 Wake Forest L. Rev. 415, 415 (2003).

29. *See Federalist* No. 51 (Madison) (expounding upon the structure of checks and balancing that would come to define our constitutional structure).

30. *See Federalist* No. 48 (Madison) (claiming that "assembling all power in the same hands" "must lead to . . . tyranny"); *Federalist* No. 62 (Madison) (describing "the propensity of all single and numerous assemblies to yield to the impulse of sudden and violent passions, and to be seduced by factious leaders into intemperate and pernicious resolutions").

31. Larry Cata Backer, From Constitution to Constitutionalism: A Global Framework for Legitimate Public Power Systems, 113 Penn. St. L. Rev. 671, 679-80 (2009) (defining constitutionalism as "(1) a system of classification, (2) the core object of which is to define the characteristics of constitutions (those documents organizing political power within an institutional apparatus), (3) to be used to determine the legitimacy of the constitutional system as conceived or as implemented, (4) based on rule of law as the fundamental postulate of government (that government be established and operated in a way that limits the ability of individuals to use government power for personal welfare maximizing ends), and (5) grounded on a metric of substantive values derived from a source beyond the control of any individual.")

32. For reasons to be explained later, constitutions that do not formally provide a countermajoritarian check to majoritarian power by way of a politically unaccountable judiciary are more likely to devolve into illegitimacy. But even nations that do not employ this system of constitutionalism can operate legitimate constitutional governance, even if it is not "constitutional" in the American sense of the word.

33. *See, e.g.,* David S. Law & Versteeg, The Declining Influence of the United States Constitution, 87 N.Y.U. L. Rev. 762 (2012); Law & Versteeg, *supra* note 13, at 1188 (in an empirical study, counting as constitutionalist any regime with written law that could be designated "constitutional," including both legal con-

stitutionalist regimes like the United States and diffuse political constitutionalist regimes like the United Kingdom).

34. John Ferejohn & Lawrence Sager, Commitment and Constitutionalism, 81 Tex. L. Rev. 1929, 1929 (2003).

35. David S. Law, The Paradox of Omnipotence: Courts, Constitutions, and Commitments, 40 Ga. L. Rev. 407, 416 (2006). *See also* Frank Michelman, What Do Constitutions Do That Statutes Don't (Legally Speaking)? *in* The Least Examined Branch: The Role of Legislatures in the Constitutional State 273 (Richard Baumann & Tsvi Kahana, eds., 2006) (arguing that even systems with written constitutions invariably rely on unwritten constitutions to find their rules of recognition).

36. Robin West, Katrina, the Constitution and The Legal Question Doctrine, 81 Chi.-Kent L. Rev. 1127, 1128–29 (2006): constitutionalism "should be understood as entailing that states are obligated to ensure that all citizens enjoy those basic capabilities necessary to lead a decent life."

37. *See* Law & Versteeg, *supra* note 33, at 873.

38. *See* Vasiliy A. Vlasihin, Political Rights and Freedoms in the Context of American Constitutionalism: A View of a Concerned Soviet Scholar, 84 Nw. U. L. Rev. 257, 258 (1989): "Making up the core of [American] constitutionalism are the ideas of 'popular sovereignty' and a social contract as the source of the government; the principles of republicanism, federalism, separation of powers, and government limited by law; respect for the rights and liberties of citizens and the protection of private property; the rule of law and the supremacy of the Constitution; and independence of the judiciary and judicial review."

39. *Federalist* No. 78 (Hamilton): "[Judicial review] is an excellent barrier to the despotism of the prince; in a republic it is no less excellent barrier to the encroachments and oppressions of the representative body. . . . [T]he courts of justice are to be considered as the bulwarks of a limited Constitution against legislative encroachments."

40. U.S. Const. Art. III § 2.

41. Some have argued that just by setting forth both a Bill of Rights and an article devoted to establishing a judiciary, the Constitution implicitly established judicial review for the primary purpose of rights enforcement. *See* Frank B. Cross, Institutions and Enforcement of the Bill of Rights, 85 Cornell L. Rev. 1529, 1534–35 (2000).

42. U.S. Const. Amend. V; U.S. Const. Amend. XIV.

43. *See* Martin H. Redish & Lawrence Marshall, Adjudicatory Independence and the Values of Procedural Due Process, 95 Yale L.J. 455 (1986).

44. U.S. Const. Art. VI cl. 2.

45. *See* Herbert Wechsler, Toward Neutral Principles of Constitutional Law, 73 Harv. L. Rev. 1, 4–5 (1959).

46. *Id.* at 5.

47. *See Federalist* No. 78 (Hamilton).

48. *See Federalist* No. 10 (Madison).

49. Prophylaxis need not necessarily be activist. *See* John F. Manning, The Supreme Court 2013 Term—Foreword: The Means of Constitutional Power, 128 Harv. L. Rev. 1 (2014). Professor Manning argues that the Constitution cre-

ates a sort of deference regime in favor of congressional interpretation. He says the Constitution affords great discretion to Congress to do what is "necessary and proper" to effectuate its delegated power, so the courts should not step in to police the boundaries of congressional power unless Congress has applied a "clearly violative" interpretation of necessary and proper. This may or may not be right, but even if it is assumed to be correct, Professor Manning's approach still charges the judiciary with the duty to determine when another branch's interpretation is "clearly violative" of the Constitution. Thus, whether or not the judiciary is deferential to congressional or executive interpretation, even a deference regime necessarily implies that the judiciary retains the last word on issues of constitutional interpretation.

50. *See* Ackerman, The Civil Rights Revolution, *supra* note 2; Young, *supra* note 2.

51. *See* Paulsen, *supra* note 2; Kramer, *supra* note 2; Tushnet, *supra* note 9.

52. *See* discussion *supra* at 20–26.

53. See Jack N. Rakove, The Super-Legality of the Constitution, or, a Federalist Critique of Bruce Ackerman's Neo-Federalism, 108 Yale L.J. 1931 (1999): "Fixated as [Madison] was on the belief that the interested, opinionated, and impassioned impulses of the people would be the preponderant sources of constitutional disequilibria, the last possibility that he wanted to contemplate was that the people would ever be called upon to speak so vigorously again. In the womb of time, no one could predict what future decades, generations, or centuries would produce; but to the extent that Madison gazed into the future, he seemed to hope that all future constitutional change would occur within the exclusio alterius of Article V."

54. Von Holst, *supra* note 15, at 63–64.

55. Frederick Grimke, Considerations upon the Nature and Tendency of Free Institutions, 123 (1856). *See* Belz, *supra* note 14, at 111.

56. Karl N. Llewellyn, The Constitution as an Institution, 34 Colum. L. Rev. 1 (1934).

57. *Id.* at 12.

58. *Cf.* Paul Brest, The Misconceived Quest for Original Understanding, 60 B.U. L. Rev. 204, 225 (1980) (voicing the political scientist's view of constitutionalism writ large, that despite the Supremacy Clause's declaration that the Constitution is supreme law, "it is only through a history of continuing assent or acquiescence that the document could become law," and our constitutional tradition is not concerned "with the document alone").

59. Llewellyn, *supra* note 56, at 17–18.

60. *See* U.S. Const. Art. V.

61. In other words, the last time that the United States implemented dramatic social or federal governmental change by way of the Article V amendment process was the period from 1865 to 1870, through the Thirteenth, Fourteenth, and Fifteenth Amendments.}

62. U.S. Const. Amend. XVI.

63. U.S. Const. Amend. XVII.

64. U.S. Const. Amend. XIX.

65. U.S. Const. Amend. XVIII.

66. U.S. Const. Amend. XXI.

67. U.S. Const. Amend. XX.

68. U.S. Const. Amend. XXII.

69. U.S. Const. Amend. XXIII.

70. U.S. Const. Amend. XXV.

71. *See, e.g.*, Voting Rights Act, 42 U.S.C. § 1973; Civil Rights Act of 1964, 42 U.S.C. § 2000.

72. *See, e.g.*, UN General Assembly, Universal Declaration of Human Rights, 217 A (III) (Dec. 10, 1948), http://www.refworld.org/docid/3ae6b3712c.html (last visited Aug. 6, 2016).

73. *See, e.g.*, Lawrence v. Texas, 539 U.S. 558 (2003) (applying rational basis review but nonetheless determining that sodomy laws violate the Fourteenth Amendment's guarantee of equal protection); Griswold v. Connecticut, 381 U.S. 479 (1965) (holding that the Constitution protects an individual's right to privacy); Brown v. Bd. of Ed. of Topeka, 347 U.S. 483 (1954) (holding that public school segregation violates equal protection).

74. *See generally* Thomas W. Merrill & Kathryn T. Watts, Agency Rules with the Force of Law: The Original Convention, 116 Harv. L. Rev. 467 (2002).

75. This is not uniformly true, inasmuch as the Nineteenth, Twenty-fourth, and even the Twenty-sixth Amendments each arguably served to enshrine new individual rights or civil liberties. Yet even these amendments are illustrative: Certainly the Civil Rights Act of 1964 did more for the rights of African Americans than did the Twenty-fourth Amendment, and although the Nineteenth Amendment provided for women's suffrage, the Equal Rights Amendment never quite made the cut. Ultimately, most advances in minority rights over the last 150 years occurred outside of Article V amendment.

76. *See* Bruce Ackerman, 1 We the People: Foundations (1991).

77. *See, e.g.*, Young, *supra* note 2; Matthew S. R. Palmer, Using Constitutional Realism to Identify the Complete Constitution: Lessons from an Unwritten Constitution, 54 Am. J. Comp. L. 587 (2006); Ackerman, The Civil Rights Revolution, *supra* note 2.

78. Todd E. Pettys, The Myth of the Written Constitution, 84 Notre Dame L. Rev. 991, 1001–02 (2009).

79. Ackerman, The Civil Rights Revolution, *supra* note 2, at 14.

80. Bruce Ackerman, 2 We the People: Transformations (1998).

81. *Id.* at 115.

82. Ackerman, The Civil Rights Revolution, *supra* note 2, at 127.

83. *Id.* at 34.

84. Young, *supra* note 2, at 454.

85. *Id.*

86. *Id.*

87. *Id.*

88. Professors McGinnis and Rappaport argue that the requirement of bicameralism and presentment is itself a tool of supermajoritarian rulemaking. *See* McGinnis & Rappaport, *supra* note 11, at 712, 770–73. It may be true that the requirement of bicameralism and presentment require more than a straight up-or-down democratic vote, but to the extent that supermajoritarian effort is needed to enact

ordinary legislation, it is of an altogether different character from the superma-joritarian movement necessary to amend the entrenched written Constitution and thereby safeguard a rule against easy repeal or revision.

89. Indeed, Professors Ackerman and Pettys have argued as much. *See* Acker-man, *supra* note 2, at 37; Pettys, *supra* note 78, at 1001–02; *supra* notes 78–83 and accompanying text.

90. Shelby County, Ala. v. Holder, 570 U.S., 133 S. Ct. 2612, 2630–31 (2013).

91. *See* Paul Horwitz, Honor's Constitutional Moment: The Oath and Presi-dential Transitions, 103 Nw. U. L. Rev. 1067, 1067 (2009) ("Constitutional mo-ments are momentous, but they are not irregular. To the contrary, they are *routine*. In particular, the changeover of executive power that we are undergoing right now bears witness to a simple proposition: *every presidential transition is a constitutional moment*").

92. This is not to suggest that the approach advocated here dictates a histori-cally based or originalist mode of interpretation. It means only that to have "con-stitutional" status, a dictate or precept must have grounding in the terms of the document.

93. *See* District of Columbia v. Heller, 554 U.S. 570, 625 (2008).

94. *See* Griswold v. Connecticut, 381 U.S. 479 (1965).

95. *See, e.g.,* Lochner v. New York, 198 U.S. 45 (1905).

96. *See, e.g.,* Ferguson v. Skrupa, 372 U.S. 726 (1963).

97. *Id.* at 485.

98. Erin F. Delaney, Judiciary Rising: Constitutional Change in the United Kingdom, 108 Nw. U. L. Rev. 543, 548 (2014). *See also* Paul P. Craig, Political Con-stitutionalism and Judicial Review, in Effective Judicial Review 19, 32 (Christo-pher Forsyth et al. eds., 2010) (political constitutionalism employs "non-judicial mechanisms for securing accountability").

99. *See* William N. Eskridge Jr. & John Ferejohn, *Super-Statutes*, 50 Duke L.J. 1215 (2001).

100. *But see* Ackerman, The Civil Rights Revolution, *supra* note 2, at 112.

101. *But see* Young, *supra* note 2, at 454.

102. *See discussion supra* at 27–36.

103. Although he is perhaps the best known among them, Michael Stokes Paulsen is not the only champion of departmentalism, though different scholars often advocate different forms of the theory. *See, e.g.,* Keith E. Whittington, Extra-Judicial Constitutional Interpretation: Three Objections and Responses, 80 N.C. L. Rev. 773, 783 (2002); Steven G. Calabresi, Caesarism, Departmentalism, and Professor Paulsen, 83 Minn. L. Rev. 1421, 1423 (1999); Christopher L. Eisgruber, The Most Competent Branches: A Response to Professor Paulsen, 83 Geo. L.J. 347, 352 (1994). It remains unclear, however, whether Paulsen would view other so-called "departmentalists" as such, given that many of them either express disbe-lief in judicial review (Paulsen does not) or reject presidential authority to refuse enforcement of judicial decrees in particular cases (which Paulsen refers to as the *Merryman* power and views as a valid exercise of executive interpretive power).

104. *See* Kramer, *supra* note 2; Robert Post & Reva Siegel, Popular Consti-tutionalism, Departmentalism, and Judicial Supremacy, 92 Calif. L. Rev. 1027, 1034 (2004); Tushnet, *supra* note 9. As Professors Prakash and Yoo have noted,

the line between departmentalism and popular constitutionalism is blurry, in large part because the scholars who worked to formulate these theories have often only vaguely defined them. Saikrishna Prakash & John Yoo, Against Interpretive Supremacy (Book Review: Larry D. Kramer, The People Themselves (2004), 103 Mich. L. Rev. 1539, 1543–44 (2005).

105. Marbury v. Madison, 5 U.S. (1 Cranch) 137, 177 (1803).

106. Paulsen, *supra* note 2, at 241–45.

107. *Id.* at 221. *See also* Eisgruber, *supra* note 103, at 348 (agreeing with Paulsen that Chief Justice Marshall's logic in *Marbury* can be said to justify executive review just as capably as it explains judicial review, and that judicial supremacy is thus not the exclusive outcome of his reasoning).

108. Paulsen, *supra* note 2, at 221. *See also* Sanford Levinson, Constitutional Protestantism in Theory and Practice: Two Questions for Michael Stokes Paulsen and One for His Critics, 83 Geo. L.J. 373, 373–74 (1994) (agreeing that the logic of judicial review applies in equal measure to executive review). *Cf.* Geoffrey P. Miller, The President's Power of Interpretation: Implications of a Unified Theory of Constitutional Law, 56 L. & Contemp. Probs. 35, 40 (1993): "The Constitution itself does not subordinate the president to the courts in matters of constitutional interpretation. On the contrary, the text and structure of the Constitution establish the president as head of a coordinate branch of the government."

109. Paulsen, *supra* note 2, at 229: "It is the idea of coordinacy, even more than the cognate concept of separation on which it depends and builds, that fuels the system of "checks and balances" that guards against "a tyrannical concentration of all the powers of government in the same hands."

110. This recalls the maxim *nemo iudex in sua causa*, the oft-recited axiom that "no man should be a judge in his own case." *See* Dr. Bonham's Case, (1610) 77 Eng. Rep. 638 (C.P.) 652; 8 Co. Rep. 107a, 118a (Coke, C.J.). *See also* Calder v. Bull, 3 U.S. (3 Dall.) 386, 388 (1798); Marbury v. Madison, 5 U.S. (1 Cranch) 137, 176 (1803) ("To what purpose are powers limited, and to what purpose is that limitation committed to writing, if these limits may, at any time, be passed by those intended to be restrained?"). Professor Adrian Vermeule has challenged whether this mantra espouses a "bedrock principle of natural justice and constitutionalism." Adrian Vermeule, Nemo Iudex in Sua Causa: The Limits of Impartiality, 122 Yale L.J. 384, 384 (2012). But considering the core principle of skeptical optimism we have identified as core to *American* constitutionalism—and considering the catholic devotion our Supreme Court has shown to the concept, through frequent reference to and reliance upon it—so sharp a contradiction is striking.

111. *Federalist* No. 48 (Madison).

112. *Cf. Federalist* No. 10 (Madison): "When a majority is included in a faction, the form of popular government . . . enables it to sacrifice to its ruling passion or interest both the public good and the rights of other citizens. To secure the public good and private rights against the danger of such a faction, and at the same time to preserve the spirit and the form of popular government, is then the great object to which our inquiries are directed."

113. Paulsen, *supra* note 2, at 235.

114. *Id.* at 236.

115. *Federalist* No. 49, at 255 (James Madison).

116. Paulsen, *supra* note 2, at 244.

117. *Cf.* Mcginnis & Rappaport, *supra* note 11, at 720 (arguing that Madison's primary goal in designing the structural Constitution was to establish a series of supermajoritarian lawmaking apparatuses).

118. *See generally Federalist* No. 78 (Hamilton): "By a limited Constitution, I understand one which contains certain specified exceptions to the legislative authority; such, for instance, as that it shall pass no bills of attainder, no *ex post facto* laws, and the like. Limitations of this kind can be preserved in practice no other way than through the medium of courts of justice, whose duty it must be to declare all acts contrary to the manifest tenor of the Constitution void. Without this, all the reservations of particular rights or privileges would amount to nothing."

119. *See* Marbury v. Madison, 5 U.S. (1 Cranch) 137, 176–77 (1803) (describing the Constitution as setting forth limited government, and explaining that those limits are meaningless if the majoritarian branches may transcend them at any time).

120. *See* Alexander Bickel, The Least Dangerous Branch (2d ed., 1988).

121. Paulsen, *supra* note 2, at 226.

122. *Cf.* Gary Lawson & Christopher D. Moore, The Executive Power of Constitutional Interpretation, 81 Iowa L. Rev. 1267, 1280 (1996) (examining the textual bases for executive interpretation and urging that the president is authorized to engage in constitutional interpretation independent from the judiciary's exercise of interpretive authority).

123. Bonham's Case, 8 Co. Rep. 114 (Ct. of Common Pleas [1610]).

124. The judiciary is, to some extent, an exception to this dictate, because under the model of judicial supremacy the courts retain authority to determine the constitutionality of their own actions. However, such an exception may be justified on a principle of necessity, because to vest the authority to determine the constitutionality of judicial action in the political branches would effectively destroy the countermajoritarian check on the majoritarian branches.

125. *See* Martin H. Redish, Judicial Review and the Political Question, 79 Nw. U. L. Rev. 1031, 1045 (1985).

126. Indeed, the Supreme Court nearly did pass on this issue. In Burke v. Barnes, the D.C. Circuit Court of Appeals held that the president had unsuccessfully vetoed a bill when he "pocket vetoed" legislation that would condition continued military aid to El Salvador on the president certifying El Salvador's progress towards protecting human rights. 759 F.2d 21 (D.C. Cir. 1984). Because the legislation expired before the case arrived at the Supreme Court, the Court reversed the D.C. Circuit on mootness grounds. Burke v. Barnes, 479 U.S. 361, 363–64 (1987).

127. *See* Carl McGowan, The President's Veto Power: An Important Instrument of Conflict in Our Constitutional System, 23 San Diego L. Rev. 791 (1986).

128. U.S. Const. Art. I § 7 cl. 2.

129. Even the judiciary is not *entirely* insulated from the power of popular majority, as the Appointments Clause vests the president with the authority to appoint federal judicial officers with the advice and consent of the Senate. *See* U.S. Const. Art. II § 2 cl. 2. *See also* Jack M. Balkin & Sanford Levinson, Understanding the Constitutional Revolution, 87 Va. L. Rev. 1045, 1068 (2001): "Partisan entrenchment through presidential appointments to the ju-

diciary is the best account of how the meaning of the Constitution changes over time through Article III interpretation rather than Article V amendment."

130. Paulsen, *supra* note 2, at 266.

131. U.S. Const. Art. II § 2.

132. U.S. Const. Art. I § 7 cl. 2.

133. *See* McGowan, *supra* note 127, at 795.

134. U.S. Const. Art. II § 3.

135. U.S. Const. Art. VI cl. 2.

136. Paulsen, *supra* note 2, at 270–71.

137. *See* Lujan v. Defenders of Wildlife, 504 U.S. 555 (1992).

138. Rule 11 of the Federal Rules of Civil Procedure requires an attorney of record to sign every pleading and motion certifying that "the claims, defenses, and other legal contentions are warranted by existing law or by a nonfrivolous argument for extending, modifying, or reversing existing law or for the establishing new law" [Fed. R. Civ. P. 11(b)(2)], and that the document "is not being presented for any improper purpose, such as to harass, cause unnecessary delay, or needlessly increase the cost of litigation" [Fed. R. Civ. P. 11(b)(1)].

139. *See* Fed. R. Cir. P. Rule 23(b)(2) (providing for classwide injunctive relief).

140. *See* Calabresi, *supra* note 103, at 1423. *Cf.* Thomas W. Merrill, Judicial Opinions as Binding Law and as Explanations for Judgments, 15 Cardozo L. Rev. 43, 79 (1993) (challenging the scholarly justifications supporting both executive acquiescence and executive non-acquiescence theories).

141. *See* John O. McGinnis, Models of the Opinion Function of the Attorney General: A Normative Description and Historical Prolegomenon, 15 Cardozo L. Rev. 375, 392 (1993).

142. *See* Martin H. Redish & Andrianna D. Kastanek, Settlement Class Actions, the Case-or-Controversy Requirement, and the Nature of the Adjudicatory Process, 73 U. Chi. L. Rev. 545, 567 (2006).

143. *See, e.g.*, Levinson, *supra* note 9, at 18 (arguing that the Constitution has not lived up to its promise and proposing a shift to a new constitutional regime with more limited judicial power); Larry D. Kramer, Popular Constitutionalism Circa 2004, 92 Calif. L. Rev. 959, 960 (2004); Post & Siegel, *supra* note 104. *Cf.* David E. Pozen, Judicial Elections as Popular Constitutionalism, 110 Colum. L. Rev. 2047, 2050 (2010) (advocating for popular constitutionalism based on the effectiveness of equivalent judicial majoritarianism in states with elected judiciaries).

144. Kramer, Popular Constitutionalism, *supra* note 143, at 1008.

145. *Id.* at 1005.

146. *Id.* at 1003.

147. *Id.* at 959.

148. *See* Steven P. Croley, The Majoritarian Difficulty: Elective Judiciaries and the Rule of Law, 62 U. Chi. L. Rev. 689, 694 (1995) ("[C]onstitutionalism entails, among other important things, protection of the individual and of minorities from democratic governance over certain spheres. When those charged with checking the majority are themselves answerable to, and thus influenced by, the majority, the question arises how individual and minority protection is secured.")

149. *See generally* Chapter 4, *infra* (describing the ways the majoritarian process of election and retention of state court judges runs counter to the American concept of due process of law).

150. *See* discussion *supra* at 20–26.

151. *See* Chapter 6, *infra*.

152. For a deeper treatment and critique of the popular constitutionalism espoused by Professors Kramer, Pozen, and Siegel, see Chapter 4, *infra*.

153. *See* discussion *supra* at 20–26.

154. *See* Daniel J. Boorstin, The Americans: The Democratic Experience (1973); Henry Steele Commager, The American Mind (1959).

CHAPTER TWO

1. Chapter 2 grew out of my article *Federal Judicial Independence: Constitutional and Political Perspectives*, 46 Mercer Law Review 697 (1995).

2 Martin H. Redish, Federal Jurisdiction: Tensions in the Allocation of Judicial Power 7–52 (2d ed., 1990).

3. Art III. § 1 provides that "[t]he judicial power shall be vested in one Supreme Court and in such inferior courts as Congress shall from time to time ordain and establish." Both this language and generally accepted constitutional history are widely deemed to establish that Congress need not have created lower federal courts. *See* Martin H. Redish, Federal Jurisdiction: Tensions in the Allocation of Judicial Power 29–44 (2d ed., 1990). The Supreme Court has reasoned that the power not to create the lower courts includes the power to abolish them, and that the power to abolish the lower courts subsumes the power to limit their jurisdiction. *See, e.g.,* Lockerty v. Phillips, 319 U.S. 182 (1943). Art. III § 2 narrowly confines the Supreme Court's original jurisdiction and provides that its appellate jurisdiction is subject to regulations and exceptions made by Congress. *See* Redish, *supra* note 2, at 25-29.

4. *Cf.* Lawrence Sager, Foreword: Constitutional Limitations on Congress' Authority to Regulate the Jurisdiction of the Federal Courts, 95 Harv. L. Rev. 17 (1981) (salary and tenure protections limit congressional power to control federal jurisdiction) *with* Martin H. Redish, Congressional Power to Control Federal Jurisdiction: A Reaction to Professor Sager, 77 Nw. U. L. Rev. 143 (1982) (salary and tenure protections apply only to cases left within federal court jurisdiction).

5. *See* discussion *infra* at 65–70.

6. *See* discussion *infra* at 65–70.

7. *Id.*

8. *See* discussion *infra* at 54–60.

9. Note that this study excludes consideration of the constitutional standards for judicial tenure, a subject possessing a unique history. *See generally* Report of the National Commission on Judicial Discipline and Removal (1993); Peter M. Shane, Who May Discipline or Remove Federal Judges? A Constitutional Analysis, 142 U. Pa. L. Rev. 1 (1993).

10. *See* discussion *infra* at 54–76.

11. *See* discussion *infra* at 55–59.

12. *See* discussion *infra* at 65–70.

13. *Id.*

14. *See* discussion *infra* at 62–65.

15. *See* Plaut v. Spendthrift Farms, Inc., at 514 U.S. 211 (1995).

16. *See* discussion *infra* at 54–60.

17. *Id.*

18. *See* discussion *infra* at 73–75.

19. *See generally* Martin H. Redish, The Constitution as Political Structure (1995).

20. *See* discussion infra at 71–75.

21. U.S. Const. Art. III § 1.

22. *See generally* Gail L. Heriot, A Study in the Choice of Form: Statutes of Limitations and the Doctrine of Laches, 1992 B.Y.U. L. Rev., 917.

23. *Id.*

24. *See generally* Henry Monaghan, Constitutional Adjudication and Democratic Theory, 56 N.Y.U. L. Rev. 259 (1981).

25. *See* Redish, *supra* note 19, at 113–25.

26. *See generally* Martin H. Redish & Matthew B. Arnould, Judicial Review, Constitutional Interpretation, and the Democratic Dilemma: Proposing a "Controlled Activism" Alternative, 64 Fla. L. Rev. 1485 (2012).

27. *See* discussion chapter 4.

28. *See* chapter 4, *infra*, for development of the argument that state court structure should be deemed to violate due process.

29. *See* Keith Rosenn, The Constitutional Guaranty against Diminution of Judicial Compensation, 24 UCLA L. Rev. 308 (1976).

30. *Id.* at 310 n. 9.

31. Will v. United States, 449 U.S. 200 (1980). For a more recent judicial exploration of the issue, see Beer v. United States, 696 F.3d 1174 (Fed. Cir. 2012). There the Federal Circuit held unconstitutional congressional efforts to withdraw statutorily vested cost-of-living increases, because "the . . . statutory scheme was a precise legislative bargain which gave judges an employment 'expectation' at a certain salary level." *Id.* at 1182. The court emphasized, however, that "the Compensation Clause does not require periodic increases in judicial salaries to offset inflation or any other economic forces." Id. at 1184.

32. *See* Rosenn, *supra* note 28, at 314–15.

33. 2 Max Farrand, The Records of the Federal Convention of 1787 45 (1911).

34. *See* discussion *supra* at 54–56.

35. Evans v. Gore, 253 U.S. 245 (1920).

36. Miles v. Graham, 268 U.S. 501 (1925).

37. O'Malley v. Woodrough, 307 U.S. 277, 282 (1939).

38. *Id.*

39. *Id.*

40. *See* discussion *supra* at 55–57.

41. *See* Smith v. Oregon, 494 U.S. 872 (1990).

42. *Cf.* Booth v. United States, 291 U.S. 339 (1934) (provision of federal statute specifically reducing pensions of federal judges held unconstitutional).

43. *See* discussion *supra* at 54–56.

44. *See generally* chapter 1, *supra*.

45. Marbury v. Madison, 5 U.S. (1 Cranch) 137 (1803).

46. *Id.*

47. *See* U.S. Const. Art. III § 2; Valley Forge Christian College v. Americans United for Separation of Church & State, Inc., 454 U.S. 464 (1982).

48. 28 U.S.C. § 1652.

49. The statute precludes the fashioning by the federal courts of purely substantive common law, Erie R. Co. v. Tompkins, 304 U.S. 64 (1938), and certain rules that implicate both substantive and procedural concerns. *See generally* Martin H. Redish & Carter G. Phillips, *Erie* and the Rules of Decision Act: In Search of the Appropriate Dilemma, 91 Harv. L. Rev. 356 (1977).

50. *See, e.g.*, Boyle v. United Technologies Corp., 487 U.S. 500, 506–08 (1988); Wallis v. Pan Am. Petroleum Corp., 384 U.S. 63, 69 (1966).

51. Martin H. Redish & Lawrence C. Marshall, Adjudicatory Independence and the Values of Procedural Due Process, 95 Yale L.J. 455, 476 (1986).

52. *See Id.* at 476–91.

53. U.S. Const. Amend. V. The same, of course, is true of the Fourteenth Amendment.

54. *See, e.g.*, Paul v. Davis, 424 U.S. 693 (1976).

55. Compare Tumey v. Ohio, 273 U.S. 510, 532 (1927) (mere possibility of financial temptation of adjudicator violates due process) *with* Withrow v. Larkin, 421 U.S. 35, 47 (1975) (in order to overcome presumption of honesty and integrity of administrative officials, a party must "convince the court that, under a realistic appraisal of psychological tendencies and human weakness[es]" a combination of investigatory with adjudicative functions poses undue risk of partiality.). *See also* Weiss v. United States, 114 S. Ct. 752 (1994) (lack of fixed term of office for military judges does not violate due process).

56. U.S. Const. Art. III § 1.

57. The dictates of formalism in the separation-of-powers context have been described in the following manner: Any exercise of governmental power, and any governmental institution exercising that power, must either fit within one of the three formal categories [legislative, executive, or judicial] . . . or find explicit constitutional authorization for such deviation. The separation of powers principle is violated whenever the categorizations of the exercised power and the exercising institution do not match and the Constitution does not specifically permit such blending. Gary Lawson, Territorial Governments and the Limits of Formalism, 78 Cal. L. Rev. 853, 858 (1990) (footnote omitted).

58. *Id.*

59. *See* Paul Brest, The Misconceived Quest for the Original Understanding, 60 B.U. L. Rev. 204 (1980); Note, Mistretta v. United States: Mistreating the Separation of Powers Doctrine?, 27 San Diego L. Rev. 209 (1991).

60. Lee S. Liberman, Morrison v. Olson: A Formalistic Perspective on Why the Court Was Wrong, 38 Am. U. L. Rev. 313, 343 (1989).

61. *See, e.g.*, Thomas O. Sargentich, The Contemporary Debate About Legislative-Executive Separation of Powers, 72 Cornell L. Rev. 430 (1987).

62. *See* Martin H Redish, The Constitution as Political Structure 99–134 (1995).

63. *Id.* at 455 (footnote omitted).

64. For example, the Appointments Clause of Art. II § 2 provides that Congress may vest the appointment of "inferior officers" in "the Courts of Law," even though performance of such a function does not implicate adjudication of a case or controversy. *See* Morrison v. Olson, 487 U.S. 654, 655 (1988).

65. Lawson, *supra* note 57, at 853.

66. Redish, *supra* note 62, at 125.

67. *Id.*

68. *See, e.g.*, Morrison v. Olson, 487 U.S. 654 (1988); Mistretta v. United States, 488 U.S. 361 (1989).

69. Redish, *supra* note 62, at 125.

70. *Id.*

71. Art. III § 1 provides that the judicial power shall be vested in such inferior courts as Congress may from time to time ordain and establish. The Supreme Court has reasoned that since Congress need not have created lower federal courts, it may also abolish them once created, and that this greater power of abolition logically includes the lesser power of curbing jurisdiction. *See* Lockerty v. Phillips, 319 U.S. 182 (1943); Sheldon v. Sill, 49 U.S. (8 How.) 441 (1850). While not everyone has agreed that Congress's power should be construed this broadly as a doctrinal matter, the existence of such power appears well established. *See, e.g.*, Akhil Amar, A Neo-Federalist View of Article III: Separating the Two Tiers of Federal Jurisdiction, 65 B.U. L. Rev. 205 (1985).

72. *See, e.g.*, Bartlett v. Bowen, 816 F.2d 695 (D.C. Cir. 1987).

73. *See, e.g.*, Lockerty v. Phillips, 319 U.S. 182 (1943).

74. *See, e.g.*, Claflin v. Houseman, 93 U.S. 130 (1876).

75. U.S. Const. Art. VI cl. 2.

76. Testa v. Katt, 330 U.S. 386, 391 (1947).

77. The Supreme Court made clear in Erie R. Co. v. Tompkins, 304 U.S. 64 (1938), however, that Congress lacks authority in diversity cases to vest purely substantive rulemaking power in the federal courts.

78. For this reason, it appears clear that apart from nondelegation questions, resolved in *Mistretta* the congressional provision of sentences does not unconstitutionally invade the judicial province.

79. *See* discussion *supra* at 20–26.

80. *See, e.g.*, Henry M. Hart, Jr., The Power of Congress to Limit the Jurisdiction of Federal Courts: An Exercise in Dialectic, 66 Harv. L. Rev. 1362 (1953).

81. *See* Redish, *supra* note 61, at 136.

82. 491 U.S. 110 (1989).

83. Cal. Evid. Code § 621 (West 1966 & Supp. 1994).

84. *Id.*

85. *Id.*

86. 491 U.S. at 119–20.

87. *Id.* at 120.

88. *Id.*

89. Cal. Evid. Code § 621.

90. *See, e.g.*, Lockerty v. Phillips, 319 U.S. 182 (1943) (discussed in note 2 *supra*).

91. *See* Jonathan R. Macey, Promoting Public-Regarding Legislation Through Statutory Interpretation: An Interest Group Model, 86 Colum. L. Rev. 223 (1986).

92. *See* discussion *supra* at 64–65.

93. U.S. Const. Art. I § 9 cl. 3.

94. 514 U.S. 211 (1995).

95. Securities Exchange Act of 1934, § 27A (amended by Pub. L. No. 102–242, Dec. 19, 1991, codified at 15 U.S.C. § 78aa-1).

96. Lampf, Pleva, Lipkind, Prupis & Petigrow v. Gilbertson, 501 U.S. 350, 364 (1991).

97. James B. Beam Distilling Co. v. Georgia, 501 U.S. 529, 544 (1991).

98. Securities Exchange Act of 1934, § 27A (amended by Pub. L. No. 102–242, Dec. 19, 1991, codified at 15 U.S.C. § 78aa-1).

99. 997 F.2d 39 (5th Cir. 1993), *aff'd*, 114 S. Ct. 1827 (1994).

100. 997 F.2d at 52–54.

101. *Id.* at 53.

102. *Id.*

103. *See generally* Axel Johnson, Inc. v. Arthur Andersen & Co., 6 F.3d 78 (2d Cir. 1993); Freeman v. Laventhol & Horwath, 34 F.3d 333 (6th Cir. 1994); Anixter v. Home-Stake Prod. Co., 977 F.2d 1533 (10th Cir. 1992).

104. 1 F.3d 1487 (6th Cir. 1993).

105. *Id.* at 1493.

106. 2 U.S. (2 Dall.) 408 (1792).

107. 1 F.3d at 1493.

108. 2 U.S. (2 Dall.) at 410.

109. *Id.*

110. 1 F.3d at 1493.

111. This issue is beyond the scope of the present inquiry.

112. 511 U.S. at 218.

113. *Id.* at 218–19 (emphasis in original) (quoting Frank Easterbrook, *Presidential Review*, 40 Case W. Res. L. Rev. 905, 926 (1990)).

114. *See* discussion *supra* at 53.

115. 380 U.S. 460 (1965).

116. U.S. Const. Art. I § 8 cl. 9.

117. U.S. Const. Art. I § 8 cl. 18.

118. 380 U.S. at 471–72.

119. *See* discussion *supra* at 64–65.

120. *See* Hanna v. Plumer, 380 U.S. at 471–72.

121. *See, e.g.*, Valley Forge Christian College v. Americans United for Separation of Church & State, Inc. 454 U.S. 464 (1982); Antonin Scalia, The Doctrine of Standing as an Essential Element of the Separation of Powers, 17 Suffolk U. L. Rev. 881, 882 (1983).

122. *See* Linda S. Mullenix, Unconstitutional Rulemaking: The Civil Justice Reform Act and Separation of Powers, 77 Minn. L. Rev. 1283, 1288 (1993).

123. This power is, of course, subject to the Seventh Amendment's requirement of jury trial in certain cases.

124. *See* discussion *supra* at 69–70.

125. It should be recalled that Congress is widely thought to possess power to remove even constitutional cases from the lower federal courts. However, this power is premised on the assumed availability of the state courts as adequate judi-

cial forums to enforce federal constitutional rights. *See* Hart, *supra* note 79. A denial of any independent forum for the adjudication of constitutional rights would almost certainly violate due process. *See* Bartlett v. Bowen, 816 F.2d 695 (D.C. Cir. 1987).

CHAPTER THREE

1. Chapter 3 represents a modified synthesis of two of my prior works, *Judicial Discipline, Judicial Independence, and the Constitution: A Textual and Structural Analysis,* 72 Southern California Law Review 673 (1999), and *Good Behavior, Judicial Independence, and the Foundations of American Constitutionalism,* 116 Yale Law Journal 139 (2006). Reproduced with permission of the publishers.

2. *See,* e.g., Alexis de Tocqueville, Democracy in America 55 (R. Heffner, ed., 1956): "Wherever the political laws of the United States are to be discussed, it is with the doctrine of the sovereignty of the people that we must begin." *See also* Gordon S. Wood, The Creation of The American Republic 1776–1787, at 330 (1969) (noting that in the prerevolutionary period, "[t]he people were the undisputed, ubiquitous source that was appealed to by both the advocates and the opponents of independence"; Michael J. Perry, The Constitution, The Courts and Human Rights 9 (1982): "We in the United States are philosophically committed to the political principle that governmental policymaking . . . ought to be subject to control by persons accountable to the electorate."

3. See U.S. Const. Arts. I and II.

4. Marbury v. Madison, 5 U.S. (1 Cranch) 137 (1803).

5. *See Federalist* No. 78 (Hamilton) at 15 (Clinton Rossiter, ed., 1961): "The complete independence of the courts of justice is peculiarly essential in a limited Constitution. . . . Limitations of this kind can be preserved in practice no other way than through the medium of courts of justice, whose duty it must be to declare all acts contrary to the manifest tenor of the Constitution void. Without this, all the reservations of particular rights or privileges would amount to nothing."

6. *See Federalist* No. 79 (Hamilton).

7. *See* Raoul Berger, Impeachment: The Constitutional Problems 224–30 (1973).

8. *See* Judge's Rejection of Evidence Is Criticized, N.Y. Times, Jan. 29, 1996, at B5; Norimitsu Onishi, Judge to Be Asked to Rethink Drug Ruling, N.Y. Times, Feb. 1, 1996, at B2.

9. See Don Van Natta, Jr., Drug Case Reversal, N.Y. Times, Apr. 3, 1996, at B3.

10. *See* discussion *infra* at 81–93.

11. *See* U.S. Const. Art. II § 4: "The President, Vice President and all civil Officers of the United States, shall be removed from Office on Impeachment for, and Conviction of, Treason, Bribery, or other high Crimes and Misdemeanors."

12. U.S. Const. Art. III § 1.

13. Saikrishna Prakash and Steven D. Smith, How to Remove a Federal Judge, 116 Yale L.J. 72 (2006).

14. *See* discussion *infra* at 81–84.

15. *See* discussion *infra* at 105–7.

16. *See* discussion *infra* at 102–3.

17. It should be noted that an important ambiguity exists concerning the extent to which either temporary suspensions or diversions of caseloads are properly

thought to affect tenure for purposes of Article III, as long as the affected judge continues to retain both her official status and salary.

18. U.S. Const. Art. II § 4.

19. U.S. Const. Art. III § 1.

20. U.S. Const. Art. III § 1.

21. Prakash & Smith, *supra* note 13, at 75.

22. *Id*. at 77.

23. *Id*. at 78 n. 15.

24. *See* U.S. Const. Art. III §1.

25. But see discussion *infra* at 85–88 (challenging the implications drawn by Prakash and Smith from their historical analysis).

26. *See* discussion *infra* at 90–93 for an elaboration on the point.

27. Prakash and Smith appear to equate textualism with originalism, and they express puzzlement that one could claim to be one without simultaneously being the other. Saikrishna Prakash & Steven D. Smith, Reply: (Mis) Understanding Good-Behavior Tenure, 116 Yale L.J. 159, 159 n. 2 (2006). But surely there must exist some alternative between the straitjacket of an interpretative model restrained by a usually fruitless effort to ascertain the narrow understanding of a group of drafters some 200 years ago, on the one hand, and utter linguistic chaos, on the other. Language need not be devoid of any restraining impact on an interpreter for one to reject an arid, largely futile attempt to constrain words by some narrow and unchanging historical perspective. For a detailed discussion of this argument see Martin H. Redish & Matthew B. Arnould, Judicial Review, Constitutional Interpretation, and the Democratic Dilemma: Proposing a "Controlled Activism" Alternative, 64 Fla. L. Rev. 1485 (2012).

28. *See* Prakash & Smith, *supra* note 13, at 79.

29. Prakash and Smith suggest that, absent the Good Behavior Clause, it would be impossible to determine what federal judicial tenure would be. Prakash & Smith, *supra* note 13, at 168. However, this ignores the hypothetical and contingent nature of the inquiry. It would be absurd to assume that if the drafters had not included the good-behavior language, they would not have inserted substitute language in its place providing for life tenure.

30. *See* discussion infra at 84–93.

31. *See* discussion *infra* at 84–93.

32. Prakash & Smith, *supra* note 13, at 92–109.

33. *Id*. at 75.

34. *Id*. at 75 n. 8

35. *Id*. at 86.

36. *Id*. at 90.

37. *Id*.

38. *See Federalist* No. 15 (Hamilton).

39. U.S. Const. Art. I §8 cl. 18, granting Congress power to "make all Laws which shall be necessary and proper for carrying into Execution the foregoing Powers, and all other Powers vested by this Constitution in the Government of the United States, or in any Department or Officer thereof."

40. Prakash & Smith, *supra* note 13, at 128–30. See, e.g., M'Culloch v. Maryland, 17 U.S. (4 Wheat.) 316, 324 (1819).

41. *See, e.g.*, M'Culloch v. Maryland, 17 U.S. (4 Wheat.) 316, 324 (1819).

42. Neither the congressional power to create lower federal courts under Art. I §8 cl. 9 nor the Good Behavior Clause itself would seem to qualify, as the former provides no removal power while the latter provides no power at all to any branch of the federal government. While arguably the power to create courts logically implies the power to abolish them, removal of an individual judge while leaving the existing judicial structure unaffected would seem to constitute a far more sweeping extension of this congressional power.

43. Prakash & Smith, *supra* note 13, at 92–109.

44. *See id.* at 92–102.

45. This point concededly may not apply to historical extension of the good-behavior standard to private officeholders, but for purposes of judicial independence and separation-of-powers theory—which are all we are considering in the present context—it is absolutely true.

46. *Federalist* No. 78 (Hamilton): "The standard of good behavior for the continuance in office of the judicial magistracy is certainly one of the most valuable of the modern improvements in the practice of government. In a monarchy it is an excellent barrier to the despotism of the prince; in a republic it is a no less excellent barrier to the encroachments and oppressions of the representative body. And it is the best expedient which can be devised in any government to secure a steady, upright, and impartial administration of the laws."

47. Prakash and Smith note that there is little specific reference to the "good Behaviour" language in the Convention debates. Prakash & Smith, *supra* note 13, at 118.

48. *Federalist* No. 78 (Hamilton), *supra* note 5, at 15: "[The judiciary] is in continual jeopardy of being overpowered, awed, or influenced by its co-ordinate branches; and that as nothing can contribute so much to its firmness and independence as permanency in office, this quality may therefore be justly regarded as an indispensable ingredient in its constitution, and, in a great measure, as the citadel of the public justice and the public security."

49. *E.g.*, *Federalist* No. 81 (Hamilton), *supra* note 5, at 452–53: "[It may be inferred that] the supposed danger of judiciary encroachments on the legislative authority, which has been upon many occasions reiterated is in reality a phantom. . . . [T]he inference is greatly fortified by the consideration of the important constitutional check which the power of instituting impeachments in one part of the legislative body, and of determining upon them in the other, would give to that body upon the members of the judicial department. This is alone a complete security."

50. *Federalist* No. 79 (Hamilton): "The precautions for their responsibility are comprised in the article respecting impeachments. They are liable to be impeached for malconduct by the House of Representatives and tried by the Senate; and, if convicted, may be dismissed from office and disqualified for holding any other. This is the only provision on the point which is consistent with the necessary independence of the judicial character, and is the only one which we find in our own Constitution in respect to our own judges." *See also Federalist* No. 81 (Hamilton).

51. *See* David P. Currie, The Constitution in Congress: The Most Endangered Bra*n*ch, 1801–1805, 33 Wake Forest L. Rev. 219, 249–59 (1998).

52. *See* Prakash & Smith, *supra* note 13, at 123.

53. Prakash and Smith argue that Congress strategically chose to use the impeachment strategy in attempting to remove Justice Chase from office because reliance on the Good Behavior Clause would have required resort to the judicial process, which they sought to avoid. *Id.* at 125. However, they provide no evidence that any Republican strategist at the time actually employed such reasoning, or even considered the possibility. In any event, once the impeachment strategy failed, resort to the Good Behavior Clause strategy would have surely been better than nothing.

54. Steven G. Calabresi & Saikrishna B. Prakash, The President's Power to Execute the Laws, 104 Yale L.J. 541, 550–59 (1994).

55. Prakash & Smith, *supra* note 13, at 125–26.

56. *See generally*, chapter 1, *supra*.

57. U.S. Const. Art. V.

58. *Federalist* No. 78 (Hamilton), *supra* note 5, at 15: "This independence of the judges is equally requisite to guard the Constitution and the rights of individuals from the effects of those ill humors which . . . have a tendency . . . to occasion dangerous innovations in the government, and serious oppressions of the minor party in the community." *See also Federalist* Nos. 47, 48, and 51 (Madison).

59. In re Murchison, 349 U.S. 133, 136 (1955), quoting Offutt v. United States, 348 U.S. 11, 14 (1954).

60. Tumey v. Ohio, 273 U.S. 510 (1927). The concept was famously invoked by Lord Coke in Dr. Bonham's Case, (1610) 77 Eng. Rep. 646 (K.B.).

61. *Federalist* No. 78 (Hamilton), *supra* note 5, at 15: "The interpretation of the laws is the proper and peculiar province of the courts. A constitution is, in fact, and must be regarded by the judges as a fundamental law. It therefore belongs to them to ascertain its meaning as well as the meaning of any particular act proceeding from the legislative body."

62. Marbury v. Madison, 5 U.S. (1 Cranch) 137 (1803).

63. *Id.* at 178.

64. *Id.*

65. The constitutional standard, according to the Court, is "possible temptation to the average man as a judge." *Tumey,* 273 U.S. at 532. For a detailed examination of this precept in Supreme Court doctrine, see Martin H. Redish & Lawrence C. Marshall, Adjudicatory Independence and the Values of Procedural Due Process, 95 Yale L.J. 455, 494–500 (1986).

66. *See* Redish & Marshall, *supra* note 65, at 494–95.

67. U.S. Const. Art. III §1. See generally *Federalist* No. 79 (Hamilton), *supra* note 50, at 440–41 (emphasizing the importance of Article III salary protections as a guarantee of judicial independence).

68. U.S. Const. Art. III §1; *id.* Art. II §4. I make no reference here to the controversial issue of judicial discipline short of removal. On the general issue, see Harry T. Edwards, Regulating Judicial Misconduct and Divining "Good Behavior" for Federal Judges, 87 Mich. L. Rev. 765 (1989).

69. Prakash & Smith, *supra* note 13, at 134.

70. *Id.* at 90–91.

71. In Nixon v. United States, 506 U.S. 224 (1993), the Supreme Court found the basis for invoking the political-question doctrine in the language of Art. II §4 vesting "the power to try" officials in the Senate. For an attack on this extension of the political-question doctrine, see Martin H. Redish, Judicial Review and the Political Question, 79 Nw. U. L. Rev. 1031 (1985). For support of this extension, see Michael J. Gerhardt, The Federal Impeachment Process 118–38 (1996).

72. *See Federalist* No. 81 (Hamilton), at 449–59.

73. *See Federalist* No. 79 (Hamilton), at 440–43.

74. Prakash and Smith contend that "good Behaviour" could not properly be construed to include simple disagreement with judicial decisions. Prakash & Smith, *supra* note 13, at 162. However, because they fail to provide a coherently confined, historically grounded definition of the phrase in the first place, it is difficult to understand how they can reach this conclusion with any level of confidence. Moreover, because our form of strong judicial review, combined with a binding supermajoritarian written constitution, never existed when "good Behaviour" developed in preconstitutional times, it is impossible to know with any certainty how a judicial invalidation of legislative action deemed not to be reasonably grounded in text or original intent would be treated.

75. Prakash & Smith, *supra* note 13, at 79.

76. *Id.* at 76–77.

77. Prakash and Smith criticize me for "effectively reading [the Good Behavior Clause] out of the Constitution as an independent constraint on judges." Prakash & Smith, *supra* note 13, at 163. But this criticism completely begs the question, for the entire subject of our debate is whether that clause is, in fact, "an independent constraint on judges" or instead merely a textual cross-reference to impeachment, as I argue.

78. *See* discussion *supra* at 84–88.

79. *See* Martin H. Redish & Matthew B. Arnould, Judicial Review, Constitutional Interpretation, and the Democratic Dilemma: Proposing a "Controlled Activism" Alternative, 64 Fla. L. Rev. 1485 (2012).

80. *See* U.S. Const. Art. II § 4.

81. It should be noted that the interpretive need to reconcile seemingly conflicting provisions is inapplicable when one of those provisions is contained in a constitutional amendment. In such situations, since the very purpose of an amendment is to amend (to alter or change) the existence of such a textual conflict should not be surprising. In these cases, any conflict is naturally resolved in favor of the amendment.

82. *See* discussion *supra* at 81–93.

83. *See* Gerhardt, *supra* note 71, at 106–07.

84. *Id.* Gerhardt offers further elaboration on this point:

> [A] federal judge might be impeached for a particularly controversial law review article or speech, because these actions undermine confidence in the judge's neutrality and impugn the integrity of the judicial process. In contrast, an executive official who has done the same thing may not be impeached, because neutrality is not necessarily important to his or her job. . . . *Id.* at 107.

85. It might be thought that this analysis ignores the presence of the language in Article III confining life tenure to periods of "good Behaviour." For reasons discussed earlier, however, the "good Behaviour" language should not be construed to restrain life tenure above and beyond the manner in which the impeachment power does.

86. *See* Gerhardt, *supra* note 71, at 107.

87. *See* discussion *supra* at 82; 86–87.

88. This point is similar to the criticism make earlier of the Prakash-Smith originalist construction of the "Good Behavior" Clause.

89. In this context, it is worth noting that one of the express complaints made against the British Crown in the Declaration of Independence concerned the Crown's power over the judges in the Colonies. See The Declaration of Independence ¶ 11 (U.S. 1776).

90. *See* Berger, *supra* note 7; Gerhardt, *supra* note 71, at 103–09.

91. *See, e.g.*, Wickard v. Filburn, 317 U.S. 111 (1942) (providing modernized, expansive view of scope of congressional power under the Commerce Clause, U.S. Const. Art. I § 8 cl. 3).

92. U.S. Const. Amend. VII: "In Suits at common law, where the value in controversy shall exceed twenty dollars, the right of trial by jury shall be preserved."

93. *See, e.g.*, Dairy Queen, Inc. v. Wood, 369 U.S. 469 (1962); Beacon Theaters, Inc. v. Westover, 359 U.S. 500 (1959).

94. Of course, one might point to this history to demonstrate that the concern expressed here is more theoretical than real. Even if this were true, however, one must shape constitutional interpretation to deal with problems that theoretically may arise. In any event, Judge Baer's experience arguably demonstrates that the dangers to which I refer are more than theoretical.

95. *Federalist* No. 10 (Madison).

96. *See* 15 James Wm. Moore and Martin H. Redish, Moore's Federal Practice § 100.04 [2] (3d ed. 1997): "It is well established that an Article III judge may be indicted and prosecuted for criminal activity before being impeached." See United States v. Claiborne, 765 F.2d 784, 789 (9th Cir. 1985) (holding that the U.S. Constitution does not immunize a federal judge from prosecution before impeachment).

97. *See* Report of the National Commission on Judicial Discipline and Removal 72–82 (1993) (offering, among others, the example of a federal judge "sentenced in 1984 to two years in jail, which he served while still holding office and receiving his federal salary").

98. *See* O'Malley v. Woodrough, 307 U.S. 277, 281–82 (1939) (ruling that judges appointed after income tax was enacted could constitutionally be subject to that tax). *See also* Atkins v. United States, 556 F.2d 1028, 1045 (Ct. Cl. 1997), cert. denied, 434 U.S. 1009 (1997) (holding that indirect decreases in judicial compensation that are unconnected to independence of judiciary are not constitutionally prohibited). But see Hatter v. United States, 64 F.3d 647 (Fed. Cir. 1995) (ruling that withholding of social security taxes from the salaries of judges who took office before those taxes were imposed violates Compensation Clause).

99. This application of criminal law threatens judicial independence not because imprisonment fails to constitute constructive removal (indeed, imprisonment in a practical sense probably does constitute constructive removal), but rather because the application of criminal law is conducted in a neutral manner that has nothing to do with the status of the judge. Such laws therefore cannot be viewed as congressional efforts to intimidate the federal judiciary.

100. A possible exception to the noncontextual nature of this analysis would be the fact that even where a federal judge is prosecuted for violation of a generally applicable prohibition, she would be permitted to attempt to establish selective discrimination in her particular prosecution. In such a situation, the aberration from a noncontextual approach would have the effect of protecting, rather than undermining, judicial independence.

101. In certain instances, whether a particular form of discipline does, in fact, affect either salary or tenure may be the subject of debate. The analysis that follows proceeds on the assumption that the forms of discipline in question do not affect either salary or tenure.

102. *See* U.S. Const. Amend. V; Art. III § 1: "The judicial Power of the United States shall be vested in one Supreme Court, and in such inferior courts as the Congress may from time to time ordain and establish."

103. *See* Redish & Marshall, *supra* note 65, at 475–91. Of course, if enactment of the legislation had been threatened *prior* to a decision, it is at least arguable that the losing litigant could claim that his due process right had been violated. The scenario described in text, however, focuses on a retributive enactment of paralyzing legislation *following* issuance of an unpopular judicial decision.

104. 273 U.S. 510 (1927) (holding that a system in which a judge is paid more for convictions than acquittals violates the Due Process Clause).

105. 475 U.S. 813 (1986) (ruling that due process was violated by failure of state supreme court justice to recuse himself in suit brought against insurance company that alleged bad-faith failure to pay claims, especially where justice had himself filed two state court suits against insurance companies also alleging bad-faith failure to pay claims).

106. Perhaps one could make an argument that the federal judges should be allowed to exercise third-party standing in order to raise the constitutional issue that would at some point in the future affect private litigants. However, third-party standing is heavily disfavored in the federal courts. *See, e.g.*, Valley Forge Christian College v. Americans United for Separation of Church and State, Inc., 454 U.S. 464, 474 (1982); Singleton v. Wulff, 428 U.S. 106, 113–14 (1976). Nevertheless, where the litigant has suffered actual injury, has a close relationship to the third party, and there exists some hindrance to the third party's ability to protect her own interests, third-party standing is allowed. *See, e.g.*, Caplin & Drysdale, Chartered v. United States, 491 U.S. 627 (1989). Whether federal judges would meet this standard, however, is open to doubt.

107. *See, e.g.*, Goldberg v. Kelly, 397 U.S. 254 (1970).

108. *See* Arnett v. Kennedy, 416 U.S. 134, 153–54 (1974) (Rehnquist, J., dissenting).

109. *See* Plaut v. Spendthrift Farm, Inc., 514 U.S. 211 (1995); Hayburn's Case, 2 U.S. (2 Dall.) 408 (1792).

110. *See* discussion *supra* at 61–66.

111. *See* discussion *supra* at 62–66.

CHAPTER FOUR

1. Chapter 4 derives from *The* Real *Constitutional Problem with State Judicial Selection: Due Process, Judicial Retention, and the Dangers of Popular Constitutionalism,* 56 William & Mary Law Review 1 (2014), an article I coauthored with Jennifer Aronoff. © 2014 by the *William & Mary Law Review.* Reproduced with permission of the publisher.

2. 556 U.S. 868 (2009).

3. *Id.* at 872–73, 884.

4. *Id.*

5. *Id.* at 884.

6. *Id.* at 886–87 (speaking, *e.g.,* of an "unconstitutional probability of bias").

7. Professor Karlan incisively noted this retrospective/prospective distinction in the wake of *Caperton. See* Pamela S. Karlan, Electing Judges, Judging Elections, and the Lessons of Caperton, 123 Harv. L. Rev. 80, 81 (2009).

8. The primary exception would probably be cases of quid pro quo bribery, which are already deemed unacceptable and, indeed, criminal.

9. *See, e.g., id.* at 795 (Kennedy, J., concurring) (noting—without explaining why—that although there is "general consensus" Article III protections have "preserved the independence of the federal judiciary," states are free to select their judges through elections). However, concern for federalism in this context begs the constitutional question, because if due process is being violated, the Fourteenth Amendment quite intentionally trumps federalism.

10. *See, e.g., id.* at 796: "By condemning judicial elections across the board, we implicitly condemn countless elected state judges and without warrant."

11. *See* discussion *supra* at 47–50.

12. *See* discussion *infra* at 135–36.

13. U.S. Const. Art. V.

14. U.S. Const. Art. III §1.

15. *Federalist* No. 78 (Hamilton).

16. *Id.*: "That inflexible and uniform adherence to the rights of the Constitution, and of individuals, which we perceive to be indispensable in the courts of justice, can certainly not be expected from judges who hold their offices by a temporary commission. Periodical appointments, however regulated, or by whomsoever made, would, in some way or other, be fatal to their necessary independence. If the power of making them was committed either to the Executive or legislature, there would be danger of an improper complaisance to the branch which possessed it; if to both, there would be an unwillingness to hazard the displeasure of either; if to the people, or to persons chosen by them for the special purpose, there would be too great a disposition to consult popularity, to justify a reliance that nothing would be consulted but the Constitution and the laws."

17. *See, e.g.*, Symposium, Judicial Ethics and Accountability, 42 McGeorge L. Rev. 1 (2010); Symposium, Fair and Independent Courts: A Conference on the State of the Judiciary, 95 Geo. L.J. 895 (2007); Symposium, Perspectives on Judicial Independence, 64 Ohio St. L.J. 1 (2003); Judicial Independence and Accountability Symposium, 72 S. Cal. L. Rev. 311 (1999); Symposium, Judicial Review and Judicial Independence: The Appropriate Role of the Judiciary, 14 Ga. St. L. Rev. 737 (1998). *See also* David E. Pozen, The Irony of Judicial Elections, 108 Colum. L. Rev. 265, 269 (2008): "So much has been written about this subject that to proffer yet another disquisition risks being redundant or worse."

18. *See, e.g.*, Charles Gardner Geyh, Judicial Selection Reconsidered: A Plea For Radical Moderation, 35 Harv. J.L. & Pub. Pol'y 623 (2012); Paul M. Carrington, Judicial Independence and Democratic Accountability in Highest State Courts, 61 Law & Contemp. Probs. 79, 107 (1998): "In some form, judicial elections are here to stay." *But see also* Charles Gardner Geyh, Why Judicial Elections Stink, 64 Ohio St. L.J. 43 (2003).

19. *Federalist* No. 78 (Hamilton), describing judicial independence as "an essential safeguard against the effects of occasional ill humors in the society."

20. *See, e.g.*, Michael R. Dimino, Sr., The Worst Way of Selecting Judges—Except All the Others That Have Been Tried, 32 N. Ky. L. Rev. 267, 303 (2005).

21. Martin H. Redish & Lawrence C. Marshall, Adjudicatory Independence and the Values of Procedural Due Process, 95 Yale L.J. 455, 457,479 (1986).

22. *See* Mathews v. Eldridge, 424 U.S. 319, 333 (1976); Goldberg v. Kelly, 397 U.S. 254, 267–68 (1970).

23. See http://www.uscourts.gov/JudgesAndJudgeships/FederalJudgeships.aspx (last visited Aug. 6, 2016); *Federalist* No. 78 (Hamilton).

24. Indeed, there are likely many more state judges. However, conclusive figures are difficult to come by. These numbers come from calculating data available at *Judicial Selection in the States—Method of Selection*, American Judicature Society, http://www.judicialselection.us/judicial_selection/methods/selection_of_judges.cfm?state= (last visited Aug. 6, 2016). Another 8 percent face pure legislative or executive branch reappointment. Even most states that initially appoint their judges require regular retention elections for judges to hold onto their seats.

25. *See, e.g.*, Nancy J. King, Fred L. Cheesman, II, & Brian J. Ostrom, Final Technical Report: Habeas Litigation in U.S. District Courts: An Empirical Study of Habeas Corpus Cases filed by State Prisoners under the Antiterrorism and Effective Death Penalty Act of 1996 3 (and generally) (2007), *available at* https://www.ncjrs.gov/pdffiles1/nij/grants/219558.pdf (last visited Aug. 6, 2016) (finding that habeas review is slower, less robust and less likely to end in a grant of the writ in the wake of AEDPA); Habeas Relief for State Prisoners, 41 Geo. L.J. Ann. Rev. Crim. Proc. 948 (2012) (detailing the labyrinthine hurdles prisoners must surmount to obtain habeas relief); Samuel R. Wiseman, Habeas after Pinholster, 53 B.C. L. Rev. 953, 953 (2012), noting "a long line of U.S. Supreme Court opinions . . . making it more difficult for state prisoners to obtain federal habeas relief under [AEDPA]." *See also* 28 U.S.C. § 1441 *et seq.* (federal removal statute).

26. For example, imagine Justice Benjamin deciding the case in *Caperton* with an eye on securing Blankenship's financial support in a future election, instead of after having already received it.

27. Karlan, *supra* note 7, at 81.

28. *In re* Murchison, 349 U.S. 133, 136 (1955).

29. *See Federalist* No. 79 (Hamilton); Steven P. Croley, The Majoritarian Difficulty, 62 U. Chi. L. Rev. 689, 694 (1995).

30. Methods of Judicial Selection, American Judicature Society, http://www.judicialselection.us/judicial_selection/methods/selection_of_judges.cfm?state= (last visited Aug. 6, 2016).

31. *Id.*

32. Larry C. Berkson, Judicial Selection in the United States, American Judicature Society, http://www.judicialselection.us/uploads/documents/Berkson_1196091951709.pdf (2010), at 1 (last visited Aug. 6, 2016). Eight of the original thirteen states vested appointment power in one or both houses of the legislature, while the other five used appointment by a governor and his council.

33. *Id.* Jed Handelsman Shugerman, The People's Courts 10 (2012).

34. *Id.*

35. Berkson, *supra* note 32, at 1.

36. Shugerman, *supra* note 33, at 10.

37. *Id.* at 10–11; Berkson, *supra* note 32, at 1.

38. Berkson, *supra* note 32, at 1–2.

39. *Id.* at 2.

40. *Id.*

41. Methods of Judicial Selection, *supra* note 30.

42. *Id.*

43. *Id.* The numbers in this section alone add up to fifty states because some states use more than one type of selection mechanism, depending on the type of court.

44. *Id.* Maine and New Jersey both use gubernatorial appointment to fill all judgeships for seven-year terms, while the legislature appoints and reappoints all judges in South Carolina and Virginia. (South Carolina technically has a judicial merit selection commission to make initial appointments, but six of the commission's ten members are members of the same legislature that makes the ultimate decision on the nominees the commission selects. The state legislature also selects the four members of the general public that make up the rest of the commission.) Vermont's judges are retained by a vote of the state's general assembly.

45. *Id.* Judges in Connecticut, Delaware, and Hawaii are all effectively reappointed by merit commissions. For instance, in Connecticut, the merit commission reviews incumbents' performance on a noncompetitive basis; the governor will then re-nominate worthy judges and the legislature will confirm them. New York's high and intermediate courts also rely on a merit commission for reappointment.

46. *Id.*

47. *Id.* Massachusetts and Rhode Island use merit selection to pick judges initially, while New Hampshire relies on gubernatorial appointment, with approval of a five-member executive council.

48. Shugerman, *supra* note 33, at 240.

49. *Id.* at 240, 252.

50. *Id.* at 252–53.

51. *Id*. at 257–58.

52. Geyh, *Why Judicial Elections Stink, supra* note 18, at 50.

53. Though, to be sure, it still matters in other ways—especially in terms of qualifications. Longer, nonrenewable terms arguably create more pressure to pick capable candidates upfront precisely because there is no going back once a judge is picked, short of removal for misconduct.

54. *See, e.g.*, Geyh, *Why Judicial Elections Stink, supra* note 18.

55. Shugerman, *supra* note 33, at 257.

56. *Id*. at 257–59. "However, as the bar has become increasingly diverse, so too have the nominations by the bar leadership on merit commissions."

57. 536 U.S. 765 (2002).

58. *Id*. at 784.

59. *Id*. Justice Scalia describes this as "precisely why the election of state judges became popular," which is arguably inaccurate.

60. *White*, 536 U.S. at 784. Under the Rules of Decision Act (codified today as 28 U.S.C. § 1652), federal judges are not supposed to make common law. However, rightly or wrongly, a number of categories of federal common law exist. *See, e.g.*, Texas Industries, Inc. v. Radcliff Materials, Inc., 451 U.S. 630, 640 (1981), noting that "the Court has recognized the need and authority in some limited areas to formulate what has come to be known as 'federal common law.'" In addition, federal courts shape the law in myriad other ways simply by virtue of being part of a system that relies on binding precedent.

61. *See, e.g.*, John Chipman Gray, The Nature and Sources of the Law 114 (2d ed. 1921): "The essence of a judge's office is that he shall be impartial, that he is to sit apart, is not to interfere voluntarily in affairs, is not to act *sua sponte*, but is to determine cases which are presented to him."

62. As the Court's Fourteenth Amendment jurisprudence makes clear.

63. *White*, 536 U.S. at 782.

64. *See, e.g., id*. at 813 (Ginsburg, J., dissenting): "[J]udicial obligation to avoid prejudgment corresponds to the litigant's right, protected by the Due Process Clause of the Fourteenth Amendment, to an 'impartial and disinterested tribunal in both civil and criminal cases'" (internal citations omitted). Justice O'Connor's concurrence also recognizes the danger that judicial reelection poses, although it does not *explicitly* cast it in due process terms. *E.g.*, "Elected judges cannot help being aware if the public is not satisfied with the outcome of a particular case, it could hurt their reelection prospects." *Id*. at 789 (O'Connor, J., concurring).

65. *Id*. at 815–16 (Ginsburg, J., dissenting) (internal citations omitted).

66. *Id*. at 815–16 (internal citations omitted).

67. *Id*. at 800 (Stevens, J., dissenting).

68. *Id*.

69. Caperton v. A. T. Massey Coal Co., 556 U.S. 868, 884 (2009). Blankenship spent $3 million on Benjamin's behalf in the run-up to the election and appeal, more than the total amount spent by all other Benjamin supporters, and $1 million more than the total amount spent by the campaign committees of both candidates combined. *Id*. at 873.

70. *Id*. at 874.

71. *Id.* at 883, citing Tumey v. Ohio, 273 U.S. 510, 532 (1927); Mayberry v. Pennsylvania, 400 U.S. 455, 465–66 (1971); and Aetna Life Ins. Co. v. Lavoie, 475 U.S. 813, 825 (1986).

72. *Id.*

73. 273 U.S. at 532.

74. *Id.* at 522, 531.

75. Caperton, 556 U.S. at 877–87.

76. Mayberry, 400 U.S. 455.

77. Among other things, the defendant called the judge a "dirty sonofabitch" and a "dirty, tyrannical old dog," told the judge to "go to hell," and referred to the proceedings as "bullshit." *Id.* at 456–62.

78. *Id.* at 466–67.

79. *Id.* at 456: "Petitioner's conduct at the trial comes as a shock to those raised in the Western tradition that considers a courtroom a hallowed place of quiet dignity as far removed as possible from the emotions of the street."

80. *See, e.g.,* Caperton, 556 U.S. at 881.

81. Tumey v. Ohio, 273 U.S. 510, 531 (1927).

82. *Id.* at 519–20, 523–24.

83. *Id.* at 532.

84. 409 U.S. 57, 57–58 (1972).

85. *Id.* at 60. *See also* Dugan v. Ohio, 277 U.S. 61 (1928) (mayor's court upheld when mayor was paid a fixed salary regardless of conviction rate).

86. 475 U.S. 813, 822–24 (1986).

87. *Id.* at 824.

88. *Id.* at 825. *See* Dr. Bonham's Case, 77 Eng. Rep. 646, 8 Coke 114a (C.P. 1610).

89. *See* Connally v. Georgia, 429 U.S. 245 (1977) (overturning Georgia system that paid justices of the peace based on the number of search warrants they issued); Gibson v. Berryhill, 411 U.S. 564 (1973) (pecuniary interest of members of state optometry board, optometrists themselves, sufficient to bar them from adjudicating a law that would put half of their competitors out of business).

90. Caperton v. A. T. Massey Coal. Co., 556 U.S. 868, 882 (2009) (Kennedy, J., paraphrasing petitioner's briefs/argument).

91. *Id.* at 884.

92. *Id.* at 873, 876 (Benjamin was elected in 2004 and last refused to recuse in 2008; West Virginia's high court judges serve twelve-year terms).

93. Indeed, as the *Caperton* opinion notes, nearly every state has adopted judicial conduct codes to guard against this type of appearance of impropriety, requiring judges to disqualify themselves from hearing cases in which their impartiality "might reasonably be questioned." *Id.* at 888. Two other West Virginia Supreme Court of Appeals justices recused themselves from rehearing the *Caperton* appeal on these grounds; Justice Benjamin refused. *Id.* at 874–75. In dissent, two of his fellow justices assailed him for participating in the decision. *Id.* at 875.

94. *See, e.g.,* Charles Gardner Geyh, The Endless Judicial Selection Debate and Why It Matters for Judicial Independence, 21 Geo. J. Legal Ethics 1259, 1276 (2008): "[T]he primary threat to independence arises at the point of re-selection, when judges are put at risk of losing their jobs for unpopular decisions that they previously made."

95. *Caperton*, 556 U.S. at 883–84, 887, quoting Withrow v. Larkin, 421 U.S. 35, 47 (1975).

96. *Id*. at 893–98 (Roberts, C.J., dissenting).

97. U.S. Const. Art. III. For instance, federal judges routinely hear cases involving challenges to statutes passed by, and decisions made by, the administration that appointed them, including the 2012 health care decision (Nat'l Fed'n of Indep. Bus. v. Sebelius, 567 U.S.) (with Obama-appointed Justices Kagan and Sotomayor participating). For a mundane but representative example, *see, e.g.*, Papazoglou v. Napolitano, No. 1:12-cv-00982, 2012 WL 1570778 (N.D. Ill. May 3, 2012) (federal district judge, an Obama appointee, ruling on an Obama administration Department of Homeland Security decision).

98. *Caperton*, 556 U.S. at 885.

99. It is true, of course, that even insulated federal judges could conceivably shape their decisions to curry favor with those empowered to promote them to a higher court or to raise their salaries. The only means of preventing these possibly skewing incentives, however, would be to prohibit either promotion or salary or salary increases—for a variety of obvious reasons, an untenable result.

100. Bush v. Gore, 531 U.S. 98 (2000).

101. 520 U.S. 681 (1997) (holding that a sitting president is not immune from civil suits against him for actions taken before he became president, and unrelated to the office of the presidency).

102. *See* Redish & Marshall, *supra* note 21, at 498–99.

103. *See* discussion infra at 158–62.

104. Redish & Marshall, *supra* note 21, at 492.

105. *Id*.

106. *Id*. at 492, 500.

107. *Id*. at 492.

108. *Id*. at 494, 496.

109. *Federalist* No. 79 (Hamilton).

110. Tumey v. Ohio, 273 U.S. 510, 531 (1927).

111. *Id*. at 533.

112. *See generally* Shugerman, *supra* note 33.

113. To wit: It has now been more than twenty-five years since a state has amended its constitution to replace contested judicial elections with a merit selection system. American Judicature Society, Responding to the 2010 Judicial Elections, 68 Bench and Bar of Minnesota 33 (Jan. 2011).

114. 551 U.S. 449 (2007).

115. Citizens United v. FEC, 558 U.S. 310 (2010).

116. Henry Paul Monaghan, The Confirmation Process: Law or Politics?, 101 Harv. L. Rev. 1202, 1211 (1988).

117. *See* Michael R. Dimino, Sr., We Have Met the Special Interests, and We Are They, 74 Mo. L. Rev. 495, 500 (2009), proposing lengthy, nonrenewable terms for state court judges, because the "pressure on judges to decide cases consistently with popular opinion, rather than with the law, may be too great in a system where judges' jobs depend on someone else's evaluation of their decisions."

118. Steven G. Calabresi & James Lindgren, Term Limits for the Supreme Court: Life Tenure Reconsidered, 29 Harv. J.L. & Pub. Pol'y 769, 843 (2006), cit-

ing James E. DiTullio & John B. Schochet, Note, Saving This Honorable Court: A Proposal to Replace Life Tenure on the Supreme Court With Staggered, Nonrenewable Eighteen-Year Terms, 90 Va. L. Rev. 1093, 1128 (2004).

119. DiTullio & Schochet, *supra* note 118, at 1128–29.

120. Methods of Judicial Selection, *supra* note 30.

121. *Id.* Alternately, states uncomfortable with life tenure could instead impose a mandatory retirement age, as in Massachusetts and New Hampshire, where judges must step down at age seventy.

122. *See generally* Martin H. Redish, Good Behavior, Judicial Independence, and the Foundations of American Constitutionalism, 116 Yale L.J. 139, 152–53 (2006) (setting out why both the micro and macro levels of analysis "represent essential elements of American political and constitutional theory").

123. *Id.* at 152.

124. Redish & Marshall, *supra* note 21, at 488.

125. *See, e.g.,* Tracey L. Meares, Everything Old Is New Again: Fundamental Fairness and the Legitimacy of Criminal Justice, 3 Ohio St. J. Crim. L. 105, 108 (2005).

126. *Id.*; John R. Allison, Combinations of Decision-Making Functions, Ex Parte Communications, and Related Biasing Influences: A Process-Value Analysis, 1993 Utah L. Rev. 1135, 1158 (1993).

127. Redish & Marshall, *supra* note 21, at 483.

128. Tumey v. Ohio, 273 U.S. 510, 531–32, 535 (1927).

129. *Id.*

130. *Id.* at 535.

131. 349 U.S. 133, 136 (1955), citing Offutt v. United States, 348 U.S. 11, 14 (1954).

132. *See, e.g.,* Joanna M. Shepherd, Money, Politics, and Impartial Justice, 58 Duke L.J. 623, 623 (2009), providing "empirical evidence that elected state supreme court judges routinely adjust their rulings to attract votes and campaign money" and "evidence that judges change their rulings when the political preferences of their voters change." This speaks to the need for prophylactic protection: The fact that there is even a *debate* about whether this is the case should be enough to answer the question of whether judicial retention elections are unconstitutional.

133. Carey v. Piphus, 435 U.S. 247, 259 (1978).

134. Reva B. Siegel, Dignity and the Politics of Protection: Abortion Restrictions Under Casey/Carhart, 117 Yale L.J. 1694, 1736 (2008): "The United States Constitution does not have a dignity clause, but Supreme Court opinions regularly and increasingly invoke dignity as a lens through which to make sense of the document's structural and individual rights guarantees."

135. Redish & Marshall, *supra* note 21, at 457, 476, 479: "Once that protection is dispensed with, the provision of all other procedural safeguards cannot cure the violation of fundamental fairness." *See also* Ellen E. Sward, Values, Ideology and the Evolution of the Adversary System, 64 Ind. L.J. 301, 308 (1989) (describing an impartial decision maker as the first requirement of a fair adjudication, because it "helps to ensure that the decision is based on the merits of the controversy"); Henry J. Friendly, "Some Kind of Hearing," 123 U. Pa. L. Rev. 1267, 1278–79 (1975) (calling an unbiased tribunal the most important factor in ensuring a fair hearing).

136. Redish & Marshall, *supra* note 21, at 476.

137. *Id*. at 476–77.

138. *Id*. at 479.

139. *See, e.g.*, Jerry L. Mashaw, Administrative Due Process: The Quest for a Dignitary Theory, 61 B.U. L. Rev. 885, 886 (1981).

140. *See* Meares, *supra* note 125, at 111.

141. Redish & Marshall, *supra* note 21, at 482–83.

142. *Id*. at 486.

143. *See id*.

144. *Id*. at 490.

145. *See, e.g.*, Marbury v. Madison, 5 U.S. (1 Cranch) 137, 176 (1803): "The distinction, between a government with limited and unlimited powers, is abolished, if those limits do not confine the persons on whom they are imposed." *See generally* chapter 1, *supra*.

146. U.S. Const. Art. III. *See also Federalist* No. 78 (Hamilton), noting that "[t]he complete independence of the courts of justice is peculiarly essential in a limited Constitution," and that life tenure is necessary if "the courts of justice are to be considered as the bulwarks of a limited Constitution against legislative encroachments."

147. *Federalist* No. 78 (Hamilton).

148. David E. Pozen, Judicial Elections as Popular Constitutionalism, 110 Colum. L. Rev. 2047, 2124–25 (2010) (citations omitted).

149. Republican Party of Minnesota v. White, 536 U.S. 765, 803–04 (2002) (Ginsburg, J., dissenting), quoting Chisom v. Roemer, 501 U.S. 380, 411 (1991) (Scalia, J., dissenting). In contrast, "judge[s] represen[t] the Law," deciding individual cases based on the law and facts before them, and are expected to "refrain from catering to particular constituencies" or prejudging cases.

150. *See, e.g.*, Martin H. Redish, Constitutional Limitations on Congressional Power to Control Federal Jurisdiction: A Response to Professor Sager, 77 Nw. U. L. Rev. 143, 156 (1982) (describing a "constitutional history which has always assumed that state courts could ultimately stand as the equal of the federal courts as protectors of constitutional rights").

151. An example is the rights of criminal defendants.

152. U.S. Const. Art. V (requiring complex supermajoritarian process for amendment).

153. Croley, *supra* note 29, at 693–94.

154. *Id*. at 694.

155. *See* 179–82 , *infra*.

156. *See, e.g.*, Larry D. Kramer, The People Themselves: Popular Constitutionalism and Judicial Review 107 (2004).

157. Larry Alexander & Lawrence B. Solum, Popular? Constitutionalism? 118 Harv. L. Rev. 1594, 1598 (2005) (reviewing Kramer, The People Themselves, and paraphrasing its arguments at, *e.g.*, 83–84, 105).

158. *See, e.g.*, Erwin Chemerinsky, In Defense of Judicial Review: The Perils of Popular Constitutionalism, 2004 U. Ill. L. Rev. 673, 676 (decrying the failure of popular constitutionalists "to define the concept with any precision").

159. Pozen, *supra* note 148, at 2052.

160. This, admittedly, could also serve as a criticism of popular constitutionalism more broadly.

161. Pozen, *supra* note 148, at 2129.

162. *Id.* at 2131, citing Robert Post & Reva Siegel, Popular Constitutionalism, Departmentalism, and Judicial Supremacy, 92 Cal. L. Rev. 1027, 1036 (2004).

163. Kramer, *supra* note 156, at 45.

164. *See, e.g.,* Kramer, *supra* note 156, at 78. *Cf.* Martin H. Redish, The Federal Courts in the Political Order 4 (1991): "[O]ur system is far from a total or unlimited representative democracy. . . . Both practically and theoretically . . . the Constitution provides counter-majoritarian (at least counter-*simple*-majoritarian) limits on democratic government."

165. *Id.* at 242–43.

166. *Id.* at 243.

167. *See, e.g.,* Mortimer Sellers, An Introduction to the Rule of Law in Comparative Perspective, in The Rule of Law in Comparative Perspective 5 (Mortimer Sellers & Tadeusz Tomaszewski, eds., 2010).

168. Alexis de Tocqueville, Democracy in America, vol. 1, pt. 2, ch. 8 (p. 247 in 1966 English trans., J. P. Mayer & Max Lerner, eds.).

169. Post & Siegel, *supra* note 162, at 1035.

170. Redish, *supra* note 164, at 5.

CHAPTER FIVE

1. Chapter 5 derives from *Legislative Deception, Separation of Powers, and the Democratic Process: Harnessing the Political Theory of United States v. Klein,* 100 Northwestern Law Review 437 (2006), an article I coauthored with Christopher Pudelski.

2. Lochner v. New York, 198 U.S. 45 (1905), is perhaps the best illustration of this subcategory. *See,* e.g., David A. Strauss, Why Was Lochner Wrong? 70 U. Chi. L. Rev. 373 (2003).

3. United States v. Klein, 80 U.S. (13 Wall.) 128 (1872).

4. *See, e.g.,* Richard A. Doidge, Note, Is Purely Retroactive Legislation Limited by the Separation of Powers?: Rethinking United States v. Klein, 79 Cornell L. Rev. 910 (1994); William F. Ryan, Rush to Judgment: A Constitutional Analysis of Time Limits on Judicial Decisions, 77 B.U. L. Rev. 761 (1997); Lawrence G. Sager, Klein's First Principle: A Proposed Solution, 86 Geo. L.J. 2525 (1998); Gordon G. Young, Congressional Regulation of Federal Courts' Jurisdiction and Processes: United States v. Klein Revisited, 1981 Wis. L. Rev. 1189.

5. For example, in United States v. Sioux Nation, 448 U.S. 371, 404 (1980), the Court described *Klein* in the following manner: "[T]he [congressionally enacted] proviso was unconstitutional in two respects: First, it prescribed a rule of decision in a case pending before the courts, and did so in a manner that required the courts to decide a controversy in the Government's favor. . . . Second, the rule prescribed by the proviso 'is also liable to just exception as impairing the effect of a pardon and thus infringing the constitutional power of the Executive.'" *Id.* quoting *Klein,* 80 (13 Wall.) at 147. As subsequently explained, neither of these holdings makes the slightest constitutional sense.

6. U.S. Const. Art. III § 2: "In all cases affecting ambassadors, other public ministers and consuls, and those in which a State shall be party, the Supreme

Court shall have original jurisdiction. In all the other cases before mentioned, the Supreme Court shall have appellate jurisdiction, both as to law and fact, with such exceptions, and under such regulations as the Congress shall make."

7. For a detailed description of the facts and holding of *Klein*, see discussion *infra* at 143–44.

8. The Sherman Antitrust Act, 15 U.S.C. § 1 (2000), provides a good illustration of this process of substantive legislative delegation. *See, e.g.*, Standard Oil Co. v. United States, 221 U.S. 1, 51 (1911), analyzing the statutory term "restraint of trade" by reference to use of these words in the common law evolutionary tradition.

9. This analytical dichotomy parallels the one employed in chapter 4.

10. For a discussion of how one may operationalize the concept of a law's DNA, *see* discussion *infra* at 158–62.

11. *See* discussion *infra* at 158–62.

12. *See* discussion *infra* at 143–49.

13. *See* discussion *infra* at 143–49.

14. *See* United States v. Sioux Nation, 448 U.S. 371, 402–03 (1980).

15. *See* Robertson v. Seattle Audubon Soc'y, 503 U.S. 429 (1992).

16. *See* discussion *infra* at 143–48.

17. *See* discussion *infra* at 149–53.

18. *See* discussion *infra* at 158–62.

19. *See* discussion *infra* at 162–64.

20. Act of July 12, 1870, ch. 251, 16 Stat. 230 (1870). For an excellently detailed history of the act, see Young, *supra* note 4.

21. The original proposal of the act explicitly required that "the Supreme Court shall on appeal reverse" judgments where a pardon established innocence in the Court of Claims; however, it was later reworded to use the "softer" language requiring the Court to "dismiss the cause" of action entirely. *See* Young, *supra* note 4, at 1208.

22. *Id*. at 1205. As the Supreme Court explained in United States v. Klein: "The substance of this enactment is that an acceptance of a pardon, without disclaimer, shall be conclusive evidence of the acts pardoned, but shall be null and void as evidence of the rights conferred by it, both in the Court of Claims and in this court on appeal." 80 U.S. (13 Wall.) 128, 144 (1872).

23. U.S Const. Art. III §2 cl. 2.

24. Admittedly, the *Klein* opinion itself is a terse read, and it is difficult to distinguish the Court's dictum from its actual holding. A fair reading recognizes, however, that at least one clear and agreeable ground for decision can be drawn from the opinion.

25. *Klein*, 80 U.S. (13 Wall.) at 146.

26. *Id*.

27. *Id*. at 147. The Court went on to say, "We must think that Congress has inadvertently passed the limit which separates the legislative from the judicial power." *Id*.

28. *Id*. at 145.

29. *Id*.

30. *Federalist* No. 78; Michael Stokes Paulsen, *The Irrepressible Myth of Marbury*, 101 Mich. L. Rev. 2706 (2003).

31. *See, e.g.*, Paulsen, *supra* note 30.

32. *See* Yakus v. United States, 321 U.S. 414, 468 (1944) (Rutledge, J., dissenting): "It is one thing for Congress to withhold jurisdiction. It is entirely another to confer it and direct that it be exercised in a manner inconsistent with constitutional requirements or, what in some instances may be the same thing, without regard to them."

33. *Klein*, 80 U.S. (13 Wall.) at 146.

34. *Id.*

35. U.S. Const. Art. I § 1.

36. *See, e.g.*, United States v. Schooner Peggy, 5 U.S. (1 Cranch) 103, 110 (1801).

37. The modern-day Supreme Court has said as much. See Plaut v. Spendthrift Farm, Inc., 514 U.S. 211, 218 (1995), noting that "later decisions have made clear" that *Klein's* prohibition on congressional prescription of rules of decision in pending cases "does not take hold when Congress 'amends applicable law,'" quoting Robertson v. Seattle Audubon Soc'y, 503 U.S. 429, 441 (1992).

38. 59 U.S. (18 How.) 421 (1855).

39. *Klein*, 80 U.S. at 146.

40. *Id.* at 147.

41. *Id.*

42. *See* discussion *supra* at 147.

43. *See, e.g.*, United States v. Sioux Nation, 448 U.S. 371 (1980).

44. *See* Plaut v. Spendthrift Farm, Inc., 514 U.S. 211, 218 (1995), noting that Congress may not overrule specific decisions of the federal courts.

45. *See* discussion *supra* at 145–46.

46. *See* discussion *supra* at 145.

47. *See* Martin H. Redish & Elizabeth J. Cisar, *"If Angels Were to Govern": The Need for Pragmatic Formalism in Separation of Powers Theory*, 41 Duke L.J. 449 (1991).

48. *See, e.g.*, Frank H. Easterbrook, *Substance and Due Process*, 1982 Sup. Ct. Rev. 85.

49. In situations where a court has already issued a final decision, legislative action seeking to reopen that litigation would be unconstitutional. See Plaut, 514 U.S. 211. However, where—as in *Wheeling Bridge*—the judicial relief that had been issued was ongoing, the court must adhere to a change in the governing substantive law. Pennsylvania v. Wheeling and Belmont Bridge Co., 59 U.S. (18 How.) 421 (1855).

50. *See* discussion *supra* at 147–48.

51. *Id.*

52. U.S. Const. Art. II § 2.

53. Whether this was actually the case in the *Klein* context is by no means clear. However, for reasons I subsequently explain, it would be unwise to have application of the legislative-deception model turn on an empirical assessment of the extent to which the public was actually deceived in the particular case.

54. *See* discussion *infra* at 145.

55. *See* discussion *infra* at 147–48.

56. H. B. Mayo, An Introduction to Democratic Theory 103 (1960). *See also* J. Roland Pennock, Democratic Political Theory 310 (1979): "Elections are thought to constitute the great sanction for assuring representative behavior, by showing what the voters consider to be their interests by giving them the incentive to pursue those objectives."

57. Cass R. Sunstein, *Beyond the Republican Revival*, 97 Yale L.J. 1539, 1545–46 (1988). In the words of Sunstein, "[i]n any representative democracy, there is simply too much slippage between legislative outcomes and constituent desires." *Id.* at 1546.

58. Robert A. Dahl, A Preface to Democratic Theory 131–32 (1956). As democratic theorist Robert Dahl has stated in response to such a line of argumentation that "[e]lections and political competition do not make for government by majorities in any very significant way, but they vastly increase the size, number, and varieties of minorities whose preferences must be taken into account by leaders in making policy choices." *Id.* at 132.

59. *See, e.g.*, Hanna Fenichel Pitkin, The Concept of Representation 14–20 (1967), discussing Hobbes's political theory, which advocated a significant amount of implied authority to elected officials. *See generally* Joseph A. Schumpeter, Capitalism, Socialism, and Democracy (1942).

60. For different uses of the political commitment principle, see Martin H. Redish, The Constitution as Political Structure 137–38, 156–61 (1995).

61. The position taken here is that nothing should turn on whether the nonsubstantive modification comes contemporaneously or subsequently, though in *Klein* the modification came subsequently.

62. 491 U.S. 110 (1989).

63. *See* John C. P. Goldberg, Twentieth-Century Tort Theory, 91 Geo. L.J. 513, 529–31 (2003), contrasting differences among alternative theories of tort.

64. *See* Jerry L. Mashaw, Prodelegation: Why Administrators Should Make Political Decisions, 1 J.L. Econ. & Org. 81, 95 (1985), asserting that "[a]ll we need do is not forget there are also presidential elections and that . . . presidents are heads of administrations." As Professor Mashaw has argued, the dynamics of accountability apparently involve voters willing to vote upon the basis of their representative's record in the legislature. *Id.* Assuming that our current representatives in the legislature vote for laws that contain vague delegations of authority, we are presumably holding them accountable for that at the polls. How is it that we are not being represented?

65. 491 U.S. 110 (1989).

66. It is possible, of course, that Congress could direct resolution of a particular case in exactly the same way that the adjudicating court would have resolved it even absent congressional direction. We cannot know this at the outset of the litigation, however, and in any event, if it is true then there was no point to the congressional direction in the first place.

67. *See* discussion *supra* at 153–54.

68. 503 U.S. 429 (1992).

69. Seattle Audubon Soc'y v. Robertson, 914 F.2d 1311 (9th Cir. 1990). These acts included the Oregon and California Lands Act, 43 U.S.C. § 1181 (2000), the

Federal Land Policy and Management Act, 43 U.S.C. §§ 1701–1782 (2000), and the Migratory Bird Treaty Act, 16 U.S.C. §§ 703–711 (2000).

70. Dep't of the Interior and Related Agencies Appropriations Act for Fiscal Year 1990, Pub. L. No. 101–121, § 318, 103 Stat. 701, 745–50 (1989).

71. *Seattle Audubon*, 914 F.2d at 1313: "Without passing on the legal and factual adequacy of [prior agreements that defined timber sales] . . . the Congress hereby determines and directs that management of areas according to subsections (b)(3) and (b)(5) of this section . . . is adequate consideration for the purpose of meeting the statutory requirements that are the basis for the consolidated cases captioned Seattle Audubon Society et al., v. F. Dale Robertson, Civil No. 89–160 and Washington Contract Loggers Assoc. et al., v. F. Dale Robertson, Civil No. 89–99 . . . and the case Portland Audubon Society et al., v. Manuel Lujan, Jr., Civil No. 87–1160-FR. The guidelines adopted by subsections (b)(3) and (b)(5) of this section shall not be subject to judicial review by any court of the United States."

72. *Id.* at 1316–17.

73. *Id.* at 1316: "Section 318 does not, by its plain language, repeal or amend the environmental laws underlying this litigation, even though some subsections add additional requirements."

74. Robertson v. Seattle Audubon Soc'y, 503 U.S. 429 (1992).

75. *Id.* at 440.

76. *Id.* at 438.

77. Indeed, commentators have argued that the essence of a substantive right created by a legislative body necessarily includes the procedural baggage imposed by that body on the enforcement of that right. *See* Easterbrook, *supra* note 48.

78. *See, e.g.*, Donnelly v. Illini Cash Advance, Inc., No. 00C094, 2000 WL 1161076 (N.D. Ill. Aug. 16, 2000), asserting that an affirmative statement on front of contract that no security interest is taken defeats boilerplate language to the contrary on back of the contract.

79. It may well be true, e.g., that in *Klein* it was widely understood how Congress was actually attempting to alter substantive law.

80. It is certainly conceivable that the *Klein* case itself was an instance in which widespread political debate existed, yet the Court proceeded on the implicit assumption of lack of public awareness.

81. 28 U.S.C. § 2072(b).

82. *See* discussion *supra* at 147–48.

83. 28 U.S.C. § 2072.

84. U.S. Const. Art. III § 1.

85. Plaut v. Spendthrift Farm, Inc., 514 U.S. 211, 219 (1995), citing Gordon S. Wood, The Creation of the American Republic, 1776–1787, at 154–55 (1969).

86. *Federalist* No. 48, at 251 (Madison) (Gary Wills, ed., 1982); *see also* Gordon S. Wood, The Radicalism of the American Revolution 322–23 (1992): "As early as the 1780s many were already contending that only the judiciary in America was impartial and free enough of private interests to solve [the] problem [of protecting private property and minority rights]. . . . These efforts to carve out an exclusive sphere of activity for the judiciary, a sphere where the adjudicating of private rights was removed from politics and legislative power, contributed to the remarkable

process by which the judiciary in America suddenly emerged out of its colonial insignificance to become by 1800 the principal means by which popular legislatures were controlled and limited. The most dramatic institutional transformation in the early Republic was the rise of what was called an 'independent judiciary.'"

87. As the Supreme Court has stated, "[t]he Framers of our Constitution lived among the ruins of a system of intermingled legislative and judicial powers, which had been prevalent in the colonies long before the Revolution, and which after the Revolution had produced factional strife and partisan oppression." *Plaut*, 514 U.S. at 219.

88. U.S. Const. Art. III § 1; see Martin H. Redish, Federal Judicial Independence: Constitutional and Political Perspectives, 46 Mercer L. Rev. 697, 700–706 (1995).

89. *See, e.g.*, Lockerty v. Phillips, 319 U.S. 182 (1943); Sheldon v. Sill, 49 U.S. (8 How.) 441 (1850); *see also* Martin H. Redish, Federal Jurisdiction: Tensions in the Allocation of Judicial Power 24–47 (2d ed., 1990).

90. Henry M. Hart, Jr., The Power of Congress to Limit the Jurisdiction of Federal Courts: An Exercise in Dialectic, 66 Harv. L. Rev. 1362, 1372–73 (1953); *see also* Yakus v. United States, 321 U.S. 414, 467 (1944) (Rutledge, J., dissenting), raising doubt as to whether "Congress can confer jurisdiction upon federal and state courts in the enforcement proceedings [under the Emergency Price Control Act of 1942], more particularly the criminal suit, and at the same time deny them jurisdiction or power to consider the validity of the regulations for which enforcement is thus sought" (internal citations omitted). To Justice Rutledge, it was "one thing for Congress to withhold jurisdiction. It is entirely another to confer it and direct that it be exercised in a manner inconsistent with constitutional requirements, or, what in some instances may be the same thing, without regard to them." *Id.* at 468. In delimiting the scope of judicial independence from the legislative branch of the federal government, it is important to distinguish the unconstitutional restrictions on judicial power from the constitutionally valid congressional power to engage in generalized lawmaking. The danger to which the legislative-deception model is directed is that instead of engaging in such generalized substantive lawmaking, Congress will employ the federal judiciary as an instrument of deception through the use of seemingly nonsubstantive devices that alter the essence of that substantive law.

91. *See* discussion *supra* at 144.

92. Hart, *supra* note 90, at 1372–73.

CHAPTER SIX

1. Chapter 6 derives from *Habeas Corpus, Due Process and the Suspension Clause: A Study in the Foundations of American Constitutionalism*, 96 Virginia Law Review 136 (2010), an article I coauthored with Colleen McNamara. Reproduced with permission of the publisher; permission conveyed through Copyright Clearance Center, Inc.

2. Daniel John Meador, Habeas Corpus and Magna Carta: Dualism of Power and Liberty 4 (1966).

3. Youngstown Sheet & Tube Co. v. Sawyer, 343 U.S. 579, 650 (1952) (Jackson, J., concurring).

4. U.S. Const. Art. I §9 cl. 2. The text of the clause does not specify which branch or branches holds the power to suspend the writ. The Supreme Court has generally reasoned that the clause's placement in Article I implies that the power rests solely with Congress. *See* Hamdi v. Rumsfeld, 542 U.S. 507, 537 (2004), alluding to Congress's power to suspend the writ; *see also* Ex Parte Merryman, 17 F. Cas. 144, 148–49 (Taney, Circuit Justice, C.C.D. Md. 1861) (No. 9,487). President Lincoln, however, asserted and maintained the writ as an executive function. Youngstown, 343 U.S. at 637 n 3. For a general discussion of the locus of the authority to suspend the writ, see David L. Shapiro, Habeas Corpus, Suspension, and Detention: Another View, 82 Notre Dame L. Rev. 59, 70–73 (2006).

5. *See* Gerald L. Neuman, Habeas Corpus, Executive Detention, and the Removal of Aliens, 98 Colum. L. Rev. 961, 977–78 (1998), describing the four suspensions. The first suspension of habeas corpus under the U.S. Constitution occurred during the Civil War, when President Lincoln authorized his military leaders to suspend the writ to protect particular areas that were critical to the defense of the union. Amanda L. Tyler, Suspension as an Emergency Power, 118 Yale L.J. 600, 637 (2009). After Congress officially authorized the suspension by passing the Habeas Corpus Act of 1863, Lincoln soon suspended the writ nationwide. Trevor W. Morrison, Suspension and the Extrajudicial Constitution, 107 Colum. L. Rev. 1533, 1562 (2007). In 1871, President Grant suspended habeas corpus in parts of South Carolina to combat a rebellion by the Ku Klux Klan. See Proclamation No. 4 of 1871, 17 Stat. 951, 951–52 (1871). He had been authorized to do so by the Ku Klux Klan Act of 1871, ch. 22, §4, 17 Stat. 13, 14–15. In 1905, the Civil Governor of the Philippines suspended habeas pursuant to authority granted to him and the president by the Act of July 1, 1902, ch. 1369, §5, 32 Stat. 691, 692. Fisher v. Baker, 203 U.S. 174, 179–81 (1906). Finally, immediately following the Japanese attack on Pearl Harbor, the governor of Hawaii suspended the writ pursuant to the Hawaiian Organic Act of 1900, ch. 339, §67, 31 Stat. 141, 153. Duncan v. Kahanamoku, 327 U.S. 304, 307–08 (1946).

6. Various sources suggest that the original draft of the USA PATRIOT Act included a provision calling for the suspension of habeas corpus. *See, e.g.,* Jonathan Alter, Keeping Order in the Courts, Newsweek, Dec. 10, 2001, at 48. *See* also Tyler, *supra* note 5, at 603 n.7 (collecting citations to additional sources).

7. *Cf.* Shapiro, *supra* note 4, at 90, arguing that the "very purpose of the suspension" would be undermined if the executive was deterred from authorizing detentions that might subsequently lead to financial liability or an alleged violation of the presidential oath, and Tyler, *supra* note 5, at 682, arguing that a valid suspension "does in fact expand the scope of executive power to arrest and detain," with Morrison, *supra* note 5, at 1541, arguing that suspension does not affect the legality of the detention or the availability of post-detention remedies.

8. Both history and psychology clearly demonstrate that this is a likely consequence of a national crisis. In his recent historical analysis of American responses to past crises, Geoffrey Stone describes the nation's historical tendency to exercise extreme deference to executive measures purportedly designed to further national security interests when we are in the midst of a national emergency. Geoffrey R. Stone, War and Liberty 167 (2007). He also notes that such measures are almost universally viewed as regrettable and unjustified after the fact. *Id.*

9. Tyler, *supra* note 5, at 609; *see also* Shapiro, *supra* note 4, at 88, describing the due process right to challenge executive detention and the remedy of habeas corpus as, in a practical sense, "not just interdependent but inseparable."

10. *See* Morrison, *supra* note 5, at 1609, arguing that "the executive can (and should) implement core facets of due process even during a period of suspension."

11. *See* discussion *infra* at 173–74.

12. *See* U.S. Const. Amend. XXI (repealing U.S. Const. Amend. XVIII).

13. *See* discussion *infra* at 178–79.

14. U.S. Const. Amend. V.

15. *Id.*

16. *See* discussion *infra* at 174–76.

17. *See* discussion *infra* at 173–76.

18. R. J. Sharpe, The Law of Habeas Corpus 8–15 (1976); *see, e.g.,* Chambers's Case, (1629) 79 Eng. Rep. 717 (K.B.) (using habeas corpus to question the validity of detention by the king).

19. See Rollin C. Hurd, A Treatise on the Right of Personal Liberty, and on the Writ of Habeas Corpus and the Practice Connected With It: With a View of the Law of Extradition of Fugitives 144 (1858). Chancery, King's Bench, Common Pleas, and Exchequer all had authority to issue the writ. Robert Searles Walker, Habeas Corpus Writ of Liberty: English and American Origins and Development 80 (2006).

20. Sir Edward Coke, The Second Part of the Institutes of the Laws of England 50 (5th ed., 1671). Modern scholars have noted that Coke dramatically overstated, if not invented, the historical link between the writ and Magna Carta. *See, e.g.,* Meador, *supra* note 2, at 21–24. Nevertheless, Sir William Blackstone later invoked Coke's ideas in his own Commentaries on the Laws of England and described the writ of habeas corpus as the "great bulwark" of the British Constitution. Blackstone, Commentaries, at 438. This statement by Blackstone was later quoted by Hamilton in *Federalist* No. 84, at 512 (Clinton Rossiter, ed., 1961).

21. 31 Car. 2, c.2 (1679) (Eng.).

22. *See* Meador, *supra* note 2, at 4; Walker, *supra* note 19, at 107, noting that while "England had supremely important legal documents" like Magna Carta and the Habeas Corpus Act, its system did not "point to a single, supreme originating instrument" that could impose constraints on Parliament.

23. *See* Rex A. Collings, Jr., Habeas Corpus for Convicts—Constitutional Right or Legislative Grace?, 40 Cal. L. Rev. 335, 339 & nn. 23–28 (1952).

24. Shapiro, *supra* note 4, at 83.

25. Parliament passed suspension legislation in 1688, 1696, 1714, 1722, 1744, and 1777, the last of which was renewed annually through the end of the American Revolution. Collings, *supra* note 23, at 339; Amanda L. Tyler, Is Suspension a Political Question? 59 Stan. L. Rev. 333, 344 (2006).

26. The suspensions during the American Revolution, for example, only applied to persons detained on charges of high treason, suspicion of high treason, or piracy. *See* 17 Geo. 3, c. 9 (1777) (Eng.); *see also* Gerald L. Neuman, The Habeas Corpus Suspension Clause after INS v. St. Cyr, 33 Colum. Hum. Rts. L. Rev. 555, 563–64 (2002), emphasizing that the characteristic form of parliamentary suspen-

sion was not a total suspension, but rather suspension for a designated category of detentions.

27. Tor Ekeland, Note, Suspending Habeas Corpus: Article I, Section 9, Clause 2, of the United States Constitution and the War on Terror, 74 Fordham L. Rev. 1475, 1482 (2005).

28. Professor Shapiro suggests that habeas corpus was, in fact, the only remedy for detention, as his research uncovered no cases in which a plaintiff used a different procedural vehicle to obtain his release. *See* Shapiro, *supra* note 4, at 84.

29. In *Federalist* No. 84, for example, Hamilton invoked Blackstone to support his argument that the availability of the writ of habeas corpus rendered an enumerated Bill of Rights unnecessary: "[A]s a remedy for this fatal evil [of arbitrary imprisonment, Blackstone] is everywhere peculiarly emphatical in his encomiums on the habeas corpus act, which in one place he calls 'the bulwark of the British Constitution.'" *Federalist* No. 84 (Hamilton), *supra* note 20, at 512.

30. William F. Duker, A Constitutional History of Habeas Corpus 115 (1980).

31. The North Carolina, Georgia, Massachusetts, New Hampshire, and Pennsylvania constitutions contained provisions explicitly guaranteeing the privilege of habeas corpus. See Zechariah Chafee, Jr., The Most Important Human Right in the Constitution, 32 B.U. L. Rev. 143, 145–46 (1952), reprinting and citing the relevant provisions.

32. *See* Neuman, *supra* note 26, at 564.

33. Mass. Const. pt. 2, ch. VI, art. VII.

34. *See* Tyler, *supra* note 5, at 623–24

35. Eric M. Freedman, The Suspension Clause in the Ratification Debates, 44 Buff. L. Rev. 451, 459 (1996).

36. *See* Walker, *supra* note 19, at 104–05: "[T]he proposed constitution recognized the pre-existence of the citizen's right to be free from arbitrary imprisonment by limiting the government's authority to suspend the operation of the writ."

37. Duker, *supra* note 30, at 129.

38. 17 Geo. 3, c. 9 (1777), authorizing the detention "without Bail or Mainprize" of persons "who have been, or shall hereafter be seised or taken in the Act of High Treason . . . or who are or shall be charged with or suspected of the Crime of High Treason . . . and who have been, or shall be committed . . . for such crimes . . . or for suspicion of such crimes."

39. These acts generally empowered the governor and his officials to arrest and detain suspected Crown sympathizers. *See* Tyler, *supra* note 5, at 622–28, discussing pre-Convention American suspensions.

40. Commonwealth of Massachusetts, An Act for Suspending the Privilege of the Writ of Habeas Corpus, ch. X (1786), in Acts and Laws Passed by the General Court of Massachusetts 510, 510 (Boston, Course & Adams, 1786)

41. Tyler, *supra* note 5, at 626

42. *See* Leonard L. Richards, Shays's Rebellion: The American Revolution's Final Battle 19–21 (2002).

43. The original text of the Suspension Clause provided that "[t]he privileges and benefit of the writ of habeas corpus shall be enjoyed in this government in the most expeditious and ample manner: and shall not be suspended by the Legislature except upon the most urgent and pressing occasions, and for a limited time

not exceeding [X] months." The Records of the Federal Convention of 1787 (Max Farrand, ed., rev. ed., 1966 [hereafter Farrand's Records]), at 2: 334.

44. *Id.,* at 438.

45. *Id.*.

46. Duker, *supra* note 30, at 131.

47. *Id.*

48. 15 The Documentary History of the Ratification of the Constitution 433–34 (John P. Kaminski & Gaspare J. Saladino, eds., 1984) (emphasis in original removed).

49. *See* Thomas Jefferson to James Madison, Dec. 20, 1787, in The Papers of Thomas Jefferson (Julian P. Boyd, ed.), 12 (1955): 438, 440, opposing omission of a bill of rights "providing clearly and without the aid of sophisms for . . . the eternal and unremitting force of the habeas corpus laws"; Jefferson to Madison, July 31, 1788, *id.,* 13 (1956): 440, 442, arguing that a suspension power was unnecessary and undesirable because "for the few cases wherein the suspension of the hab. corp. has done real good, that operation is now become habitual, and the minds of the nation almost prepared to live under it's *[sic]* constant suspension."

50. *See Federalist* No. 47 (Madison defining "tyranny" as the concentration of power within one person or branch.

51. At the time of the ratification debates, the role of the courts within the new federal system had not been fully articulated. The available records of the Convention debates contain little reference to a discussion of judicial review in general, so the Framers likely did not ascertain the possibility of providing for judicial review of a suspension. The institution of judicial review would not officially emerge for another sixteen years, when Chief Justice Marshall issued his seminal opinion in Marbury v. Madison, 5 U.S. (1 Cranch) 137 (1803).

52. Three state delegations dissented from permitting Congress ever to suspend the writ. Neuman, *supra* note 26, at 566.

53. See 2 Farrand's Records, *supra* note 43, at 438, citing the original proposal, the text of which was eventually ratified in Art. I § 9 of the U. S. Constitution. Neuman notes that the reasons for the disappearance of Pinckney's proposal to guarantee the writ "in the most expeditious and ample manner" are uncertain, but he suggests that the wording might have been "too indeterminate to be effective and too difficult to make precise." Neuman, *supra* note 26, at 566.

54. *Id.* at 566–67.

55. 2 Farrand's Records, *supra* note 43, at 576.

56. It also changed the word "where" to "when." *Id.* at 596.

57. "Due process doctrine subsists in confusion," according to Richard H. Fallon, Jr., Some Confusions about Due Process, Judicial Review, and Constitutional Remedies, 93 Colum. L. Rev. 309, 309 (1993).

58. Cynthia R. Farina, Conceiving Due Process, 3 Yale J.L. & Feminism 189, 189 (1991), arguing that beneath the "smooth, plausible skin of the doctrine . . . lies turmoil, contradiction, and . . . destructiveness."

59. Edward L. Rubin, Due Process and the Administrative State, 72 Cal. L. Rev. 1044, 1046 (1984), arguing that the Supreme Court has "clearly fail[ed] to . . . provide a coherent, realistic doctrine for applying our notion of pro-

cedural due process to the recently developed features of the administrative state."

60. *See, e.g.*, Bd. of Regents of State Colls. v. Roth, 408 U.S. 564, 578 (1972), holding that an assistant professor with no tenure rights had no property interest in continued employment at a university; Perry v. Sindermann, 408 U.S. 593, 601–03 (1972), holding that an implied tenure system does create a constitutionally protected property interest in ongoing employment.

61. *See, e.g.*, Goldberg v. Kelly, 397 U.S. 254, 260 (1970) (defining the constitutional issue to be decided as "whether the Due Process Clause requires that the recipient [of welfare benefits] be afforded an evidentiary hearing before the termination of benefits").

62. *See* discussion *infra* at 175.

63. *See* discussion *infra* at 175–76.

64. U.S. Const. Amend. V.

65. The Court most clearly articulated this operational principle in Cleveland Board of Education v. Loudermill, 470 U.S. 532, 541 (1985), in which it stated that "the Due Process Clause provides that certain substantive rights—life, liberty, and property—cannot be deprived except pursuant to constitutionally adequate procedures." *See also* Mathews v. Eldridge, 424 U.S. 319, 333 (1976) (proceeding directly from the recognition of a "property" interest to a determination of what procedures are required); Bd. of Regents, 408 U.S. at 569–70: "When protected interests are implicated, the right to some kind of prior hearing is paramount"; Bell v. Burson, 402 U.S. 535, 542 (1971): "While '[m]any controversies have raged about . . . the Due Process Clause,' . . . it is fundamental that . . . when a State seeks to terminate [a protected] interest . . . , it must afford 'notice and opportunity for hearing appropriate to the nature of the case' before the termination becomes effective" (quoting Mullane v. Cent. Hanover Bank & Trust Co., 339 U.S. 306, 313 (1950).

66. *See, e.g.*, Zinermon v. Burch, 494 U.S. 113, 125 (1990): "In procedural due process claims, the deprivation by state action of a constitutionally protected interest in 'life, liberty, or property' is not in itself unconstitutional; what is unconstitutional is the deprivation of such an interest without due process of law."

67. *See, e.g.*, Connecticut v. Doehr, 501 U.S. 1, 12 (1991) (concluding that a temporary lien on real property merits due process protection); Fusari v. Steinberg, 419 U.S. 379, 387–89 (1975) (noting that the length of the deprivation is relevant in the determination of how much process is "due" in a given case).

68. Fuentes v. Shevin, 407 U.S. 67, 86 (1972).

69. *See* Zadvydas v. Davis, 533 U.S. 678, 690 (2001) ("Freedom from imprisonment—from government custody, detention, or other forms of physical restraint—lies at the heart of the liberty that Clause protects."); Foucha v. Louisiana, 504 U.S. 71, 80 (1992) ("Freedom from bodily restraint has always been at the core of the liberty protected by the Due Process Clause from arbitrary governmental action."); United States v. Salerno, 481 U.S. 739, 755 (1987) ("In our society liberty is the norm, and detention . . . without trial is a carefully limited exception."); Jones v. United States, 463 U.S. 354, 361 (1983) ("It is clear that 'commitment for any purpose constitutes a significant deprivation of liberty that requires due process protection.'"); Parham v. J.R., 442 U.S. 584, 600 (1979)

(finding a "substantial liberty interest in not being confined unnecessarily"); O'Connor v. Donaldson, 422 U.S. 563, 576 (1975) (concluding that the state's confinement of a nondangerous individual violated his "constitutional right to freedom").

70. Hamdi v. Rumsfeld, 542 U.S. 507, 529–30 (2004) (internal citations omitted).

71. Richard H. Fallon, Jr. & Daniel J. Meltzer, Habeas Corpus Jurisdiction, Substantive Rights, and the War on Terror, 120 Harv. L. Rev. 2029, 2067–70 (2007).

72. *See, e.g.*, Frank H. Easterbrook, Substance and Due Process, 1982 Sup. Ct. Rev. 85, 87–100 (discussing the historical connection between the phrase "due process of law" and the individual's "liberty" interest in remaining free from imprisonment).

73. Sniadach v. Family Fin. Corp. of Bay View, 395 U.S. 337, 341–42 (1969).

74. N. Ga. Finishing v. Di-Chem, Inc., 419 U.S. 601, 608 (1975).

75. Goldberg v. Kelly, 397 U.S. 254, 261 (1970).

76. Fuentes v. Shevin, 407 U.S. 67, 70, 84, 89–90 (1972).

77. 424 U.S. 319, 335 (1976).

78. Cleveland Bd. of Educ. v. Loudermill, 470 U.S. 532, 542 (1985) (quoting Mullane v. Cent. Hanover Bank & Trust Co., 339 U.S. 306, 313 (1950)); *see also* Mathews, 424 U.S. at 333 ("This Court consistently has held that some form of hearing is required before an individual is finally deprived of a property interest"); Fuentes, 407 U.S. at 80; Armstrong v. Manzo, 380 U.S. 545, 550 (1965) (holding that lack of notice "violated the most rudimentary demands of due process of law"); Baldwin v. Hale, 68 U.S. (1 Wall.) 223, 233 (1863); Morrison, *supra* note 5, at 1611 (describing the three core requirements of notice, hearing, and a neutral adjudicator as a "reasonably concrete operative proposition").

79. *See, e.g.*, Hamdi v. Rumsfeld, 542 U.S. 507, 538 (2004) (holding that an individual detained by the government was entitled to a neutral adjudicator "as a matter of due process of law"); Ward v. Vill. of Monroeville, 409 U.S. 57, 61–62 (1972) (concluding that due process requires "a neutral and detached judge in the first instance"); Bell v. Burson, 402 U.S. 535, 542 (1971): "While '[m]any controversies have raged about . . . the Due Process Clause,' . . . it is fundamental that except in emergency situations (and this is not one) due process requires that when a State seeks to terminate [a protected] interest . . . , it must afford 'notice and opportunity for hearing appropriate to the nature of the case' before the termination becomes effective" (quoting Mullane, 339 U.S. at 313); Tumey v. Ohio, 273 U.S. 510, 522 (1927): "That officers acting in a judicial or quasi-judicial capacity are disqualified by their interest in the controversy to be decided is, of course, the general rule."

80. Fuentes, 407 U.S. at 80 (quoting Baldwin, 68 U.S. at 233).

81. Hamdi, 542 U.S. at 538 (quoting Concrete Pipe & Prods. of Cal. v. Const. Laborers Pension Trust, 508 U.S. 602, 617–18 (1993)); *see also* Caperton v. A. T. Massey Coal Co., 129 S.Ct. 2252, 2259 (2009); Aetna Life Ins. Co. v. Lavoie, 475 U.S. 813, 821–22 (1986); Tumey, 273 U.S. at 523; Martin H. Redish & Lawrence C. Marshall, Adjudicatory Independence and the Values of Procedural Due Process,

95 Yale L.J. 455, 476 (1986) (arguing that other procedural safeguards are of no real value "if the decisionmaker bases his findings on factors other than his assessment of the evidence before him").

82. Hamdi, 542 U.S. at 533: "At the same time, the exigencies of the circumstances may demand that, aside from these core elements [notice, hearing, and neutral adjudicator], enemy-combatant proceedings may be tailored to alleviate their uncommon potential to burden the Executive at a time of ongoing military conflict."

83. *See* discussion *infra* at 177–78.

84. Compare, e.g., Goldberg v. Kelly, 397 U.S. 254, 266–68 (1970) (prescribing a full hearing, which included the opportunity to present and cross-examine witnesses, prior to the termination of welfare benefits), with Mathews v. Eldridge, 424 U.S. 319, 340 (1976) (holding that an oral evidentiary hearing was not required prior to discontinuation of social security disability benefits).

85. *See* Hamdi, 542 U.S. at 563–64 (Scalia, J., dissenting); Morrison, *supra* note 5, at 1577 (acknowledging that suspension "does remove all means of obtaining contemporaneous relief from the detention itself—that is, discharge"); Shapiro, *supra* note 4, at 80 ("No one would doubt that the effect of the suspension is, at a minimum, to require dismissal of a habeas petition if the return establishes that the particular custody is within the scope of the statute."); Tyler, *supra* note 5, at 609 (arguing that the "purpose and 'immediate effect of a suspension is the facilitation of detaining individuals during times of crisis,'" and that allowing judicial remedies would "undercut 'the underlying premise of the legislative decision' to suspend").

86. *See* Hamdi, 542 U.S. at 563–64 (Scalia, J., dissenting) ("When the writ is suspended, the Government is entirely free from judicial oversight."); Morrison, *supra* note 5, at 1578–79; Tyler, *supra* note 25, at 386.

87. Tyler, *supra* note 25, at 386–87.

88. Professor Morrison argues that during a suspension, responsibility for enforcing individual due process rights falls to the executive branch. See Morrison, *supra* note 5, at 1602–15 (describing executive branch implementation of the Due Process Clause during a suspension). Absent supervision from a coordinate branch, however, there is no guarantee that the executive will make a good-faith effort to provide detainees with constitutionally adequate procedure. While the executive branch might, as Morrison suggests, attempt to set up neutral tribunals that provide detainees with a meaningful opportunity to rebut the evidence against them, it seems just as likely that the executive will provide detainees with no process at all. History shows us that even in the absence of a suspension, the executive is all too happy to lock individuals up and throw away the key unless the courts step in and mandate individual hearings.

89. *See* the All Writs Act, 28 U.S.C. §1651 (2006).

90. Trevor W. Morrison, *Hamdi's* Habeas Puzzle: Suspension as Authorization? 91 Cornell L. Rev. 411, 433 n. 134 (2006).

91. *Id.*; *see also* Shapiro, *supra* note 4, at 89–90 (arguing that the suspension power frees the executive from any legal restraints on the detention, including any writ that provides a remedy analogous to that of habeas corpus).

92. For a fictional description of a scenario ominously reminiscent of this hypothetical situation, see generally Sinclair Lewis, It Can't Happen Here (1935).

93. Thus, this argument is no way meant to suggest that a subsequently enacted statute supersedes a prior constitutional provision.

94. *Federalist* No. 78 (Hamilton), *supra* note 20, at 468 (emphasis added).

95. Wood v. United States, 41 U.S. (16 Pet.) 342, 363 (1842).

96. 451 U.S. 259, 266 (1981); see Mercantile Nat'l Bank v. Langdeau, 371 U.S. 555, 565 (1963) (noting that a later statute can implicitly repeal an earlier statute in cases of "manifest inconsistency" or "positive repugnance" between the two laws); Georgia v. Pa. R.R. Co., 324 U.S. 439, 457 (1945): ("Only a clear repugnancy between the old law and the new results in the former giving way and then only pro tanto to the extent of the repugnancy" (citing United States v. Borden Co., 308 U.S. 188, 199 (1939).

97. Black's Law Dictionary 89 (8th ed., 2004).

98. For example, before holding that the Eleventh Amendment superseded Congress's power to authorize suits by private parties against unconsenting states, the Court noted that the Eleventh Amendment "stood for the constitutional principle that state sovereign immunity limited the federal courts' jurisdiction under Article III." Seminole Tribe of Fla. v. Florida, 517 U.S. 44, 64 (1996).

99. In this sense, cases of constitutional implied repeal are fundamentally different from cases of implied statutory repeal. Although the same general rule—that a later provision implicitly repeals an earlier one in cases of "manifest inconsistency"—governs both cases, the Court often declines "to read the statutes as being in irreconcilable conflict without seeking to ascertain the actual intent of Congress." Watt, 451 U.S. at 266. By contrast, the Court did not consult any legislative history to determine whether the Eleventh and Fourteenth Amendments conflicted in Fitzpatrick v. Bitzer, 427 U.S. 445, 456 (1976), or whether Congress's Article I powers conflicted with the Eleventh Amendment in Seminole Tribe, 517 U.S. at 66–67. The difference is most likely attributable to the fact that the designation of a provision as an amendment in itself indicates an intent to modify all earlier provisions.

100. *See* Fitzpatrick, 427 U.S. at 456 (holding that principle of state sovereignty embodied by the Eleventh Amendment is limited by the enforcement provisions of §5 of the Fourteenth Amendment).

101. 517 U.S. 44 (1996).

102. U.S. Const. Amend. XI.

103. U.S. Const. Art. I §8 cl. 3.

104. U.S. Const. Art. I §8 cl. 18.

105. Seminole Tribe, 517 U.S. at 72–73. For a discussion of *Seminole Tribe*, see Martin H. Redish & Daniel M. Greenfield, Bankruptcy, Sovereign Immunity and the Dilemma of Principled Decision Making: The Curious Case of Central Virginia Community College v. Katz, 15 Am. Bankr. Inst. L. Rev. 13, 22–28 (2007).

106. U.S. Const. Amend. V.

107. *See* Martin H. Redish & Abby Marie Mollen, Understanding Post's and Meiklejohn's Mistakes: The Central Role of Adversary Democracy in the Theory of Free Expression, 103 Nw. U. L. Rev. 1303, 1353–66 (2009).

108. *See, e.g., Federalist* No. 41 (Madison).

109. Professor Morrison has suggested that substantive constitutional rights continue to exist during a suspension, even though they may not be enforced at the time. He asserts, however, that once the suspension has been revoked the victim may sue for damages in order to vindicate his constitutional rights. See Morrison, *supra* note 5, at 1588.

110. 71 U.S. (4 Wall.) 2, 125 (1866).

111. *See* Leonard W. Levy, Bill of Rights, in Essays on the Making of the Constitution 258, 275–78 (Leonard W. Levy, ed., 2d ed., 1987) (noting that "the Constitution was ratified only because crucial states, where ratification had been in doubt, were willing to accept the promise of a bill of rights in the form of subsequent amendments to the Constitution").

112. *See* U.S. Const. Art. III §1.

113. Chafee, *supra* note 31, at 143.

114. *See supra* note 5.

115. *Cf.* Brown v. Bd. of Educ., 347 U.S. 483, 495 (1954) (voiding separate-but-equal doctrine), with Plessy v. Ferguson, 163 U.S. 537, 550–52 (1896) (enshrining separate-but-equal doctrine as constitutionally sound).

116. *See* Va. State Bd. of Pharmacy v. Va. Citizens Consumer Council, 425 U.S. 748, 762–65 (1976).

117. *See* Shaffer v. Heitner, 433 U.S. 186, 213–17 (1977).

118. *See* Roe v. Wade, 410 U.S. 113, 152–56 (1973); Griswold v. Connecticut, 381 U.S. 479, 484–86 (1965).

119. *See* Abraham Lincoln, Message to Congress in Special Session (July 4, 1861), in 4 Collected Works of Abraham Lincoln 421, 430 (Roy P. Basler, ed., 1953) (asserting that "[i]t was not believed that any law was violated" when he unilaterally suspended the writ).

120. Many justices have endorsed this view, including Chief Justice Marshall in Ex parte Bollman, 8 U.S. (4 Cranch) 75, 101 (1807), Chief Justice Taney in Ex parte Merryman, 17 F. Cas. 144, 151–52 (Taney, Circuit Justice, C.C.D. Md. 1861), and Justice Scalia in Hamdi v. Rumsfeld, 542 U.S. 507, 562 (2004) (Scalia, J., dissenting).

121. *See, e.g.*, Samuel Issacharoff & Richard H. Pildes, Between Civil Libertarianism and Executive Unilateralism: An Institutional Process Approach to Rights during Wartime, 5 Theoretical Inquiries in Law 1, 44 (2004).

122. *See* discussion *supra* at 173–79.

123. *Cf.* Vincent Blasi, The Pathological Perspective and the First Amendment, 85 Colum. L. Rev. 449, 456 (1985).

124. *See, e.g.*, Tyler, *supra* note 5, at 672 (arguing that the suspension power accomplishes nothing if it does not "free the executive to act quickly and decisively, and without fear of repercussion" during "extraordinary occasions").

125. *See* discussion *supra* at 176–78.

126. *See* discussion *supra* at 176–78.

127. These labels are not intended to coincide with labels used by other scholars to differentiate between constitutional and factual questions. *See, e.g.*, Issacharoff & Pildes, *supra* note 121, at 7 (discussing the Court's analysis of "first-order" claims of rights).

128. *See* discussion *supra* at 177–78.

129. Cleveland Bd. of Educ. v. Loudermill, 470 U.S. 532, 542 (1985), quoting Mullane v. Cent. Hanover Bank & Trust Co., 339 U.S. 306, 313 (1950).

130. It should be noted that while I refer here to this due process inquiry being performed by an *Article III* federal court, it is arguable that, under generally accepted precepts of congressional authority to regulate federal court jurisdiction, Congress could replace the federal courts with state courts. See Martin H. Redish, Federal Jurisdiction: Tensions in the Allocation of Judicial Power 7–52 (2d ed., 1990). However, because Congress possesses the power to control neither state judicial tenure nor state judicial salaries, those courts would also satisfy the neutrality requirements of due process. *See id.* at 43–44.

131. *See* Morrison, *supra* note 5, at 1613.

132. Moreover, the interest at stake for the detainee is roughly analogous to the interest at stake for a criminal defendant. These arguments parallel the ones made by the alleged "enemy-combatant" in Hamdi v. Rumsfeld, who had also been denied any procedural rights. See 542 U.S. 507, 511–12 (2004).

133. Cafeteria & Rest. Workers Union, Local 473 v. McElroy, 367 U.S. 886, 895 (1961).

134. 424 U.S. 319, 334–35 (1976).

135. Scholars have argued that the narrow, utilitarian focus of this test overlooks the individual's "dignitary values," which could be fostered by the use of additional procedures that only minimally increase decision-making accuracy. See Coleen E. Klasmeier, Towards a New Understanding of Capital Clemency and Procedural Due Process, 75 B.U. L. Rev. 1507, 1527 n.117 (1995); *see also* Jerry L. Mashaw, The Supreme Court's Due Process Calculus for Administrative Adjudication in Mathews v. Eldridge: Three Factors in Search of a Theory of Value, 44 U. Chi. L. Rev. 28, 47–48 & n.61 (1976). Standing alone, the test also fails to establish a constitutional floor for the definition of due process, see Redish & Marshall, *supra* note 81, at 472–74, and fails to recognize the value of litigant autonomy, see Martin H. Redish & Nathan D. Larsen, Class Actions, Litigant Autonomy, and the Foundations of Procedural Due Process, 95 Cal. L. Rev. 1573, 1578–79 (2007).

136. *See, e.g.*, Farina, *supra* note 58, at 234: "If due process is to mark out and defend a sphere in which the individual is reliably preserved from the demands of the collective, how can the extent of the protection the individual receives turn on some calculus explicitly designed to maximize aggregate welfare?"); Rubin, *supra* note 59, at 1138: "Establishing three distinct factors, two of which operate in opposition to each other, seems impressive, but it is unclear how to resolve the inevitable conflicts between them."

137. Hamdi, 542 U.S. at 532.

138. *Id.* at 531.

139. In *Hamdi*, the government conceded that "given its unconventional nature, the current conflict is unlikely to end with a formal cease-fire agreement." *Id.* at 520. The Court then concluded that "[t]he prospect [of indefinite detention that] *Hamdi* raises is therefore not farfetched." *Id.*

140. Although it is not essential to the central argument made here, it should be noted that the detainees might also be able to claim a viable liberty interest in the damage that the government would do to their reputations through this wrongful imprisonment. See Goss v. Lopez, 419 U.S. 565, 574 (1975) ("The Due Process

Clause also forbids arbitrary deprivations of liberty," including deprivation of "a person's good name, reputation, honor, or integrity").

141. *See* Mathews v. Eldridge, 424 U.S. 319, 340 (1976) (finding ability of full retroactive relief a significant factor in the determination that the Due Process Clause does not mandate a full evidentiary hearing prior to the termination of the plaintiff's social security disability benefits); Goldberg v. Kelly, 397 U.S. 254, 267–68 (1970) (holding that a full evidentiary hearing is necessary before the termination of welfare benefits).

142. Compare *Cf.* Morrison, *supra* note 5, at 1539 ("Suspension does not displace any post-detention remedies, nor does it alter a detention's legality"), with Shapiro, *supra* note 4, at 89 (arguing that suspension of the writ "frees the Executive from the legal restraints on detention that would otherwise apply").

143. While the Court has never directly addressed this issue, analogies to previous rights that the Court has deemed "irreparable" provide ample support for the argument advanced here. In Fuentes v. Shevin, the Court held that no later monetary award could compensate the plaintiff for the arbitrary repossession of her gas stove. 407 U.S. 67, 82 (1972); *see also* Sniadach v. Family Fin. Corp. of Bay View, 395 U.S. 337, 341–42 (1969) (concluding that a prejudgment garnishment of wages may do irreparable harm by "as a practical matter driv[ing] a wage-earning family to the wall").

144. Fuentes, 407 U.S. at 82, quoting Stanley v. Illinois, 405 U.S. 645, 647 (1972).

145. *See, e.g., Mathews*, 424 U.S. at 347.

146. *See* Hamdi v. Rumsfeld, 542 U.S. 507, 531–32 (2004) (summarizing the government's argument that its interest in reducing process available to detainees is "heightened by the practical difficulties that would accompany a system of trial-like process. In its view, military officers who are engaged in the serious work of waging battle would be unnecessarily and dangerously distracted by litigation half a world away, and discovery into military operations would both intrude on the sensitive secrets of national defense and result in a futile search for evidence buried under the rubble of war").

147. *See id.* at 534: "We think it unlikely that this basic process will have the dire impact on the central functions of warmaking that the Government forecasts."

148. The Supreme Court entertained Hamdi's habeas petition nearly three years after the attacks precipitating the detention took place. At that point, he had been in custody for nearly two years. *See id.* at 512–13.

149. The Court has never explicitly addressed this question in the context of a liberty deprivation. It has, however, noted that certain exceptional circumstances may justify a delay in providing a hearing in cases involving deprivations of property. *See, e.g.,* Connecticut v. Doehr, 501 U.S. 1, 16–18 (1991) (noting that the possibility that Doehr was about to transfer or encumber the property at issue would have been an "exigent circumstance permitting postponing any notice or hearing until after the [deprivation] had been affected," but later clarifying that "[w]e do not mean to imply that any given exigency requirement protects an attachment from constitutional attack").

150. *See* discussion *supra* at 175–76.

151. *See* Hamdi, 542 U.S. at 535.

152. 424 U.S. 319, 335 (1976).

153. *See* the detailed discussion of *Tumey* in chapter 4, *supra* at 122–23.

154. Withrow v. Larkin, 421 U.S. 35, 47 (1975) (holding that "[t]he contention that the combination of investigative and adjudicative functions necessarily creates an unconstitutional risk of bias in administrative adjudication [is] a . . . difficult burden of persuasion to carry" because it "must overcome a presumption of honesty and integrity in those serving as adjudicators").

155. 273 U.S. 510, 523 (1927).

156. *Id*. at 532; *see also* Aetna Life Ins. Co. v. Lavoie, 475 U.S. 813, 825 (1986); Ward v. Vill. of Monroeville, 409 U.S. 57, 61 (1972).

157. Cf. Caperton v. A. T. Massey Coal Co., 129 S. Ct. 2252, 2263 (2009): "There are instances when the introspection that often attends this process may reveal that what the judge had assumed to be a proper, controlling factor is not the real one at work."

158. *Id*.

159. *Id*.

160. *See, e.g.*, Withrow v. Larkin, 421 U.S. 35, 46 (1975) (reviewing constitutional question of whether a state medical examining board could function as a neutral adjudicator for purposes of the Due Process Clause).

161. Fallon & Meltzer, *supra* note 71, at 2101.

162. This hypothetical legislation represents a simplified version of the Habeas Corpus Act of 1863, ch. 81, 12 Stat. 755 (1863). The Court in Ex parte Milligan did not evaluate the constitutionality of the Act because Justice Davis mistakenly viewed any suspension as presumptively valid. See 71 U.S. (4 Wall.) 2, 114–15 (1866). It should be noted that these restrictions were not actually enforced during the Civil War. See Mark E. Neely, Jr., The Fate of Liberty: Abraham Lincoln and Civil Liberties 175–79 (1991).

163. As a practical matter, the threat of even temporary imprisonment might suffice to silence political opposition and allow an ambitious president to accrete more power.

164. Ex parte Milligan, 71 U.S. at 122.

165. *Id*. at 127.

166. This chapter has avoided issues involving arrest of non-citizens or enemy combatants—issues which are beyond the scope of the inquiry.

167. *See* discussion *supra* at 191.

168. *See* discussion *supra* at 191–92.

169. Tyler, *supra* note 5, at 603. Professor David Shapiro also endorses this view of the suspension power, arguing that because the writ was originally understood as the method for challenging the lawfulness of executive detention, the Framers (by including the Suspension Clause in the Constitution) were "willing to allow Congress to abridge [the underlying right to challenge the basis for the detention] during times of crisis." *See* Shapiro, *supra* note 4, at 93.

170. Tyler, *supra* note 25, at 386; *see also* Shapiro, *supra* note 4, at 90 (worrying that the "very purpose of the suspension" might be undermined if the executive could be subject to ex post financial liability or allegations of violating the oath to support the Constitution and its laws).

171. Tyler, *supra* note 5, at 604. While at certain points Professor Tyler advocates recognition of an unlimited congressional suspension power, *see, e.g.*, Tyler, *supra*

note 25, at 386, arguing that the "very purpose of suspension is to permit Congress to override core due process safeguards during times of crisis," at other points she appears to qualify this position, see *id.* at 390–92, noting that "[t]here exists a formidable argument that even in the event of a valid suspension, equal protection principles at a minimum would have something to say about [a hypothetical involving Congress suspending the writ in Muslim neighborhoods]."

172. Shapiro, *supra* note 4, at 91–92.

173. *See* Tyler, *supra* note 25, at 382–83; *see also* Shapiro, *supra* note 4, at 91–92.

174. Tyler, *supra* note 25, at 382–83; *see also* Shapiro, *supra* note 4, at 87 (noting that Blackstone described Magna Carta as establishing a "substantive commitment[] of compliance with law" and the writ of habeas corpus as requiring "that a reason be given for every commitment").

175. *See* discussion *supra* at 170–73.

176. *See* Tyler, *supra* note 5, at 618.

177. Tyler, *supra* note 25, at 382; *see also* Shapiro, *supra* note 4, at 93: "Rather, in both its inception and its development (though recent years have seen some significant expansion), the writ was understood as the method of challenging the lawfulness of detention. Thus, in my view, it was that particular aspect, and only that aspect, of due process that the Founders were willing to allow Congress to abridge during times of crisis."

178. It should once again be emphasized that while the Due Process Clause is surely not unambiguous as to its outer frontiers, it most definitely is unambiguous that summary and indefinite coercive confinement without the provision of any form of meaningful opportunity to be heard most certainly fails to qualify as due process.

179. *See, e.g.,* Bartlett v. Bowen, 816 F.2d 695 (D.C. Cir. 1987) (Due Process Clause limits congressional power over federal court jurisdiction under Article III); Battaglia v. General Motors Corp., 169 F.2d 254 (2d Cir.), cert. denied, 335 U.S. 887 (1948) (same).

180. One scholar argues that the Due Process Clause was redundant because "[d]ue process was constitutional shorthand for many particular rights that other clauses of the Fifth and Sixth Amendments explicitly protected," and that "[i]nclusion of the clause showed conventional deference to Magna Carta" Levy, *supra* note 111, at 305.

181. *See* discussion *supra* at 170–73.

182. Neuman, *supra* note 26, at 566.

183. *See Federalist* Nos. 47 and 48 (both Madison) (arguing that the "mere demarcation on parchment of the constitutional limits of the several departments, is not a sufficient guard against those encroachments which lead to a tyrannical concentration of all the powers of government in the same hands."

184. Martin H. Redish & Elizabeth J. Cisar, "If Angels Were to Govern": The Need for Pragmatic Formalism in Separation of Powers Theory, 41 Duke L.J. 449, 462 (1991).

185. James Madison, Adding a Bill of Rights to the Constitution (Speech in Congress, June 8, 1789), in Selected Writings of James Madison 164, 170 (Ralph Ketcham, ed., 2006).

186. *See* Tyler, *supra* note 25, at 337 (arguing that the "internal predicates required for a valid suspension (the existence of a 'Rebellion or Invasion') are inextricably intertwined with the core due process right to seek impartial review of the Executive's justification for a prisoner's detention").

187. *See* U.S. Const. Amend. V.

188. The Court has limited "virtual representation," a preclusion doctrine that permits a litigant to be bound by a judgment in a prior case in which she was not a party. Taylor v. Sturgell, 553 U.S. 880 (2008).

189. Martin H. Redish, Good Behavior, Judicial Independence, and the Foundations of American Constitutionalism, 116 Yale L.J. 139, 153 (2006).

Index